Clutch Leadership

Today's organizational leaders contend with a considerable array of potentially profound disruptive forces. Emerging information management and creation tools like AI and robotics, in conjunction with economic swings, global manufacturing shifts, and political instabilities, are creating immeasurable effects on business strategies and leadership practices. Transforming short-term challenges into long-term opportunities requires *rising to the occasion*, or what we call "clutch leadership." We believe that all leaders have it in them to be "clutch leaders!" Such is the thrust of this book.

Clutch leaders have the skills to manage disruptions, break down silos, and align people around a compelling vision of success that represents a shift from "strategic fit" (matching resources and capabilities with opportunities) to "strategic stretch" (leveraging industry positioning to create competitive advantage). They create a productive and motivating sense of urgency and high aspiration in the organization during times of increased stakes. Clutch leaders build consensus in support of high-stakes decisions and model the way with a combination of confidence, conviction, capability, and conviction. Focusing on impact during disruptive times enables clutch leaders to harness the full potential of organizational resources beyond strategic fit, even if it requires a temporary push of skills and behaviors to extreme or taking on additional risks and opportunities (strategic stretch).

What makes clutch leadership unique is the focus on "temporary imbalance" – the suspension of trade-offs between staying in the comfort zone versus playing to one's tried and true strengths – until the gap is closed or until the new vision and reality are realigned through innovation and leverage. Their distinctive ability to balance high-stress, big picture thinking with composure, agility, attention to detail, and strong logical reasoning with communication skills and empathy allows them to navigate fast-paced, challenging situations quickly and successfully.

Numerous case studies are also included to illustrate innovative leadership techniques and applications.

Innovative Leadership Series

AI is rapidly transforming business strategies and leadership practices. Innovative leaders thrive by fostering continuous learning, collaboration, and empowerment, leveraging new technologies for organizational success. In high-stakes moments, clutch leaders make decisive, bold moves, and then promote shared ownership and co-creation to sustain engagement. Innovative Leadership emphasizes adaptability, purposeful innovation, and balancing stress with intuition and character. It combines expertise, empathy, and the "Why" with practical "Know-How" to promote growth. This three-book series equips strategists, executives, and managers with diagnostic tools to enhance self-awareness, leverage strengths, and achieve win-win outcomes amid disruption.

Books in the series:

Brilliant Leadership: Unlocking the Power of Innovation-Communication
Edited by Alan Belasen and Nicole Pfefferman

Forthcoming books in the series:

Transparent Leadership: Bridging the Trust Gap Between Senior Executives and Middle Managers
Alan Belasen and Ariel Belasen

Clutch Leadership: Harnessing the Qualities of a Gamechanger
Edited by Alan T. Belasen and Barry Eisenberg

Clutch Leadership

Harnessing the Qualities of a Gamechanger

Edited by Alan T. Belasen, PhD and
Barry Eisenberg, PhD

Routledge
Taylor & Francis Group
A PRODUCTIVITY PRESS BOOK

Designed cover image: Shutterstock

First published 2026
by Routledge
605 Third Avenue, New York, NY 10158

and by Routledge
4 Park Square, Milton Park, Abingdon, Oxon, OX14 4RN

Routledge is an imprint of the Taylor & Francis Group, an informa business

ISBN: 978-1-041-04639-4 (hbk)
ISBN: 978-1-041-04637-0 (pbk)
ISBN: 978-1-003-62921-4 (ebk)

DOI: 10.4324/9781003629214

Typeset in Garamond
by Deanta Global Publishing Services, Chennai, India

I dedicate this book to the memory of my father, George Eisenberg. He was the most devoted father, and as time goes by, I continue to think of him as the wisest person I've ever known. As I reflect on the theme of the book – succeeding through disruption – I marvel at how my dad spent a lifetime drawing on an inner strength, resourcefulness, and commitment to virtue. His parents spoke no English when they arrived from Poland, so it was up to my dad and his siblings to navigate the family's assimilation. As a child in the Great Depression, he learned to be grateful for life's basics, and especially cherishing his family and community, values he carried for a lifetime. He is missed every day.

Barry Eisenberg

To Steven Draheim, Chef and Owner of Barrio and Shimshon restaurants in Bend, Oregon, who exemplifies the key traits of clutch leadership – character, intuition, and empowerment – excelling under moments of pressure when stakes are high, adapting and rethinking his business model to thrive after the ripple effects of the COVID-19 pandemic. Steven demonstrated the mental toughness to lead and persevere through challenges and setbacks, using them as learning opportunities for growth. He is empathetic and compassionate. An innovator with the know-how to balance the dynamic tensions between expectations for stability and the inevitable need to embrace new experiences. A clutch leader in a league of his own.

Alan Belasen

Contents

PART D INNOVATION AND ETHICS

PART E STRATEGIC DISRUPTION

PART F IN PERSPECTIVE

Acknowledgments

In addition to numerous articles, presentations, and a wealth of other professional projects, this is the third book I have had the pleasure of working on with my dear friend and colleague, Dr Alan Belasen. Alan's rich insights into leadership effectiveness have been a significant influence on my growth as a researcher of organizational behavior. He is an exceptionally prolific writer whose considerable contributions to his field are in a league of their own. I am grateful for Alan's masterful stewardship of this project and, more broadly, for our wonderful partnership over many years. Our collaborations are a true joy.

I have worked extensively with many of the authors who have contributed to this book. Each is a gifted scholar, and in this book, each has fortified our understanding of what it takes to lead under challenging circumstances. Their distinct perspectives shine a brilliant light on the subject of clutch leadership, a topic of growing importance given the increasingly complex world in which we live and the emerging technologies which offer both promise and concern.

I have the privilege of working with extremely talented students in the MBA in Healthcare Leadership program at SUNY Empire State University. I am deeply appreciative of their dedication to making the healthcare system more accessible to good quality care for all. They are role models for critical concepts presented in this book.

I could not be more thankful for my amazingly supportive family. I have the great pleasure of frequently collaborating professionally with my wife, Dr Amy Eisenberg. Collaborating in life is even better, and Amy's love and encouragement mean the world. We are immeasurably grateful for the support of our children and their partners, Kerry and Nathan, Jesse, Anna, and our grandson Banner, and Hallie and Nullah. Amy and I feel very blessed for their devotion and involvement in all we do.

Barry Eisenberg

Special thanks go to my co-editor, colleague, and research partner Dr Barry Eisenberg, whose interdisciplinary knowledge and vast professional experience, thoughtful ideas, and passion for advancing new frameworks of leadership shaped my own thinking about *Clutch Leadership*. Barry has always been a valuable sounding board for intellectually stimulating ideas and insights. My true knowledge fountain for this and my other book projects. Thank you, Barry!

I would like to acknowledge the contributors to this important book. Not only did they offer their depth of knowledge, but they also believe in the importance and universal appeal of *Clutch Leadership* and the applicability of the new framework across organizations and industries. Their diverse perspectives and rich experiences helped make this book insightful and provocative, showcasing the inner strengths of clutch leaders who navigate challenges with purpose and resilience.

I am deeply indebted to President Lisa Vollendorf and Provost Rai Kathuria, SUNY Empire State University, for granting my Sabbatical leave to pursue my scholarly work. Empire State University provides resources, mentorship, and connections that promote learning, research, and scholarly endeavours - An incubator that fosters growth, innovation, and opportunities to explore new directions. I am grateful to my colleagues at Empire's Business, Management, and Leadership program for the opportunity to collaborate on important research projects leading to this book.

Special thanks go to Kristine Mednansky, Acquisitions Editor, Taylor & Francis Group, who believed in the message and relevance of this book project. As with my previous books, Kris was instrumental in moving this book project through the various production phases.

As with my other book projects, my wife Susan provided the social and emotional support. Being surrounded by my five A's has always been rewarding and intellectually stimulating, running ideas by them and getting feedback to improve or expand my writing. Ari, PhD, an accomplished scholar and Professor of Economics at SIUE; Amy, an accomplished author, founder of ABD Creative, podcast host, digital marketing expert, and a successful travel blogger; Anat, PhD, in Ecology & Evolutionary Biology, NSF Postdoctoral Research Fellow in Biology, UT Austin Department of Integrative Bio; Amanda, MA, a client service specialist in a global organization; and Abigail, MD, a Hospitalist at Albany Medical Center. I am indebted to everyone.

Alan Belasen

Contributors

Alan T. Belasen, PhD, earned his doctorate from Rockefeller College, SUNY Albany. For over 30 years, Dr. Belasen has been involved in executive education and development programs in the United States and abroad. Dr. Belasen chaired the MBA Program at SUNY Empire University for over a decade, where he co-designed and guided the MBA in Management, MBA in Global Leadership, MBA in Healthcare Leadership, and MBA Pathway for Veterans.

Dr. Belasen has written over 150 journal articles, book chapters, and conference papers on topics such as executive education, self-managed teams, HR competencies, work motivation, women's leadership, communication innovation, corruption in business, trusted leadership, healthcare management, and leadership development. His articles appear in journals such as the *International Journal of Strategic Communication; International Journal for Quality in Health Care; Journal of Human Resource Management; International Journal of Human Resources Development and Management; Journal of Economic Modelling; Gender in Management: An International Journal; Journal of Racial and Ethnic Health Disparities; Journal of Organizational Healthcare Management; Journal of Healthcare Management; International Journal of Sport Marketing & Sponsorship; and the Journal for Advancing Business Education.*

Dr. Belasen's recent books include *Transparent Leadership - Bridging the Trust Gap Between Senior Executives and Middle Managers (2025); Brilliant Leadership: Unlocking the Power of Innovation-Communication (2024); Transforming Leadership, Improving the Patient Experience (2024); and Resilience in Healthcare Leadership: Practical Strategies and Self-Assessment Tools (2022).*

Dr. Belasen received the Outstanding Reviewer Award from the Academy of Management ten times in the past 25 years. He is also the recipient of the 2017 *John L. Green Award for Excellence in Business Education*, the International Accreditation Council for Business Education (IACBE), and the 2014–2015 *SUNY Chancellor's Award for Scholarship and Creative Activities.*

William Borgos, MD, is the Chief Medical Officer of the Hudson Headwaters Health Network, an organization of 27 Federally Qualified Health Centers in the Adirondack region of New York. Dr. Borgos has 30 years of clinical experience as a family medicine physician, and in his current role, oversees the clinical practice of more than 200 medical providers. During his career, Dr. Borgos has contributed to a number of quality and population health initiatives. In 2022, he was recognized as the recipient of the Dr. Jack Geiger Award by the Community Health Care Association of New York State for his dedication to addressing community health, poverty, and human rights. In 2012, he was the recipient of the Glens Falls Hospital Mac Depan Award for Physician Excellence. Dr. Borgos is a dedicated mentor, having served as an adjunct Clinical Instructor with Albany Medical College and a clinical Assistant Instructor with the University of Vermont Robert Larner, MD College of Medicine. Dr. Borgos earned his Doctor of Medicine (MD) degree from the Johns Hopkins University School of Medicine and a Bachelor of Arts degree in Economics from the University of Notre Dame. He completed a Family Medicine residency and served as chief resident at the University of Michigan.

Jill Borgos, PhD, MS, RN, has over 30 years of combined academic, clinical, and leadership experience in healthcare and higher education. She is an Assistant Professor and Academic Coordinator in SUNY Empire State University's MBA Healthcare Leadership program. Dr. Borgos has held academic appointments in nursing undergraduate and graduate programs where she has taught courses in Health Policy, Organizational Behavior, Leadership, and Ethics. With an interest in education as a determinant of health outcomes globally, Borgos' research spans the areas of the internationalization of higher education, policy, and healthcare. She has presented and published on cross-border medical and nursing education, social network analysis, resource dependency across geopolitical borders, and distance learning. Dr. Borgos holds a PhD from the University at Albany in Educational Policy & Leadership, a Master of Science degree from the University of Michigan, and a Bachelor of Science degree in Nursing from Boston College. In recognition of her leadership in education, Borgos was the 2013 recipient of the University at Albany's Sanford H. Levin Fellowship. She served her community on the K-12 Board of Education for 15 years.

Jenine (Nina) Buchanan, EdD, is an Associate Teaching Professor in Leadership for Educational Equity in Higher Education in the CU Denver School of Education and Human Development. Her teaching and research reflect her commitment to recognizing humanity in every individual and creating spaces to foster connection and care. Prior to her faculty role, she held leadership positions in student and academic affairs. Dr. Buchanan holds a Doctor of

Education from Widener University in Higher Education Leadership, a Master of Education from the University of Delaware in Student Affairs Practice, and a Bachelor of Arts in English from the University of Delaware.

Amy Eisenberg, DMH, consults with hospital systems with the goal of helping practitioners manage patient interactions more effectively. With her team, Dr. Eisenberg also trains health professionals in effective end-of-life conversations, including guiding ethical choices and communicating empathically. Eisenberg's model was published in *Academic Medicine*, which was based on her pilot work at Jersey Shore Medical Center/Meridian Health System and the Atlantic Health System. She has written and produced two plays: "Anna's Story," an adaptation of the Atlantic Health System short film of the same name, about the need for end-of-life decision-making, and "A Tear in the Universe," illustrating the emotional experience of medical students. Dr. Eisenberg developed "It Couldn't Happen to Me," a series of videos with a coordinated training program, sponsored by the American Medical Association, about the perils of prescription drug abuse.

Barry Eisenberg, PhD, has over 40 years of experience in healthcare leadership, consulting, and higher education. He established and directed a management development program at Memorial Sloan Kettering Cancer Center in New York and later served as Vice President of human resources and then as Vice President of administration/operations in a New Jersey-based hospital.

In addition to co-developing and serving on the SUNY Empire State University's MBA in Healthcare Leadership faculty, Dr. Eisenberg consults with health care organizations on strategic planning, mergers and acquisitions, market expansion, and board of directors' development. Dr. Eisenberg has also led crisis and disaster management planning for healthcare organizations.

Dr. Eisenberg is co-author of *Mastering Leadership: A Vital Resource for Healthcare Organizations and Transforming Leadership, Improving the Patient Experience: Communication Strategies for Driving Patient Satisfaction,* as well as many articles and book chapters on healthcare management and a novel, *Primal Calling*. He also maintains a blog with wide distribution that includes many entries on healthcare covering consumer, practitioner, leadership, and health policy perspectives: https://barryeisenbergauthor.com/blog. Dr. Eisenberg serves on nonprofit boards that focus on access to scholarships, social justice, and arts education.

Ben Fagan, MS, is a doctoral student at the University of Cincinnati and holds a bachelor's degree in multimedia journalism and a master's degree in digital media from Lynn University. His research explores individual identity and how factors such as success, social and personal expectations, and performance pressures influence people's ability to thrive in their work. Before entering academia, Ben worked in career services and led professional development programs for students, educators, and business professionals.

Heather Horowitz, EdD, is a former higher education administrator with extensive leadership and supervision experience. She is currently an Assistant Professor in the Educational Leadership and Change EdD program at Empire State University, where she teaches courses on ethical leadership, institutional culture and strategic change, and leading change for social justice and diversity. Dr. Horowitz' research focuses on inclusive teaching practices and work environments in higher education. She earned her Doctor of Education from Wilmington University, as well as a Master of Arts in Organizational Leadership and Bachelor of Arts in Political Science and History from Rider University.

Betul Lus, PhD, holds a doctorate in Industrial Engineering and Operations Research from the University of Massachusetts Amherst. Currently, she is an Associate Professor at SUNY Empire State University and the coordinator of the MS programs in Applied Analytics, Marketing Analytics, and Healthcare Analytics. Dr. Lus has more than 15 years of teaching experience in operations management, global supply chain management, and quantitative methods in decision-making. Her research interests include operations and supply chain management, sustainability, and the role of AI in higher education and business.

Daniel M. Peat, PhD, earned his doctorate from the University of Cincinnati. He is currently an Assistant Professor – Educator in Management at the Lindner College of Business at the University of Cincinnati. Peat teaches a variety of courses in management, business strategy, and leadership, and his scholarly contributions explore human capital, strategic leadership, and military veterans in organizations. His work has been published in *Sage Business Cases*, *Journal of Organizational Behavior Education*, *Journal of Veterans Studies*, *Journal of Small Business and Enterprise Development*, *Journal of Business Research*, and *The International Journal of Human Resource Management* and featured in *Forbes*.

Dr. Peat has delivered invited talks and conducted professional development workshops on change management, leadership during crises, military/veteran inclusive organizations, and workplace stress to a variety of academic and professional audiences. Prior to joining academia, he served in a number of military and government roles, culminating as a Division Chief for the Defense Technical Information Center. He continues to serve in the US Army Reserves as an Adjunct Instructor for the Command and General Staff College.

Rosilyn Sanders, PsyD, has a doctrate in Organizational Leadership Psychology with a concentration in Consulting from William James College, Newton, MA, and an MA in Counseling. She is Prosci ADKAR change management certified, certified as a Change Management Specialist, and has a Lean Six Sigma Yellow Belt certification. Dr. Sanders is an Assistant Professor in the Industrial Organizational Psychology program at Empire State University, NY, where she is responsible for creating curriculum, program design and development, and instructional design. In addition, Dr. Sanders is one of, if not the first, African American women Organizational Leadership Consulting Psychologists from Arkansas. She is the founder and owner of Sanders Consulting & Associates, LLC, a local consulting agency providing professional development, coaching, and consultation to individuals, teams, and organizations. Dr. Sanders is an active member of Blacks in I-O Psychology, American Psychological Association, Division 13 Society of Consulting Psychology, and Alpha Kappa Alpha Sorority Incorporated.

Michael A. Schwartz, MD, MBA, FAAOS, is a board-certified orthopedic Surgeon specializing in sports medicine and arthroscopic surgery. He practices at White Plains Hospital Physician Associates-Center for Orthopaedic and Spine Surgery in White Plains, NY. Dr. Schwartz also holds an appointment as Clinical Assistant Professor of Orthopaedic Surgery at Montefiore Medical Center-Albert Einstein College of Medicine.

Dr. Schwartz is a graduate of the University of Health Sciences/Chicago Medical School and completed his residency at Stony Brook University Hospital. He furthered his training with an Orthopaedic Sports Medicine Fellowship at Thomas Jefferson University Hospital/Rothman Institute. Demonstrating a commitment to leadership and healthcare management, Dr. Schwartz earned an MBA in Healthcare Leadership from Empire State University.

In addition to his clinical practice, Dr. Schwartz is actively involved in medical education as an Associate Master Instructor for the Arthroscopy Association of North America. He also serves as Team Physician and Sports Medicine Program Director for the Harrison Central School District. Dr. Schwartz has been recognized as a Top Doctor by Castle Connolly multiple times and is a member of several professional organizations, including the American Academy of Orthopaedic Surgeons and the American Orthopaedic Society for Sports Medicine. Outside of his professional endeavors, Dr. Schwartz values time spent with his family, traveling, and pursuing an active lifestyle.

Sylwia E. Starnawska, PhD, MBA, is an Associate Professor at SUNY Empire State University. She holds a PhD in Economics from the Warsaw School of Economics, Poland, EU. Currently, she is the coordinator of the Global Finance and Investment graduate certificate program. Dr. Starnawska has experience in the management of financial institutions, mainly MNEs. She has been involved in international corporate finance, global capital markets, and international investments. She has also served as a CNBC guest speaker. Her research interests and publications focus on international financial markets, multinational strategic management, value-based management and shareholder value creation, and global portfolio management.

Ruifang Hope Sun, EdD, PMP, is an Associate Professor at SUNY Empire State University's School for Graduate Studies, specializing in instructional technology, AI integration, and project management. Her research focuses on AI in education, digital equity, and AI literacy for teaching and learning. She has published extensively on AI-enhanced learning, project leadership, and open education. Dr. Sun holds certifications in Generative AI and Learning Technology Leadership and integrates emerging technologies into education. Her expertise includes LLMs, metaverse development, and chatbot applications, with practical applications in e-commerce and higher education. A former Chair of the Division of Business, Management, and Leadership, she remains committed to fostering innovative, technology-driven learning environments.

Thomas Wiese, PhD, MBA, PMP, CMRP, is an Assistant Professor of Analytics and MBA Academic Coordinator at SUNY Empire State University, specializing in AI integration, machine learning, and data analytics. With over 19 years of professional experience, Dr. Wiese has led multiple data-driven transformations across the healthcare, transportation, and energy sectors. His research centers on developing advanced AI models to automate tasks, enhance operational efficiencies, and improve organizational decision-making processes.

Dr. Wiese holds Applied Data Science, Advanced Machine Learning, Project Management, and Reliability Engineering certifications and has published research on machine learning applications, data insights, and automation. His industry expertise includes designing and deploying scalable AI-powered tools, leveraging his strong background in leadership, engineering, programming, system optimization, and enterprise solutions. A veteran of the U.S. Navy and an accomplished entrepreneur, Dr. Wiese is committed to fostering innovation and developing analytics leaders equipped for dynamic, data-centric roles.

Chapter 1

Unlocking the Strengths of Clutch Leadership

Alan T. Belasen and Barry Eisenberg

Introduction

Today's organizational leaders contend with a considerable array of potentially profound disruptive forces. Emerging information management and creation tools like artificial intelligence (AI) and robotics, in conjunction with economic swings, global manufacturing shifts, and political instabilities, are creating immeasurable effects on business strategies and leadership practices. Transforming short-term challenges into long-term opportunities requires *rising to the occasion*, or what we call "clutch leadership." We believe that all leaders have it in them to be "clutch leaders!" Such is the thrust of this book.

Clutch leaders have the skills to manage disruptions, break down silos, and align people around a compelling vision of success that represents a shift from "strategic fit" (matching resources and capabilities with opportunities) to "strategic stretch" (leveraging industry positioning to create competitive advantage). They create a productive and motivating sense of urgency and high aspiration in the organization during times of increased stakes. Clutch leaders build consensus in support of high-stakes decisions and model the way with a combination of confidence, conviction, capability, and conviction. Focusing on impact during disruptive times enables clutch leaders to harness the full potential of

DOI: 10.4324/9781003629214-1

organizational resources beyond strategic fit, even if it requires a temporary push of skills and behaviors to extreme or taking on additional risks and opportunities (strategic stretch).

This shift requires leaders with the unique ability to think intuitively and act quickly – a "Slam Dunk" leadership talent that is impactful and that energizes and inspires others to reach their full potential. These, then, are clutch leaders – those immensely capable individuals who construct highly functional teams in support of the transformation and role model how to get the job done in even the most challenging circumstances, all the while empowering those around them and cultivating a climate of trust.

Clutch leaders excel under stress when high stakes are on the line. They have the mental toughness to lead in crucial times and navigate complex situations by focusing on critical outcomes and by pushing themselves beyond the "comfort zone," leaning heavily on that special leadership aptitude required in moments of pressure.

When clutch leaders sustain peak performance by building a culture of commitment that drives success, they continuously motivate organizational members through messaging strategies and winning stories that keep the momentum going. They align brand and reputation, increase the organization's value proposition by optimizing operational and supply chain efficiencies, celebrate employee achievements to boost morale, and engage stakeholders for their input and advice to sustain brand loyalty.

What makes clutch leadership unique is the focus on "temporary imbalance" – the suspension of trade-offs between staying in the comfort zone versus playing to one's tried and true strengths – until the gap is closed or until the new vision and reality are realigned through innovation and leverage. Their distinctive ability to balance high-stress, big-picture thinking with composure, agility, attention to detail, and strong logical reasoning with communication skills and empathy allows them to navigate fast-paced, challenging situations quickly and successfully.

The key to sustaining balanced leadership is to remain within a "positive zone" – the proverbial "Sweet Spot," that represents a healthy equilibrium of skills and behaviors and facilitates common understanding with individuals and teams.

Effective clutch leaders move outside their sweet spot at times of crisis, creating a temporary imbalance that is geared toward resolving high-stakes issues. Once the issues are resolved, they bounce back by restoring balance among their leadership roles. Leadership greatness is knowing when to relinquish control and empower others to take the lead, rather than always acting at the forefront. Clutch leaders have the special talent to recognize situations that require a "slam dunk" approach at critical junctures where multiple factors align for crucial decisions or actions, then step back as the best course of action for co-creation and high involvement.

Avoiding the Trap of Quick Wins

During disruptions, the trust that employees have in their leaders shapes the interpretation of insecurity and uncertainty, as the perceived threat is reduced to the extent to which employees believe in their leadership's ability to create a safe environment. Leaders whose words and deeds are misaligned, who are overly competitive, boastful, and presenting quick wins in a grandiose way, invariably find it challenging to rebuild trust in their organizations. Without getting teams on board or neglecting to mobilize support for the change, such leaders may be susceptible to the "Quick Wins Paradox" (Van Buren & Safferstone, 2009). In pursuit of short-term results, whether sustainable or not, such leaders often resort to overconfidence, falling into arrogance traps that prevent them from generating the goodwill necessary to gain support in crucial moments.

Rather than conveying excessive self-importance and personal pride – that harmful "blind spot" that often creates negative experiences, after slam dunk wins – it would be advisable for leaders to demonstrate humility, self-control, and mindfulness. Indeed, at times of crisis, humility signifies a modest and unassuming attitude essential for sharing positive outcomes and working with team members to sustain the collective gains. Lack of humility and poor self-control (or self-regulation) may unleash an unintended consequence of fueling the atmosphere with toxicity – the dark side of leadership.

To counter the paradox of quick wins, clutch leaders lessen the urge for self-aggrandizing or for branding themselves as heroes. They resort back to non-binary or balanced leadership which integrates important personality traits – *assertiveness* with *agreeableness*, *openness* with *conscientiousness* – ensuring that no single trait becomes overly dominant. Such a leadership mode enables them to operate within the "sweet spot" – to move forward with plans and goals while considering the well-being of team members (Belasen & Frank, 2008).

Extreme events require clutch leaders to display excess assertiveness, which is much needed for critical decisions. However, they also rely on agreeableness to build consensus during emergent (and often unknown) situations (Freitag & Bauer, 2016). Once the crisis is resolved, both conscientiousness and openness become effective for developing trust. In this context, trust plays a vital role as the foundation upon which a leader can successfully rebalance these diverse, potentially mutually exclusive traits and preserve the "sweet spot."

Adaptive Personality Traits

Trust is the glue that binds followers and their leaders during disruptive times. Clutch leaders with adaptive personality traits focus on the common purpose, are inspirational, and project trustworthiness and empathy to ensure people stay calm and engaged in creative problem-solving (Bajaba, 2021). The unique talent of clutch leaders to balance high-stress, big-picture thinking with composure, agility with attention to details, and strong logical reasoning with communication skills and empathy allows them to navigate challenging events successfully.

Effective leaders have the capacity to moderate the intensity of personality traits – *assertiveness, openness, conscientiousness,* and *agreeableness* – the set of unseen characteristics that underlie behavior in routine situations or in response to extreme events (Belasen & Frank, 2012). Therefore, in this chapter, we also introduce an assessment tool of personality traits to illustrate the dynamic interplay between balanced and imbalanced leadership profiles.

Trait Extremes – Imbalance

Most trait extremes result from stressful challenges associated with disruptions, transitions, workload pressure, time urgency, uncertainty, or unachievable goals. Some executives respond by keeping a low profile or staying away, while others resort to overemphasizing their dominant trait. When trait extremes are prolonged beyond the triggered event (i.e., leaders neglect to restore balance), the leader is likely to be perceived negatively by others, often resulting in mistrust and a lack of confidence in the ability of leaders to meet stated objectives.

Assertive (take charge, challenger, competitive, extroverted) – The capacity to quickly analyze the situation and make choices with limited information; possessing the self-confidence to look beyond the immediate crisis (or quick wins) to develop long-term recovery plans and mitigate future risks.

Openness (innovative, entrepreneurial, big-picture thinking, adventurous) – The behavioral flexibility critical for adjusting strategies and plans as the crisis evolves and embracing new information in the face of changing circumstances.

Conscientious (rational, task oriented, precise, maintains order) – Being recognized as a reliable leader who is highly organized, dependable, responsible, and focused on implementing plans and achieving goals by prioritizing work ethics.

Agreeable (cooperative, friendly, good-natured, supportive) – Understanding the emotions and concerns of those affected by the crisis, demonstrating compassion and support.

Leaders fail to deliver when they experience:

- Difficulty in leading teams and work units (not assertive).
- An absence of behavioral flexibility (not open to new ideas).
- An inability to execute to meet objectives (not conscientious).
- Troubled interpersonal relationships or contentiousness (not agreeable).

Examples of imbalance in personality traits during crisis situations are adapted from Belasen (2016) and appear in the next four figures. The necessity to restore these "profiles" during stable times is evident.

The Social Cost of Getting Stuck – Toxic Leadership

Mindfulness and self-regulation are the antecedents that distinguish effective leaders from toxic leaders who "get stuck" in the "negative zone" (or "blind spot") without worrying about any gaps in their behaviors or how they are perceived by others. They often become self-absorbed and self-centered and tend to respond with exaggerated egocentricity and diminished adaptive regulation. Typically, they operate from the top of the pyramid and commonly rely on their charisma and glibness to draw attention to their goals, whether or not those align with the best interests of the organization. When followers accept the values of leaders without questioning their motives or moral reasoning, they also migrate to the leaders' sphere of influence quickly and effectively.

In turn, those leaders perpetuate the imbalance in their leadership mode by using their unmitigated power and control as important levers to continuously overcome objections or eliminate opponents. They are apt to resort to Machiavellian behavior, placing political expediency above morality to augment their power and use it for personal gain and self-promotion. More importantly, they consolidate their centralized authority by using fear and intimidation tactics that also fuel paranoia and impulsive decision-making (Padilla et al., 2007).

In the extreme version, toxic leaders epitomize narcissism. They are manipulative, selfish, and patronizing. They view themselves as the "face" of their base, which supports them blindly. Therefore, whatever incentivizes the leader has an oversized impact on those in their base, because such leaders perceive themselves as "owning" the group. These leaders are self-absorbed with an inflated sense of their personal value and are excessively preoccupied with their personal adequacy, attributes, self-importance, and growth goals.

Toxic leaders thrive on the vulnerabilities of those in their orbits. They create dependence of followers on them for survival by exploiting frailties and by reframing a worldview that is saturated with tensions, conflicts, and instability, further strengthening their value proposition as the sole "fixers." These leaders often communicate with group members through rhetoric rich with metaphors and messages containing images of hate or violence. This is accomplished by promoting the superiority and solidarity of the leader-centric primary group and by devaluing outsiders and rivals. Group members are made to feel as if they were under attack by rivals and that the only way to survive is through their continued loyalty to the leader and unquestionable support (Belasen, 2016).

Excess Assertiveness

Excessive assertiveness (Figure 1.1) is triggered by monopolizing airtime during team meetings, dominating the narratives, and not listening to others. These leaders are disrespectful of others' viewpoints and have domineering presences. They are distrusted until proven trustworthy and often are perceived by followers as ineffective.

It is quite conceivable that by simply listening more and seeking areas of commonality and paying more attention to ideas and alternatives proposed by others, the adverse consequences of assertiveness can be mitigated. To avoid prolonging this trait extreme beyond the crisis resolution, effective clutch performance avoids the tendency to start by defining problems in terms of proposed

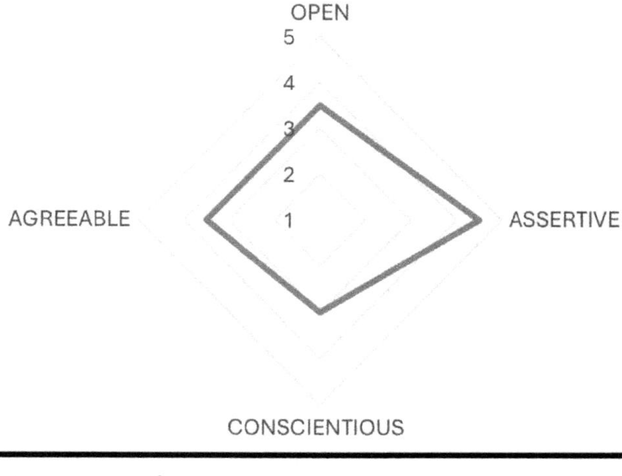

Figure 1.1 Excess assertiveness.

solutions. Asking the right questions rather than prescribing solutions is a great adjustment that can help shift the profile in Figure 1 more toward the center, that of balanced leadership.

Excess Openness

Being open to new ideas is a highly desired asset for leading during disruptive times. It allows the leader to broaden the scope of alternatives and implement the strategy with the best chances of surviving pushback or possible resistance. This is especially important since disruption constitutes either a novel set of circumstances or conditions which may have been present but are now significantly heightened in their degree of challenge – in either case, the inflow of new ideas could mean the difference between a successful outcome and failure.

Openness is associated with behavioral flexibility, permeability, and resilience. Too much creativity or an excess of innovative thinking (the paradox of "what if"), with one idea followed by another compelling idea and so on, may lead to a perception of the leader as a disorganized external or a great abstract thinker, but one without the ability to achieve closure (Figure 1.2).

Excess in this trait is often the result of perfection-seeking and the constant need to look for or experiment with more ideas. Too much abstract thinking creates unnecessary complexity and is confusing and distracting. One remedy is taking some clues from others and understanding when the pursuit of perfection becomes the needless enemy of good.

Encouraging mistakes and risk-taking by drawing on other traits or by shifting some of the excess energy from change and adaptation to stability and

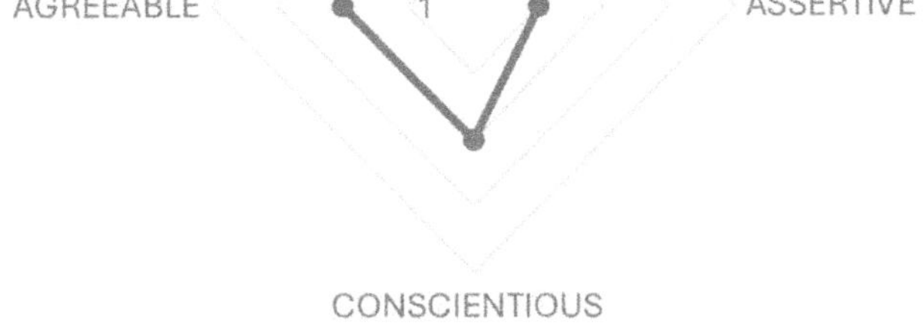

Figure 1.2 Excess openness.

control may help restore trust and shift the leader's attention to the other traits, thus recreating the balance. Widening the span of attention to include the opposite trait by becoming more conscientious or shifting sideways by reducing ambiguity (becoming more assertive) and by communicating realistic ideas and options more clearly (becoming more agreeable) will help recreate the balance.

Excess Conscientiousness

Conscientiousness reflects structure and discipline, formal logic, efficiency, and attention to detail. The conscientious leader prefers to follow rules and embrace the status quo. Excess in this trait (Figure 1.3) might create the perception that the leader is an obsessive monitor who tends to micromanage people and processes.

While conscientious behavior might get leaders some of the results they expect, in the long run, it is a losing proposition as followers, peers, and other stakeholders may resent this style or switch to questioning the validity of the leader's core assumptions. Micromanagers risk disempowering their followers, thereby increasing the risk of burnout and losing employees' confidence and trust.

A straightforward remedy is to balance the demands of this quadrant (trait) for control and details with openness (opposite quadrant), engagement (adjacent quadrant), and acceptance (agreeableness). Playing the role of devil's advocate (posing "what if" scenarios) might help balance the need for control, details, and boundaries (rather than for ideas as in the case of openness) with the need for flexibility.

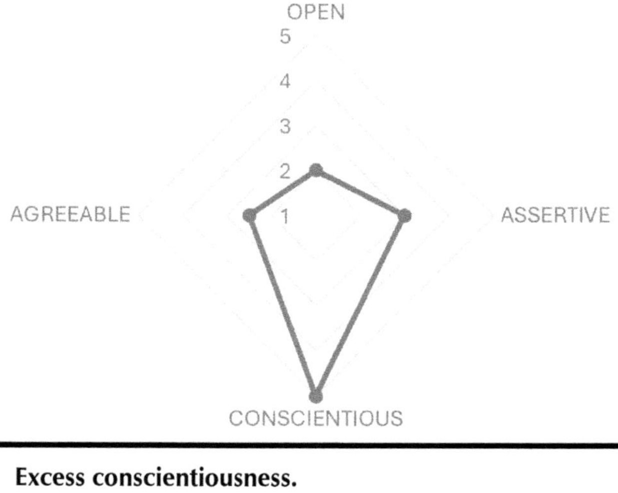

Figure 1.3 Excess conscientiousness.

Excess Agreeableness

Agreeable leaders who employ this trait to excess are non-confrontational and tend to avoid conflicts and disruptions. While they thrive in harmonious relationships, they often appear too weak and vulnerable. This is true when agreeableness is pushed to the extreme (Figure 1.4) – to the point at which the leader is perceived as too permissive, good tempered and easygoing.

Under these conditions, followers may perceive the leader as less confident and unassertive, someone who cannot be effective during times of crisis. One way to mitigate the soft tendencies of agreeableness is to become more assertive, competitive, and rational (qualities associated with the opposite trait), thus restoring balance.

Balancing the expectations of this trait with the demands of the other traits can help bring more structure and clarity and generate better ideas for solving problems. Practicing situational leadership (knowing when to intervene and when to let go) is a productive way to reduce the effects of excess in this trait and balance individual considerations with task orientation.

With their strong self-awareness skills, effective clutch leaders recognize the dynamic interplay between "sweet spots" and "blind spots" and when to get unstuck or avoid the trap of the quick wins paradox. When crises erupt, clutch leaders rise to the surface with resilience and confidence, typically drawing on a temporary imbalance in leadership style with strengths that are geared toward resolving the disruption. Once the situation calms, clutch leaders bounce back by recreating their balanced leadership style.

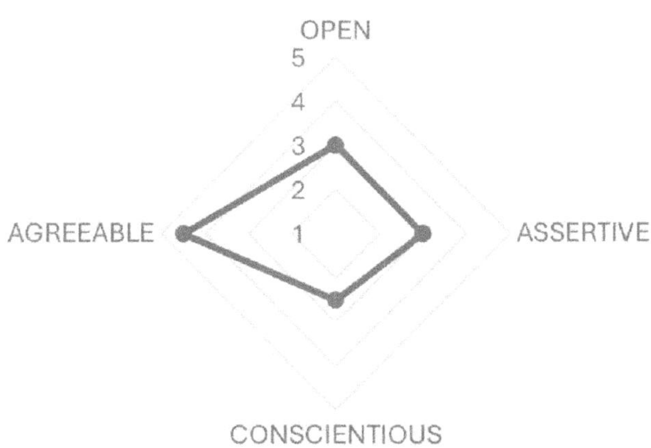

Figure 1.4 Excess agreeableness.

Balanced Leadership

Self-regulation distinguishes effective clutch leaders as having strong emotional intelligence, impulse control, and self-discipline that drive success. Evidence shows that leaders with high self-regulation were among the most successful leaders during the fight against the COVID-19 pandemic. Strong self-regulation skills create opportunities for better communication, positive team dynamics, enhanced motivation, and increased trust. Self-regulation is maintained through (1) the setting of internal standards, which can be existing standards or newly formulated ones, (2) the evaluation of discrepancies between these standards and actual or potential outcomes, and (3) the identification of intended actions for resolving these discrepancies (Gardner, et. al., 2005).

Knowing when to become unstuck, successful clutch leaders do not fall prey to the temptation to drift toward toxicity or prolong trait extremes. Operating in the positive zone of balanced leadership (Figure 1.5) allows the leader to bridge the gap between desired and undesired behaviors by using inputs from others, play to their strengths, and realign their behaviors with the generally accepted norms.

Example scenarios of balanced leadership in action include:

- A CEO acting quickly and credibly to establish project teams to address a major product recall by swiftly implementing quality control measures and transparent communication with customers.

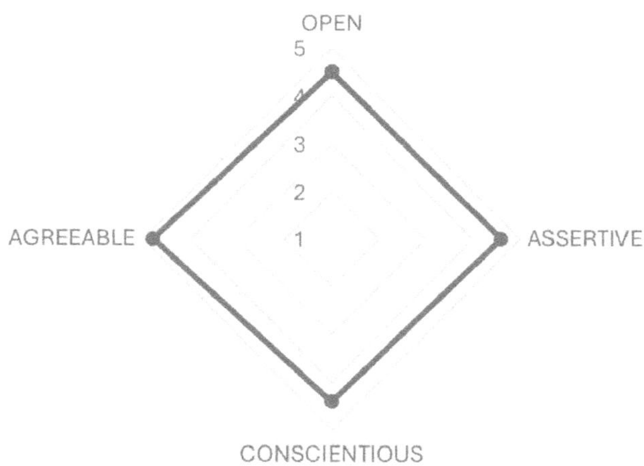

Figure 1.5 Balanced personality traits.

- A hospital executive making critical decisions which affect bed occupancy numbers while maintaining the overflow rate at a reasonable level during a health crisis, such as in a public health outbreak or mass injury, ensuring patient care while managing care teams' morale.
- A government leader projecting a calm demeanor during a natural disaster, coordinating emergency response efforts and reassuring the public with credible and transparent messages.
- A community leader stepping up to provide guidance and structure during a time of significant disruption or emergency, often setting the tone in coordinating relief efforts, disseminating vital information, updating the public, communicating a caring attitude, and ensuring the well-being of residents.

Leaders must also be adept at receiving and evaluating feedback on the effectiveness of their decisions and behaviors. Absent that, they are unlikely to change and improve. Experience demonstrates that shifting significant decision-making input to those closest to managing the health crisis improves organizational agility and enhances innovation. The Seattle-based Swedish Health Services' senior executives showed that delegating decision-making not only flattened the hierarchy but also empowered caregiver teams to develop creative responses to the unique challenges posed by COVID-19 (Dale, Welling, & Clearfield, 2020).

Structure of the Book

The leadership dynamics described in the five parts of this book demonstrate the transformative nature of clutch leadership across internal and external environments. Each part contains either one or two chapters with distinct themes that reflect the challenges faced by clutch leaders during extreme events. Taken together, the five parts and chapters in this book represent a holistic view of how and why clutch leaders shift from "Slam Dunk" to "Sweet Spot" for bigger payoffs. The assessment frameworks in this book can also be used diagnostically for further assessment and development to strengthen the new leadership mindset.

The Pentagon Framework (Figure 1.6) reflects the clutch leader's span of attention, focusing on five key areas essential for strong and well-rounded leadership. It demonstrates possibilities for self-development – from actual to a more desired behavioral pattern that are accepted and supported by others. These five areas of focus parallel the five parts in this book – "Awareness Competencies," "Trust and Reliability, Operational Efficiency," "Innovation and Ethics," and "Strategic Disruption." A Pentagon Framework represents a balanced approach

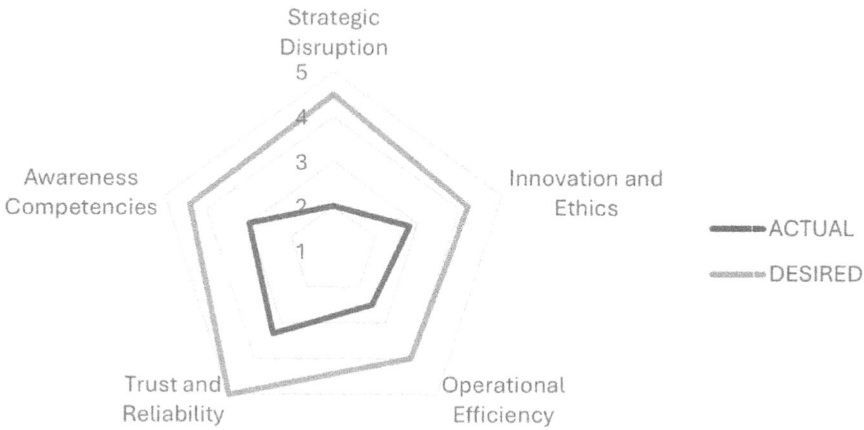

Figure 1.6 Key areas of clutch leadership.

of prioritizing all five areas equally, where no single area is neglected at the expense of another.

Awareness competencies include strong self-understanding of strengths and weaknesses and heightened social intelligence skills, which foster a culture of commitment, investments in people's growth, and empowerment of individuals to reach their full potential.

Trust and reliability reflect the consistency with which expected outcomes are achieved and the extent to which trust is preserved in and around the organization. Clutch leaders are expected to be transparent, accountable, credible, and honest – the foundation for trustworthy leadership.

Operational efficiency focuses on creating agile structures, optimizing processes, managing resources effectively, and ensuring the implementation of AI technologies and related information management tools to achieve peak performance.

Innovation and ethics center on the relationship between emerging technologies and ethical standards, demonstrating integrity and upholding principles of care and accountability in innovation implementation.

Strategic disruption focuses on balancing change and stability throughout the supply chain, developing long-term goals, and anticipating future challenges to guide the growth of the organization.

By considering all five areas holistically, clutch leaders can nurture a well-focused approach to dealing with disruptive events and rebalance their leadership mode to foster a strong, sustainable organization.

Part A – Awareness Competencies

Chapter 2 – Clutch Leadership during Disruptions

This chapter examines the relationship between vital leadership traits and building and maintaining trust, and most specifically, how their interplay influences leadership performance in the face of a crisis. When an unanticipated high-pressure situation suddenly emerges, stakeholders seek reassurance, typically by demanding transparency, honesty, credibility, and accountability. While some leaders rise to the occasion, it is not uncommon for others to succumb to a desire for a rapid way out, resorting to denial, finger-pointing, minimization of the problem's scope, and communication avoidance.

With examples from different industries, this chapter identifies how trustworthiness in organizations can be developed and preserved during a crisis. We demonstrate that the "clutch" leader is well-positioned to temporarily shift the balance among the dimensions of trustworthy leadership to successfully navigate crises. Ethical considerations through vignettes and scenario examples illustrate the significance of establishing personal integrity that drives joint accountability in and around the organizations. Moreover, we show how organizational cultures rooted in evidence-based practice are more hospitable to building the very trust necessary to mobilize support for successfully navigating disruptive waters. In so doing, clutch leaders can use disruptive experience to reinforce the mission and values of the organization to capitalize on future opportunities.

Keywords: *Crisis, Trustworthiness, Transparency, Honesty, Credibility, Accountability, Ethics, Assessment, Evidence*

Part B – Trust and Reliability

Chapter 3 – Navigating Disruption

This chapter explores the vital role of empathy in leading through disruption. In doing so, the goals and benefits of empathetic leadership are presented along with practical strategies for developing this critical skill.

Disruption is ever-present. As organizations navigate transitional challenges such as technological advancements, economic shifts, restructuring, and policy and regulatory changes, organizational leaders must not lose sight of the proposition that the work of the organization is accomplished by people. Accordingly, today's leaders must discover ways to preserve and even strengthen employee motivation and inspire a shared vision. The centerpiece of such a leadership model is *empathy*.

Empathetic leaders foster supportive and inclusive cultures because of their genuine concern and sensitivity to their employees' needs for professional gratification and belief that the organization's values are in sync with their own. Valuing employees contributes to a culture of socio-psychological safety, motivation, and collaboration, all of which are closely tied to organizational success. Therefore, it is understandable that empathetic leadership is especially important in times of uncertainty.

Special emphasis in this chapter is placed on the role of empathetic leadership in driving digital transformation. Vignettes and scenarios are employed to illustrate how empathetic leaders can advance organizations in the face of disruption. These scenario-based examples demonstrate how empathy can help leaders support their teams through specific challenges like resistance to change, fear of job loss related to AI, and learning new systems.

Moreover, clutch leaders recognize that a culture of trust and respect is essential for promoting experimentation and innovation, along with productivity and confidence enhancement. As such, this chapter provides a framework designed to equip leaders to foster transformation through employee empowerment, relationship building, and buy-in, all essential in the face of instability and flux. As disruptive forces continue to threaten institutions, empathetic leaders are best prepared to convert those threats into opportunities.

Keywords: *Leadership, Empathy, Culture, Trust, Care, Empowerment*

Chapter 4 – Lessons for Clutch Leadership

This chapter explores how High Reliability Organization (HRO) principles, cultivated within military leadership, can be applied to civilian organizations, especially those facing disruption and uncertainty. It highlights key competencies such as resilience, adaptability, risk awareness, and ethical decision-making, offering actionable strategies for leaders to foster reliability and agility.

Further, the chapter provides guidance for transitioning into a High Reliability Organization (HRO) in multiple capacities, including into positions for which direct experience from the military is appropriate, as well as for positions which indirectly benefit from skill transference. We also identify potential barriers to skill transferability, such as cultural misalignment and underutilization, while offering action pathways for addressing these challenges. Through illustrative case studies and practical examples, this framework provides clutch leaders with insights to perform under high-stress situations, cope with disruptive changes, adapt effectively, and thrive under pressure.

Keywords: *Reliability, Agility, Resilience, Adaptability, Risk Awareness, Ethical Decision-Making*

Part C – Operational Efficiency

Chapter 5 – Project Leadership in the AI Age

Integrating practical insights with strategic frameworks, this chapter provides a comprehensive roadmap for leaders aiming to thrive amid digital disruption. It underscores the qualities of empowerment, urgency, and high aspiration that define clutch leadership, offering actionable strategies for aligning organizations with the demands of an AI-driven era. By driving ethical, innovative, and inclusive AI applications, clutch leaders can foster long-term value creation and organizational resilience in an era of constant transformation.

The transformative impact of artificial intelligence (AI) on project leadership, including the challenges it imposes and the opportunities it creates, is explored in detail. Drawing on case studies from industries such as healthcare, technology, and manufacturing, it examines the successes and failures of AI-driven leadership strategies. Practical insights demonstrate how project leaders leverage AI to enhance adaptability, improve productivity, foster ethical decision-making, and achieve measurable outcomes.

The chapter also delves into the human dimensions of AI leadership, emphasizing the importance of cultivating trust in data-driven insights, fostering employee adaptability through targeted reskilling, and promoting inclusivity and equity in AI system deployment. It examines critical ethical dilemmas inherent in AI utilization, such as algorithmic bias, privacy concerns, and accountability in automated decision-making. It provides actionable frameworks to navigate these challenges effectively, including ethical AI guidelines and transparent governance structures.

As an example, the chapter highlights how algorithmic biases can disproportionately affect women in leadership roles, with recruitment algorithms potentially undervaluing soft skills and gendered language biases influencing leadership evaluations. By highlighting these challenges, the chapter emphasizes the necessity for developing inclusive AI systems through diverse datasets and rigorous testing and for leaders to adopt frameworks like the Gender Equality Principles for AI in leadership contexts.

Keywords: *Clutch Leadership, AI in Project Leadership, Digital Transformation, Inclusive Leadership, Ethical Leadership, Strategic Innovation*

Chapter 6 – Aligning Innovation Strategy with Leadership

Healthcare organizations are experiencing unprecedented challenges, driven by a confluence of forces, including rapidly evolving technological advancements, burgeoning compliance pressures, financial strains, ever-increasing expectations related to service and quality, and, of course, information tools that possess revolutionary impact potential. Drawing on established management theories and real-world examples, this chapter explores the critical leadership skills necessary for navigating momentous healthcare transformations, particularly those that challenge the status quo and, thus, require bold action.

Four action pathways to drive transformative change and foster innovation are presented along with case studies of healthcare organizations that have successfully steered through significant transformation:

- Innovation and adaptability: Today's successful leaders encourage a culture of innovation and creativity, cultivate calculated risk-taking, embrace new technologies and services, and leverage evidence-based decision-making to drive continuous organizational improvement.
- Engagement and collaboration: The essential role of emotional intelligence in healthcare leadership is highlighted, offering insights on building trust, managing conflicts, motivating teams to achieve organizational goals, and engaging effectively with patients, staff, and community partners.
- Change management and organizational coordination: Emerging challenges demand pragmatic strategies for optimal integration, fostering buy-in, implementing effective strategies to maximize resource utilization, and aligning diverse departments and stakeholders around shared goals.
- Strategic agility and stakeholder communication: Techniques for developing and communicating vision and strategy to stakeholders at all levels are provided. This section also explores methods for maintaining strategic flexibility, particularly in the face of uncertainty, and making timely strategic decisions.

Using cases and practical examples, this chapter highlights the role of clutch leaders in navigating the interplay of entrepreneurialism, operational excellence, motivational strategies, ethical wherewithal, and visionary thinking, vital for driving innovation, improving patient care, and achieving successful outcomes.

By mastering these essential leadership skills, healthcare leaders can successfully manage the complexities of organizational transformation and create a sustainable future for their organizations.

Keywords: *Leadership Skills, Healthcare, Transformation, Innovation, Strategy*

Part D – Innovation and Ethics

Chapter 7 – Ethical Leadership in an Era of AI

The 21st century is no stranger to rapidly advancing technology. Artificial Intelligence, a technology capable of mimicking human decision-making, has swiftly become the latest and most progressive technological advancement. The release of generative AI tools creates both optimism and apprehension, and some might even add fear and anxiety. In healthcare, AI offers the potential to improve research, patient care, and education in the field, which could contribute to long-term efficiencies of resources and patient outcomes.

The use of AI, large language models, and machine learning technologies gives rise to predictive outcomes and diagnoses on a more massive scale with every passing day. Moreover, the strategic implementation and ethical implications of the use of AI are both vast and open to consideration. Application of AI in clinical practice, in particular, raises concerns related but not limited to informed consent in the use of AI from patients, bias and discriminatory information produced by AI-generated content, unintentional fostering of intellectual laziness, and errors created by missed interpretations. The delivery of healthcare, with the explicit intent of optimizing speed and accuracy of diagnosis while minimizing errors and harm, has always grappled with how to best use tools that achieve those objectives.

Healthcare is not alone in wrestling with the ethical implications posed by AI and Open AI technology. For example, with respect to the legal field, the New York State Bar has cautioned attorneys to make certain that AI does not put attorney-client privilege at risk, citing the potential exposure of confidential information from lagging security issues in the use of AI.

The alarming rate at which all forms of artificial intelligence are being advanced requires clutch leaders who can move through a disruptive state with a sense of intellectual inquiry, a strong moral compass, appropriate caution, and the ability to formulate vision despite the vast unknown without fear of pivoting quickly. Hence, this chapter explores where applications of AI in healthcare are making positive inroads both clinically and administratively, where AI is ineffective with respect to patient care, and how leaders can best stay in the zone, amid the rapid advancement of AI while keeping an ethical mindset.

Keywords: *Artificial Intelligence, Ethics, Healthcare, Leadership, Clinical Practice*

Chapter 8 – Clutch Leadership and Digital Transformation

At the heart of this chapter lies the concept of trust in the context of digital transformation. To remain relevant in a competitive market, a growing number of organizations are embracing the opportunities triggered by digital transformation. These technological advancements, when applied to business operation processes, have the potential to produce more value and foster a sense of optimism and hope. However, due to its disruptive nature, implementing transformation requires cooperation and collaboration from all parties, including clients and employees, and their cooperation depends on their trust in the process.

The chapter explores the connection between digital transformation, trust, and engagement by applying empirical evidence based on expert insights from direct interviews and case studies. Actionable steps to guide the implementation of technological advances are provided in addition to highlighting practical strategies for building trust and encouraging engagement for improved business outcomes.

The chapter underscores the pivotal role of transparency and effective communication, including active listening and empathy, in fostering trust and the power of personalization in boosting engagement. It stresses the need to understand and cater to the unique needs of stakeholders and customers. Furthermore, it addresses potential barriers and ethical considerations associated with the delicate balance between digital and human-driven engagement strategies, resolving personalization data protection issues, and managing privacy and security concerns.

Keywords: *Digital transformation, trust, engagement, transparency, personalization, AI, organizational psychology, effective communication, ethics*

Part E – Strategic Disruption

Chapter 9 – Bold Leadership vs. Epic Failures

This chapter explores the dichotomy of bold leadership and epic failures within the context of global supply chain management by examining novel approaches to critical situations such as consolidation, international expansion, diversification, and the acceleration of contingency plans. It expands the concept of first-mover advantage in supply chain management by incorporating technological, ethical, and risk dimensions. Additionally, environmental, social, and governance factors, along with trends related to Sustainable Development Goals, will assist with addressing emerging challenges, including legal, environmental, and sociopolitical issues.

Through the analysis of case studies, the chapter illustrates the practical application of pioneering strategies, experimentation, and venturing into new frontiers. It explores pathways to successful operational excellence, scrutinizing the integration of reliable solutions with flexible resources to create dynamic and agile organizations. The chapter also identifies the red flags of future potential business disasters, offering valuable insights for proactive decision-making.

The chapter follows a functional perspective of leadership decisions with the vision of a future global business system driven by blockchain and AI technologies. It is written as a transformative inspiration for clutch leaders preparing for urgent and instant interventions during global disruptions. Emphasis is placed on the central role of leadership in balancing efficiency and resilience in a rapidly evolving global economy. Practical insights and actionable strategies offer a framework for addressing current and future challenges, making this chapter a vital resource for fostering sustainable and robust supply chain ecosystems.

Keywords: *Global Supply Chain Management, International Business, ESG Factors, AI Technologies, Risk Management*

Part F – In Perspective

Chapter 10 – Harnessing the Power of Character, Intuition, and Empowerment of Clutch Leaders

This concluding chapter has three purposes. The first is to recap the relevant and applicable expectations, attributes, and skills that clutch leaders use to drive disruptive innovation and mitigate the costs of change. In so doing, we demonstrate how enormously impactful events such as the COVID-19 pandemic, as well as threats to individual companies, underscore the crucial nature of leadership and give rise to an overarching question: can leadership meet extreme moments?

Major disruptions require responsible leaders to be aware of their vulnerabilities, to empower and trust others to carry out critical tasks. Acknowledging weaknesses and adjusting for them in the scope of responses to crisis situations is the essence of dependability. This leadership predilection not only enhances stakeholder perceptions of the leader's self-awareness and relational transparency but also benefits followers, paving the way for those followers to unleash their full potential. Such leaders are effective in creating safe work environments and in achieving positive and enduring outcomes when their organizations are tested.

The second purpose builds on the skills and attributes of clutch leadership that are presented throughout this book by addressing the seemingly intangible yet indispensable trait of *character*, the synergistic interplay of our mental and moral impetuses that drive our choice-making tendencies and fuel our tenacity to achieve beneficial outcomes. But clutch leaders do not exercise drive with blinder-free recklessness. Their self-confidence and risk-taking are tempered by the critical restraining qualities of self-regulation and self-discipline. And their decisiveness is balanced against a sharp eye for situationally pertinent input from others, which strengthens the decision-making probability of achieving favorable outcomes.

Third, while much of this book naturally focuses on the organizational decision-maker, we firmly believe that clutch leadership is not confined to the person at the top of the organizational chart. We posit that everyone has the capacity to be a clutch leader. In the end, clutch leadership is more about the determination and ability to make a positive difference in a challenging moment than it is about one's formal role. This book, then, is a roadmap for each of us to find our clutch leader within.

Closing Thoughts

Chapter 1 focused on profile awareness as a powerful medium for rebalancing the leader's mode of behavior. Self-assessment tools are designed to reveal personal vulnerabilities and how others perceive the behaviors and traits of clutch leaders. Executives can use these instruments to evaluate potential gaps in their own behaviors and develop plans to enhance their capacity to shift and balance their leadership style as needed.

Each chapter in the book is more than a collection of ideas. It is a part of a broader leadership framework that describes action pathways and how and why clutch leaders use winning strategies to achieve the best results for the organization. Each chapter in this book provides a unique contribution that is distinct and, at the same time, connected to other chapters through the Pentagon's organizing framework by showing how the key areas of clutch leadership are interrelated. For example, leaders cannot invest in innovative digital technology to enhance coordination ("Operational Efficiency") without considering the impact of these investments on employees and teams ("Awareness Competencies"). They cannot introduce disruptive innovation ("Strategic Disruption") without considering its impact on customers, partners, stakeholders, and employees ("Trust and Reliability").

In addition to enriching your learning about what makes a successful clutch leader, the book's chapters, which are authored by experts from diverse backgrounds, provide rich and broader perspectives for fostering a leadership profile in high-stake environments. Key benefits from this book include:

- Inspiring executives and professionals to think critically about shifting priorities.
- Mapping relevant leadership skills for dealing with high-stake environments.
- Understanding the ethics of shifting priorities in organizational operations.
- Providing strategies for regaining self-confidence after making tough choices.
- Offering insights into assessing and leveraging personal strengths.
- Sharing best practices of clutch leaders across organizations and industries.

The biggest impact of a clutch player in high-paced sports, such as basketball, in which lead swings happen quite frequently throughout the game – particularly during crucial time like the last two minutes (L2M), where a single basket, foul shot, or turnover can significantly alter the score and potential outcome, is their ability to significantly alter the outcome of a game by performing exceptionally well in high-pressure situations.

Clutch players seize the moment by believing in themselves and by knowing when to let go and get others involved. We hope that you will become the *Clutch Leader* of your organization.

References

Bajaba, A., Bajaba, S., Algarni, M., Basahal, A., & Basahel, S. (2021). Adaptive managers as emerging leaders during the COVID-19 crisis. *Frontiers in Psychology, 12*, 661628.

Belasen, A. & Frank, N. M. (2008). Competing values leadership: Quadrant roles and personality traits. *Leadership and Organizational Development Journal*, 29(2), 127–143.

Belasen, A. & Frank, N. M. (2012). Using the competing values framework to evaluate the interactive effects of gender and personality traits on leadership roles. *The International Journal of Leadership Studies*, 7(2), 192–215.

Belasen, A. (2016). Deception and failure: Mitigating leader-centric behaviors. In Belasen, A. & Toma, R. (Eds), *Confronting Corruption in Business: Trusted Leadership, Civic Engagement* (pp. 183–216), New York: Routledge.

Dale, C. R., Welling, L., & Clearfield, C. (2020). How one Seattle health system is managing the COVID-19 crisis. *Harvard Business Review*. Retrieved from https://hbr.org/2020/04/how-one-seattle-health-system-is-managing-the-covid-19-crisis

Freitag, M., & Bauer, P. C. (2016). Personality traits and the propensity to trust friends and strangers. *The Social Science Journal*, 53(4), 467–476.

Gardner, W., Avolio, B., Luthans, F., May, D., & Walumbwa, F. (2005). Can you see the real me? A self-based model of authentic leader and follower development. *The Leadership Quarterly*, 16(3), 343–372.

Padilla, A., Hogan, R., & Kaiser, R.B. (2007). The toxic triangle: Destructive leaders, vulnerable followers, and conducive environments. *Leadership Quarterly*, 18, 176–194.

Van Buren, M. E. & Safferstone, T. (2009). The quick wins paradox. *Harvard Business Review*, 87, 55–61.

AWARENESS COMPETENCIES

A

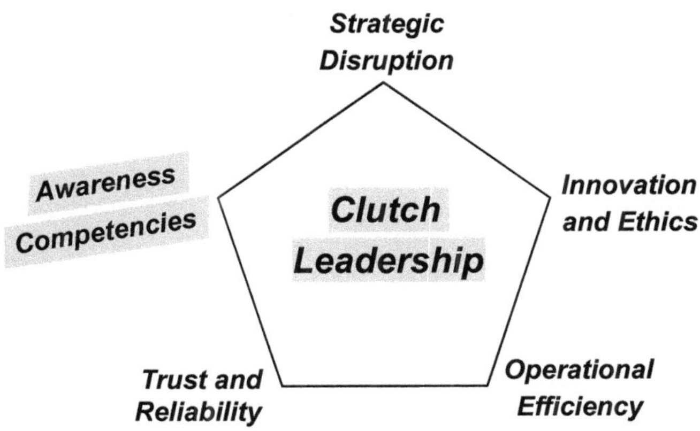

DOI: 10.4324/9781003629214-2

Chapter 2

Clutch Leadership during Disruptions: Prioritizing Ethics, Building Trust

Barry Eisenberg, Alan T. Belasen
and Amy Eisenberg

Introduction – Meeting the Moment

A crisis is a turning point in a situation in which concentrated and high-level decision-making is essential to address an urgent and generally unanticipated event. Sometimes, the incident brings strong potential for undesirable outcomes, including threats to an organization's reputation, financial status, or even survival. A crisis is often characterized as a situation that has a very low probability of occurrence, produces significant psychological impacts, shatters previously held notions that bad things cannot happen to individuals and organizations, and provides little response time.

Most organizational crises are announced by a "surprise" – an unexpected event, action, or incident that alters the public's view of the organization and which may pose a threat to human lives, property, and/or the environment. Of course, it also involves the need to respond quickly to employees, customers, and the media. How a leader manages a crisis can have significant effects

DOI: 10.4324/9781003629214-3

on the functioning of the organization, effects that have a variety of potential consequences. And the consequences can be quite serious; for example, the reputation of an organization can be damaged, its value threatened, operations disrupted, lawsuits from victimized consumers can be initiated, and swings in asset prices might be triggered. These consequences may become tipping points for stakeholders.

In this chapter, we set out to link common traits associated with clutch leadership to the ability to communicate effectively during a crisis. Clutch leaders with high efficacy tend to exert more effort toward urgent outcomes and persevere when facing unexpected challenges. A critical role of a clutch leader during a crisis is to sustain or rebuild trust in and around the organization. When information is diffused or limited, or when communication is ambiguous, the desire for *transparency, honesty, credibility,* and *accountability* – the dimensions of trustworthy leadership – increases (Belasen & Belasen, 2024). When communication is clear, empathic, transparent, and timely, internal dialogues are more positive and constructive, and people show more confidence in the ability of leaders to avert negative outcomes (Belasen & Eisenberg, 2023).

In the next sections, we describe the roles of clutch leaders in mitigating the negative consequences of crises, building and preserving trust, and creating opportunities for collaboration and joint accountability. We then discuss communication and messaging strategies, introduce important dimensions of trustworthiness, highlight ways to overcome imbalance tendencies in trustworthy leadership traits, demonstrate how trustworthiness is rooted in making ethical choices that place a premium on having built a culture rooted in evidence and employee empowerment, and conclude with defining how self-regulation and ethical mindfulness are hallmarks of balanced leadership. Self-assessment of trustworthy leadership is also featured in this chapter.

Crisis Leadership

When a crisis occurs, attention is centered on how leaders manage the crisis in the moment. Clutch leaders who frame crises as transformative are more open-minded and flexible, can adapt quickly and formulate constructive solutions for recovery, as well as validate the experiences of organizational members. Renewal is central to growth from the crisis and requires the leader to exemplify hope and optimism toward positive outcomes. They walk a fine line between operational and relational systems, addressing the recovery of both operations and employees. This may involve rebuilding trust through improved communication, updating and sharing information, advancing new knowledge, and securing resources that enable learning, and improving the capacity to assess and manage unexpected socioeconomic shocks to the organizational system.

Great crisis leaders earn the public's trust. The public views such leaders as acting with clarity, focus, transparency, and compassion (Dubrin, 2013). Without transparency, the public may sense deception, which can reduce the credibility of the leader. In the wake of the COVID-19 pandemic, Singapore's political leadership delivered a series of informative and medically accurate communications. In doing so, they succeeded in conveying clear and trustworthy advice to the public consistent with the best available public health information. The cohesive messaging and understanding that detailed knowledge matters and that the health and economic risks were asymmetrically distributed also facilitated confidence-building, enhanced leadership credibility, and strengthened public trust.

While Singapore had early cases of infection, it had been broadly effective in limiting the spread of COVID-19 despite the high level of commercial and economic engagement with China. The focus on facts and credible advice from the government played an important role in building trust and showing unity. But the soundness of advice and accuracy of information are not enough. Effective leadership requires a commitment to engage with all pertinent constituencies, driven by the belief that their understanding will prove central to their motivation to comply with that advice. The messaging was consistently clear and evidence-based, and the public had remained well-informed throughout the multiple stages of the pandemic.

Managing a Crisis

While it is challenging to plan for every crisis scenario, it is critical to identify those who will be involved in the decision-making process. Additionally, it is imperative that the roles and responsibilities of those in charge be clearly delineated to mitigate the potential for unpreparedness, ignorance, absence, silence, distance, untruthfulness, and naiveté. Unpreparedness involves the lack of a cohesive plan and/or the capacity to effectively disseminate information and updates to external audiences.

In the context of leadership, ignorance is essentially tantamount to not being attuned to the potential for a crisis, including the wealth of implications, emergent priorities, and/or the information needs of key stakeholders, including those who may appear on the periphery, such as families, the media, and the public. At this point, credibility and trust are at stake, and executives need to demonstrate accountability by disclosing important and relevant information. If they become invisible, that is, if they are absent from the situation, remain silent, or avoid tough inquiries, they run the risk of losing their grip on the flow of information or suffer the consequences of tarnished credibility from which recovery can prove dauntingly challenging. Distance may involve pulling back too soon by creating unnecessary, and even conceivably dangerous, buffers between the organization and affected populations. Untruthfulness is not responding to inquiries forthrightly and on a timely basis, creating unnecessary confusion and increasing the anxiety of affected parties.

How a leader handles a crisis can have profound implications for its relationships with stakeholders, especially consumers. With increasingly open access to multiple channels of communication, consumers have become actively engaged players in the mass consumption, creation, and distribution of information. Faster, immediate, and multidirectional communications spread messages beyond their targeted audiences, making it more difficult to trace attitudes or changes or to monitor their direction and potential impact. Therefore, the leadership role is critical in diffusing the potential negative effects of crises and in restoring the public's trust. It is also important for leaders to maintain a sense of continuity, relevance, and consistency in the dissemination of information by remaining calm, visible, truthful, trustworthy, and responsive. Accurate and timely communication is always important, of course, but is especially vital during times of uncertainty.

Communication and Messaging Strategies

An important responsibility for communication strategists during crises is to create dialogic loops with useful information to all publics, employ user-oriented and accessible forms of communication, and post relevant and regular updates on a company's website to generate return visits. Paul Polman, Unilever's CEO, is a good example of someone who successfully engaged the media in February 2017 to rebuff a takeover bid by the food industry giant Kraft Heinz, strongly asserting that it lacked relevance to Unilever's internal and external stakeholder base and was inconsistent with its core business.

Once Polman rejected the offer, he published a statement explaining to the public – and particularly the company's shareholders – the rationale for rejecting the $143 billion offer. As part of the multifaceted strategy, Polman instructed executives to contact journalists to communicate the warning that a deal would cause immeasurable harm to the long-term-focused business model. Following the takeover fiasco, he used appearances on television, print media, conferences, and social media to continue to support his objection. "Do we choose to serve a few billionaires, or do we choose to serve the billions?" he tweeted on September 10, 2017. Polman's discourse underscores the important responsibility of focused leadership – influencing the public's perception and sustaining the positive image of the corporation.

When crises strike, they tend to overwhelm the communication channels of organizations, often causing miscalculations or tendencies to fall back on inadequate or misguided responses. Communication failures may include disconnects with stakeholders, rushes to judgment, overreactions, failure to act quickly, misreads of facts, lack of empathy, deflection of responsibilities, tunnel vision, reluctance to delegate, withholding information, and inadequate preparation. The problem is compounded by the tendency of highly competitive media outlets to add flavor to the reporting, including occasional sensationalism.

As such, organizations are advised to be prepared with a communication program that is organized around strategic messaging, capable of being rapidly disseminated, tailored to the distinct needs of different stakeholder groups, and sufficiently flexible to adapt to evolving circumstances. With a proactive approach, the organization's communication is more apt to become part of the media's story; absent that, the media could be inclined to focus far more fully on the incident, adding their own interpretation, potentially wedging the organization into a defensive communication posture.

A critical episode in Zoom's recent history is quite telling. Zoom, a company whose name has become virtually synonymous with videoconferencing, experienced a crisis of confidence just as its prospects were soaring, virtually exponentially, in early 2020. The COVID pandemic dramatically accelerated the rate of videoconferencing use in both social and business contexts. Zoom was well-positioned to be the leader in this phenomenon.

And yet, not long into the pandemic, concerns about privacy, encryption methods, and data management quickly gained traction. "Zoombombing," which involved the disruptive intrusions into meetings, became a regular feature in certain arenas.

Discussions surfaced in corporate America, in schools, and in government about curtailing the use of Zoom. Once unleashed, anxieties about confidentiality can easily mushroom. Unabated, such discussion could quickly translate into action, destabilizing Zoom and threatening its leading position in the videoconferencing market.

To its credit, the company took quick action. Rather than acting defensively and minimizing or denying the basis for the outcry, Eric Yuan, Zoom's President apologized: "We recognize that we have fallen short of the community's – and our own – privacy and security expectations. For that, I am deeply sorry" (Iyengar, 2020).

That apology accomplished at least two objectives. First, it constituted a foundation for the rebuilding of trust. By admitting fault, the company could no longer easily be charged with nefariousness. Second, the apology created a credible opportunity for Zoom to take corrective actions. Among the initiatives were (1) a suspension of new feature development so that the company could focus its energies on addressing the privacy and confidentiality flaws as well as (2) the preparation of "transparency" reports that would be shared with the corporate world, including social media companies that could now be enlisted as ambassadors of Zoom's efforts to restore user confidence.

The strategy of issuing a mea culpa to reestablish credibility and trust, followed by a well-delineated action plan, all connected through a comprehensive communication program targeted to Zoom's broad stakeholder universe, proved quite effective. Zoom's 1Q 2020 revenue was approximately $400 million. Its 4Q in 2020 was approximately $1 billion. Its 2Q 2024 earnings were approximately $1.14 billion, and it remains a leader in the teleconferencing industry.

Dimensions of Trustworthiness

Disruptions in operational practices invariably expose leaders' vulnerabilities, and how they access, understand, and act on evolving events reveals much about their capacity to handle those stressful episodes. Leaders can devise a well-synchronized communication plan that includes responses to early warning signals of a threatening crisis and action pathways to deal with the unexpected. The action pathways should be credible, transparent, and carried out by leaders who convey honesty and inspire joint accountability, essential for overcoming disruptions.

Transparency enables trustworthy leaders to learn from others and be willing to revise their existing disaster preparedness plans. *Accountability* reflects the importance of complying with regulations and communicating important information or pathways to stakeholders. *Credibility* reinforces important goals and interests, and the need to actively seek and hear feedback from employees. *Honesty* enables the trustworthy leader to promote openness and participation in the decision-making process, while holding members to high standards of truthfulness (Belasen & Eisenberg, 2023).

Trustworthy leaders acknowledge uncertainty, communicate with compassion, show understanding, and are empathic. Messaging that appeals to collective values and history plays a key role in enhancing public trust and stakeholders' acceptance (Belasen & Belasen, 2019). A good example of the process for regaining stakeholder acceptance involves the discovery in 2018 that Dr José Baselga, the Chief Medical Officer of Memorial Sloan-Kettering Cancer Center (MSKCC), a world premiere healthcare organization, "failed to disclose millions of dollars in payments from drug and health care companies in recent years, omitting his financial ties from dozens of research articles in prestigious publications" (Ornstein & Thomas, 2018).

Medical ethicists frown upon such arrangements, claiming that they open the door to questions about how studies on pharmaceutical products are structured and which medications will make their way to the market. Patients rightly want to believe that the sole reason physicians prescribe their specific medications is medical necessity, not because the prescriber has a financial interest in the company that manufactured it.

On a more macro level, over its long history, MSKCC has cultivated a reputation for research and clinical excellence. If the public came to believe that the hospital's medical staff was engaged in undisclosed profit-making from companies on whose boards they sit and, therefore, presumably influence the direction of their product development, the potential for reputation damage could surely arise.

The CEO of MSKCC, Dr Craig Thompson, took action to contain potential fallout and restore integrity to the healthcare organization's reputation. He and his spokespersons assembled a broad-based communications response which acknowledged the matter involving Dr Baselga while emphasizing MSKCC's opposition to such practice (*honesty*) and convening meetings of the medical staff, board, and other internal and external groups (*accountability*). Dr Baselga resigned from the medical center.

An MSKCC Task Force developed a series of recommendations, including that senior executive officers should be prohibited from serving on the boards of directors of for-profit health- or science-related companies (*credibility*). Incidentally, this action had sweeping implications for the health industry in which such board membership was not uncommon.

Finally, to prevent a recurrence of the potential conflict-of-interest scenario, a host of initiatives was undertaken (*transparency*). These included, but were not limited to, the implementation of a website in which updated conflict-of-interest policies would be shared in open forums and the hosting by MSKCC of symposia "with experts and stakeholders from across the biomedical research community as a first step toward developing a common framework that harmonizes financial disclosures in research publications" (Berns, 2019). Notably, internal and external stakeholder audiences were included in the largely proactive efforts to prevent reputational damage from manifesting in a way that otherwise could have been long-lasting and immensely costly.

For leaders managing crises, if any one of the four traits is removed, credibility is likely to suffer. Leaders gain credibility when they project compassion and demonstrate that they understand the risks and probable impact of unanticipated consequences. They are aware of their weaknesses and have the humility to defer to experts and delegate responsibilities to competent team members

(Petriglieri, 2020). It is important to acknowledge this paradox: by acknowledging limitations, the leader gains strength.

Measuring Trustworthiness

A survey has been developed and implemented to examine individual managers' perceptions of their own behaviors and levels of self-awareness with respect to the four pillars of strong clutch leadership (Belasen & Eisenberg, 2023; Belasen & Belasen, 2024). The survey questions address the extent to which managers focus on using inclusive leadership, are sensitive to stakeholders, whether they encourage feedback and joint decision-making, and how well they hold themselves to high ethical standards. While this requires an assumed level of self-awareness on the part of the managers, inconsistencies in responses may reveal a lack in this area. The 40-item survey reflects the values associated with *transparency, credibility, accountability*, and *honesty* and consists of Likert-style response options with answers on a scale of 1 ("I do not demonstrate this behavior") to 5 ("I demonstrate this behavior to a great degree").

Respondents are asked to complete the survey two consecutive times, first as a manifestation of their "actual" behavior, and second, as a reflection of their "desired" behavior. Examples of current and desired profiles are provided in Figures 2.1 and 2.2, respectively. Figure 2.3 transposes the two profiles to provide a single view of the gaps across the four dimensions of trusted leadership. Understandably, the ratings in Figure 2.1, which denote current behaviors, are lower than the ratings in Figure 2.2, which represent desired behaviors.

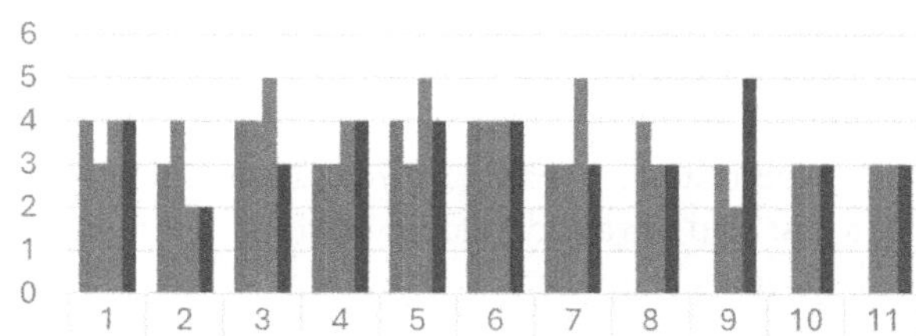

	1	2	3	4	5	6	7	8	9	10	11
■ Transparency	4	3	4	3	4	4	3				
■ Credibility	3	4	4	3	3	4	3	4	3	3	3
■ Accountability	4	2	5	4	5	4	5	3	2	3	3
■ Honesty	4	2	3	4	4	4	3	3	5	3	3

Figure 2.1 Current traits.

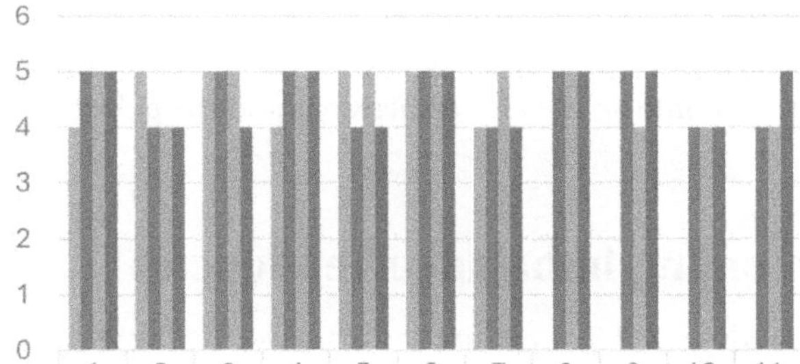

	1	2	3	4	5	6	7	8	9	10	11
Transparency	4	5	5	4	5	5	4				
Credibility	5	4	5	5	4	5	4	5	5	4	4
Accountability	5	4	5	5	5	5	5	5	4	4	4
Honesty	5	4	4	5	4	5	4	5	5	4	5

Figure 2.2 Desired traits.

Figure 2.3 Current and desired traits in perspective.

The gap between the two figures (see Figure 2.3) highlights opportunities for improvement.

To foster the alignment between actual behaviors and expectations from others, self-assessments can be used periodically to determine how well one has evolved and honed their leadership qualities over time. Another option is to obtain feedback from relevant constituents (e.g., stakeholders, executives, board members) using the same survey to assess the perceived trust of leaders.

The differences between self-assessment and assessment from others could be very revealing and should lead to a more valid and reliable understanding of gaps. Ideas and actions for improvement or self-development could be prioritized to reflect inputs from others and eventually lead to a better alignment between the leader's profile on the four dimensions and the perceptions of trust by others.

Overcoming Imbalance Tendencies

Understanding self-perceptions of trustworthy leaders' efficacy and desired behaviors helps prepare both current and future leaders to regain trust and communicate effectively. The assessment framework proposed in this chapter is based on the four attributes – transparency, credibility, accountability, and honesty – that must be present simultaneously to increase the propensity to act with trust. A deficiency in *transparency* can occur when a leader is too inwardly focused, for example, by paying disproportionate attention to operational and financial objectives as well as managing internal dynamics. While these are important matters and they cannot be ignored, the temptation among many leaders is to act with a sense of urgency rather than strategy.

This is where excess comes into play, i.e., overemphasizing certain behaviors at the expense of others. When this occurs, certain behaviors, which may be assets in non-crisis situations, now shift into weaknesses. For example, taking a more leisurely approach to decision-making, diving into precedent, and examining pros and cons from a multitude of angles may work well in non-crisis situations, but can be detrimental during a crisis. Refocusing behaviors on purposeful ideas as the basis for strengthening equity and fairness within the organization and for a good alignment of organizational values and stakeholders' views is at the core of trusted leadership.

Other leaders experience a deficiency in *accountability*. This deficiency is usually marked by a tendency to shoot from the hip, characterized by making authoritative decisions without the benefit of input from affected stakeholders or all the available information. Executives who demonstrate lower levels of accountability are advised to resist the temptation to make hasty decisions, despite the urgent pressures of the moment. Unless the matter is extremely urgent and a decision absolutely must be made on the spot, leaders should pause to consider: is there information or data to support the decision? What do we know? What don't we know? How long do we have to decide this? How long will it take to get the data? Who has it? Who is working on it? What is the risk and cost of making the wrong decision?

Deficiency in *honesty* may prove to be the most difficult to remedy, since it relies on motives associated with one's emotional intelligence and the psychosocial predisposition to empathize with others, especially followers. Supervisors and leaders have a tremendous impact on those who work in an organization. Recent surveys of employees have found higher levels of dissatisfaction with workplace environments that display dishonesty. For example, a report by Deloitte (2019) showed that 80% of business and HR leaders worldwide indicated they need to develop leadership capabilities that can help to motivate and re-engage employees. Transparency, honesty, mutual respect, and trust were highlighted as great mitigations for building social capital in organizations.

Finally, leaders deficient in *credibility* can sacrifice reputation and ability to marshal resources for the common good. They can quickly become perceived as political and manipulative and unable to mobilize support for their vision and resort to making decisions independently. These leaders tend to withhold information and resort to secrecy and closed-door decisions. Credible leaders who lead by example are not only true to themselves but also help others to become more ethical and trusted individuals.

Readiness for Crisis: Abandoning Ethics or Embracing Them?

When thinking about ethics, the temptation to apply a reductionist approach is often compelling, housing the concept in the neat binary framework of right and wrong. On the surface, this makes sense. After all, many ethical violations are easy to identify. Theft. Lies. Distortions. Harm. And, at the same time, many good deeds are also easy to identify. Charitableness. Selflessness. Empowering the weak. Humbling the privileged.

But more often than not, there are some gray elements in the sphere of ethics. For organizational leaders, whose job is to make decisions that affect the entirety of the organization, the choice spectrum may be constructed such that it appears that one stakeholder group's gain is another group's loss. How we approach those situations reveals much about the ethical orientation leaders apply to their role. One of our authors recently worked on a consulting project that demonstrates the point. The project involved Hospital A as it was becoming ready to merge into a large hospital system. In structuring a deal for their acquisition, senior leadership chose not to share its plans with middle management and staff for fear that if the information was leaked to the public, the deal could fall through.

Negotiations were delicate, and Hospital A executives were justifiably concerned that the plan could unravel, especially since the acquiring entity was actively considering other hospitals that could be brought into the fold instead. In that fiercely competitive environment, it's quite probable that Hospital A could not have survived as an independent entity had another hospital been chosen for the merger.

Hospital A's leadership was torn. They knew very well that some of their middle managers would face job insecurity in the merged environment. After all, among the principal reasons for the merger was the achievement of economy of scale. The less time those managers had to consider alternative employment plans, the more challenging it would be to obtain gainful employment elsewhere. Hospital leadership weighed that concern against the risks of announcing the merger before the deal was at the very near completion point, as this would provide competitor hospitals with time to make an attractive counteroffer. Hospital leadership determined that such a risk was too great to assume.

Thus, when the leadership finally announced the plan, just six days ahead of the signing ceremony, many middle managers were disheartened and angry. They believed they were entitled to transparency, that they should have been informed not just about the acquisition but about what the acquisition might mean in terms of their positions. They came to believe that the lack of transparency was a clear sign that leadership cared more about the acquisition prospects than about their livelihoods.

In the final weeks of the negotiations, Hospital A's leadership team became convinced that middle management, indeed all hospital staff, would understand their predicament. With discussions confined to their executive team and board of trustees group, the collective conviction was reinforced that they could manage the perceptions of middle managers effectively. In fact, they even came to believe that they were forthcoming with plans to announce the merger as soon as it reached an irreversible stage.

In this case, each group, leadership and middle management, viewed transparency quite differently. The lesson for both sides is that transparency, much like beauty, is best viewed as in the eye of the beholder. That is, we may think of transparency less as a fixed entity – that is, one is either transparent or not – but as a belief about one's behavior held by others.

That perspective – that one's transparency is a function of the other's perceptions – becomes clearer when we examine "choice-making" through different ethical lenses. A *deontological* approach would suggest a duty-bound adherence to honesty, that lying of any sort categorically constitutes an ethical transgression. Yet, if Hospital A's leadership interpreted its ethical responsibility in that way, the hospital merger may not have come to fruition, and the hospital may have suffered a fate that would have placed many more employees, perhaps even the hospital itself, in jeopardy.

The *utilitarian* view of ethics, as exemplified by leadership's actions, placed emphasis on what they believed was the greater good, that is, what was in the best interests of the largest number of people. Plainly put, this ethical philosophy suggests that the ends justify the means, provided that the ends are grounded in the best interests of many others. But the greatest lesson may lie not in an examination of how leadership handled a highly pressure-packed situation, notwithstanding whether we label it a crisis or not. Rather, the more relevant lesson relates to how leadership built and nurtured the organizational culture up until that point.

Here, we may conclude that the disconnect between leadership and middle management was an entrenched feature of their relationship well before the merger prospect arose. Consider that the rationale behind leadership's failure to prematurely disclose was understandable. After all, there was good reason for secrecy – the very deal hinged on it. And despite this, middle managers felt as though their interests had not been considered. In fact, they felt they had been double-crossed. Sure, it would be understandable to feel angry about the potential loss of their jobs. It could also conjure very legitimate feelings of being frightened about their future.

But betrayal doesn't necessarily relate to those aspects of the situation. Rather, betrayal is a function of middle managers' beliefs about leadership's *motives*. Accordingly, betrayal reveals something fundamental about the prevailing leadership-middle management relationship, the one that had been in place, woven into the very fabric of the organizational culture. Had that relationship been characterized instead by a history of leadership's forthcomingness, middle management may have still experienced apprehension and fear related to their future.

But in all likelihood, they would have understood leadership's predicament and likely would not have felt betrayed, certainly not to the extent they did. Hence, the most potent predictor of whether a crisis will be managed effectively is to examine its readiness for a crisis well before the crisis hits.

Crises, as noted throughout this book, constitute special sets of circumstances. At the very least, in a crisis, the decision-making timeframe is shortened, the risk of failure is elevated, consultation opportunites with stakeholders are compressed, and broad mobilization of support is critical. While decision-making, risk assessment, stakeholder consultation, and support are always important, crises demand highly structured and rapid coordination of those processes. If leaders pursue *deliberative* action effectively during non-crisis periods, *decisive* actions during crises have a far greater chance of yielding positive results. When that occurs, deontological and utilitarian philosophies of ethics integrate into a complementary relationship rather than remain discrete or mutually exclusive. This is primarily due to the willingness of stakeholders to subjugate personal interests for the common good. The motives of those in decision-making positions are not viewed skeptically or cynically, but as thoughtful, even though the consequences may be harmful to some.

In this framework, ethics operate within the realm of motives as much as they do behavior. And leaders who establish a culture in which readiness for a crisis – readiness which includes the welfare of all stakeholders, including and especially employees and those served by the organization – will have transcended the either/or deontological/utilitarian divide. In so doing, decisions which place an emphasis on the best interests of the organization are likely to be perceived as also being in the best interests of the employees.

Treating Thoughts as Guesses

Critically, and as discussed, managers who cultivate a leadership style characterized by transparency, accountability, honesty, and credibility during non-crisis periods will have an advantage during crisis periods. During non-crisis operations, leaders have, at least relatively speaking, some luxury of weighing possible scenarios with more time. This provides an opportunity to engage in extensive consultation and keep all stakeholders informed. If the interest is building multidirectional trusting relationships, leaders are advised to treat their own inclinations and thoughts as speculative, thereby providing space for input.

The leader who posits that employees are inherently and unmovably resistant to change will, naturally, build decision-making options with that in mind. Say the leader believes reorganization is necessary to dilute the silo culture because they believe the lack of collaboration and coordination across departments slows down work processes. Such a predisposition will influence the range of assumptions and corresponding actions that the leader will take. For one, they will undoubtedly assume they know best where the bottlenecks lie.

For another, they will probably develop the plan with limited input from those affected and delay explaining the plans until the plans have been largely set. And finally, they will implement the plan without having thoroughly analyzed the implications of the new organizational structure. If a crisis hits, that same leader will be at a distinct disadvantage. This is largely because employees have become conditioned to believe that their contribution, their perspective, is not valued. When called upon in a moment of threat, how much of their heart and spirit will be in it? And how invested are they likely to be in the organization's mission?

The leader who is likely to gain their employees' productive and active engagement is one who cultivates a climate of trust. Trust, a most precious and invaluable organizational commodity, takes time, skill, and dedication to develop. High on the list of activities in that effort is framing beliefs as assumptions that need to be tested. This concept of testing beliefs is at the core of a behavioral health field called Cognitive Behavioral Therapy, or CBT. The reality is that many of the thoughts we have are not facts. They are merely conclusions that we develop in response to a limited set of facts. Therapy Los Angeles, CBT therapists employ that premise to destabilize patterns of self-destructive thinking by encouraging clients to open their perceptions to new possibilities.

In much the same way, if the leader seeking a reorganization were to treat assumptions as guesses, they would begin by examining whether the bottlenecks are real and seeking input from employees as to why those bottlenecks occur. Whether that would necessitate a reorganization would depend on what the investigation uncovers, which leads to the role evidence plays in ethical decision-making and creating a climate of readiness for a crisis.

Evidence

As Walter Lippmann (1922) observed, "For the most part we do not first see and then define, we define first and then see." The use of evidence has both ethical and strategic importance. While its value is ever-present, it takes on special significance during crises. When employees become accustomed to their leaders providing bona fide reasons for their actions, that is, when leaders' motives are perceived to be driven by evidence rather than opinion or personal gain, they are more likely to be predisposed to lend support.

But evidence is not so simple. Just because we call something "evidence" – and, by implication, experience some satisfaction because we have convinced ourselves that we are being "objective" – it doesn't mean that such self-satisfaction is warranted. By referring to something as evidence, we may be lavishing it with a glossy ethical sheen it may not deserve. Further, what evidence is to one person may be conjecture to another. The risk of employing the term "evidence" is the implication that we have moved past bias, attitude, and belief, and are now safely – and ethically – operating in the realm of truth.

So, what exactly is an ethical use of evidence? We may typically think of evidence as a seemingly or purportedly "objective" substantiation for a claim. But the question arises: is the evidence an inherent feature of the material, or does it lie in beliefs about the material held by the person looking at it? If the latter, presumably it would be subject to interpretation. If that's the case, the evidence may be (1) refutable, (2) rooted in a leader's motive (thus, developed on an a priori basis, and presumably designed to support a predetermined conclusion), (3) a result of a flawed methodological execution, or (4) lacking sufficient relevance or application to the problem at hand. With respect to the latter, what may be appropriate evidence in one context (or organization) may not be generalizable to or appropriate for another.

In 2003, then-Secretary of State Colin Powell gave a speech to the United Nations outlining a justification for initiating a war against Iraq. In that speech, Secretary Powell identified a range of weapons of mass destruction that Iraq allegedly had developed and was prepared to use. By his own admission, Secretary Powell later admitted that the vetting of the so-called evidence was neither thorough nor sufficiently credible (Wilkerson, 2018). It has been largely concluded that the decision to invade Iraq had already been made, and the "fact-finding" was less an exercise in evidence-gathering than it was in "justification-finding."

We need not look only at the political world to find examples of such "cherry picking." Leaders anywhere and everywhere who surround themselves with subordinates who are predisposed to validate their bosses' wishes are unlikely to hear information contrary to those wishes. The oil executive who wants to drill in a particular location may get reports about the lack of environmental harm in that area from employees or consultants who seek to curry favor or avoid punishment. The pharmaceutical executive intent on advancing a drug to market may hear more about its effectiveness than its adverse effects from a boss-pleasing inner circle.

On the other hand, the executive who directs employees to put the needs of the organization and its audience first, even though they may conflict with what the executive wants to hear, is likely to receive more valid information. When the executive insists that this approach to loyalty is expected and encouraged, even and especially when the news is not favorable, we may then say that the motive is ethical and more likely based on binding evidence.

During times of crisis, the ethical leader is far less likely to have their motives questioned. Since crises demand rapid synchronization of activity, if the ethical foundation is already in place, the coordination of that activity is likely to be supported, and certainly not questioned. But if that ethical foundation is tenuous, at least one significant consequence is that employees may question the motive of the leader. Cynical employees are less likely to be supportive of such a leader, shrinking the probability of positive outcomes.

In the absence of an organizational climate characterized by transparency, accountability, honesty, and credibility, employees may develop dissonance. During crises, such cynicism may constitute the basis of dissonance, a stressful condition that occurs when it becomes nearly impossible to function when incompatible views are entrenched.

Take this example from the height of the COVID pandemic. The public was on the receiving end of mixed messages. Some political leaders discouraged the use of mitigating protocols, including, for example, wearing masks, practicing social distancing, and avoiding crowds. Notwithstanding what we have since learned regarding the questionable effectiveness of masks and other measures, the medical community did encourage mask-wearing during the 2020–2021 period, prior to and during the first year of vaccinations. Putting faith in a political leader who denounces mask-wearing while simultaneously hearing from the scientific community that wearing a mask is essential for one's health causes dissonance. This leads to the likelihood of embracing a dissonance-reducing course that neutralizes the stress produced by the incompatibility of those messages.

Options include (1) discrediting the political leader, or (2) discrediting the message that mask-wearing is necessary. If option two is chosen, the logical next step is (3) discrediting the source of the message that mask-wearing is necessary, thereby potentially discrediting the very concept of "expertise," and, by extension, (4) discrediting all those who believe the source of the pro-mask messaging. The latter choices contributed to a climate of divisiveness that characterized the political culture during the period of the pandemic.

Had the relationship among the political leadership of the nation, the states, and the scientific community been productive and respectful prior to the pandemic, chances are the messaging to the public would have been consistent. Most importantly, motives would not have been viewed as suspect. The respective roles of political leaders and the scientific community would have been clear. And critically, messaging would have been grounded in evidence that would have been perceived to be unrelated to self-serving motives.

Thus, we can see that evidence is an indispensable mechanism for securing an organization's readiness for effective management of a crisis. It moors the culture with an ethical and strategic footing. And yet, with evidence, simply put, obstacles can emerge. As much as those with influence in decision-making contexts may want to objectively investigate something, they may also be inclined to please those in positions of authority or go along with an idea that seems to have gained wide acceptance or traction.

Factoring the political winds out of the decision-making calculus is not easy, nor necessarily advisable, given the importance of remaining sensitive to organizational politics. But when those considerations drive a decision, evidence then becomes an element of secondary institutional importance. The point is that evidence-based models require a certain openness, a willingness to set aside preconceived beliefs to conduct an impartial examination. It means that leaders embrace a judicial as well as an advocacy role.

The paradox of evidence-based readiness for a crisis is that although it promotes an "objective" approach to data gathering, assessment, and decision-making – and thus makes it more reliable, at least theoretically – it also imposes a potential risk for certain leaders. That is, it could be regarded as a way of moving the decision-making judgment and/or responsibility away from the individual who holds a self-perception of infallibility. If such a self-perception exists, the systems of incentives and punishments that reinforce that perception – some explicit, some tacit – permeate the organization. The information gathered may be used to support a desired outcome. It may be contrived to have the veneer of evidence, but it is not.

On the other hand, there are chief executives who believe that their talent is in exercising good judgment, but only after all the facts are gathered. This chief executive will have a greater willingness to see where the facts lead, and those around this chief executive will be more empowered to pursue investigations that are not based on a priori decisions.

Empowerment and trust go hand in hand. In an organizational culture that values evidence, all are more apt to suspend beliefs and judgments until the relevant information has been obtained, assembled, and analyzed. In such cultures, key questions are asked: are ideas for new approaches invited and encouraged? Is feedback sought? Are front-line workers consulted (genuinely, not ceremoniously or patronizingly)? To the extent such activity characterizes the communication environments, we may consider the organization readier for a crisis than those which do not.

Conclusion

Clutch leadership involves making quick and meaningful decisions when stakes are high and time is in short supply. Clutch leaders exhibit self-confidence in the face of pressure, demonstrating conviction, mindfulness, and clarity in communication with key stakeholders and the public, in managing expectations, and in building trust.

Unsurprisingly, trustworthiness is a core characteristic of clutch leaders who understand that their success necessitates a balancing act that requires strong sensitivity and communication skills. When leaders and followers are engaged in transparent, honest, accountable, and credible behaviors, they also give more attention to self-reflection, which can result in effective behavioral change. Leaders who share information about themselves and the organization and who tie ethics and diversity to the long-term success of the organization build a culture of trust with followers and enhance organizational credibility with stakeholders.

When people are entrusted with the necessary information to make wise choices, they are likely to act responsibly and sustain a culture of higher purpose. And wise choices emanate from cultures in which evidence drives decision-making. Evidence allows organizations to transcend opinion; when opinion governs decision-making, it is most likely that the most authoritative person's opinion will prevail. In an evidence-driven culture, all are empowered to contribute. Trust, invariably, emerges as a defining feature of the relationships between leadership and employees.

Trustworthy leadership begins and ends as an important responsibility for those holding positions of organizational authority. Responsible leaders are mindful of instilling the values of honesty, transparency, credibility, and accountability in the social fabric of the organization. In the end, crisis situations require leaders who draw heavily on *self-regulation* and *ethical mindfulness*.

Mindfulness is a state of active awareness, a continual creation and refinement of values and principled behavior, an openness to new experiences and new ideas as well as a willingness to respond to and view contexts of emerging situations using multiple lenses of inquiry. Mindful leaders do not think of a binary, either-or, attaching mutually exclusive categories to people and values which are often the cause for leadership failure. Instead, clutch leaders, who are also recognized as trustworthy leaders, spark mindful learning in others as an essential part of dealing with crises and preserving trust in organizations.

References

Belasen, A. T. & Belasen, A. R. (2019). The strategic value of integrated corporate communication: Functions, social media, stakeholders. *International Journal of Strategic Communication*, 13, 4. https://doi.org/10.1080/1553118X.2019.1661842

Belasen, A. T. & Belasen, A. R. (2024). Signaling trust during disruptions: Perceived gender differences in trustworthy leadership traits. *Gender in Management: An International Journal*, 40(2), 197–214. https://doi.org/10.1108/GM-04-2024-0187

Belasen, A. T. & Eisenberg, B. (2023). Building trust for better crisis communication: Lessons for leadership development, Chapter 7. In N. Pfeffermann & M. Schaller (Eds.),, *New Leadership Communication - Inspire Your Horizon* (pp. 93–110). Switzerland, Springer. https://doi.org/10.1007/978-3-031-34314-8_7

Berns, D. (2019), A message to all employees. *MSCKK Internal Memorandum from Chief Risk Officer*. https://int.nyt.com/data/documenthelper/559-12cancermemo/e18455bae968acf91a5e/optimized/full.pdf#page=1

Deloitte Global Human Capital Trends. (2019). Retrieved from https://www2.deloitte.com/za/en/pages/human-capital/articles/2019-deloitte-global-human-capital-trends-.html

DuBrin, A. J. (2013). *Handbook of Research on Crisis Leadership in Organizations*. Edward Elgar Publishing, Cheltenham.

Iyengar, R. (2020). Zoom CEO apologizes for having 'fallen short' on privacy and security. *CNN*. https://www.cnn.com/2020/04/02/tech/zoom-ceo-apology-privacy/index.html#:~:text=%E2%80%9CWe%20recognize%20that%20we%20have,addressing%20privacy%20issues%2C%20Yuan%20said

Lippmann, W. (1922). *Public Opinion*. Good Press, NewYork.

Ornstein, C. & Thomas, K. (2018). Top cancer researcher fails to disclose corporate financial ties in major research journals. *The New York Times*. https://www.nytimes.com/2018/09/08/health/jose-baselga-cancer-memorial-sloan-kettering.html?action=click&module=RelatedCoverage&pgtype=Article&region=Footer

Petriglieri, G. (2020, April 22). The psychology behind effective crisis leadership. *Harvard Business Review*. https://hbr.org/2020/04/the-psychology-behind-effective-crisis-leadership

Wilkerson, L. (2018). I helped sell the false choice of war once. it's happening again. *The New York Times*. https://www.nytimes.com/2018/02/05/opinion/trump-iran-war.html

TRUST AND RELIABILITY

B

DOI: 10.4324/9781003629214-4

Chapter 3

Navigating Disruption: Leading with Empathy

Jenine (Nina) Buchanan and Heather Horowitz

Introduction

Disruption is everywhere. As organizations navigate transitional challenges such as technological advancements, economic shifts, policy and regulatory changes, and restructuring, organizational leaders must recognize that the work of the organization is accomplished by its people. During disruptive times, swift decision-making and clear communication are crucial, limiting opportunities for deeper reflection. Organizations must be able to quickly and efficiently share information and respond. In such dynamic environments, leaders must discover ways to preserve – and even strengthen – employee motivation and inspire a shared vision (Kouzes & Posner, 2023). The centerpiece of such a leadership model is *empathy*, which must be embedded within the organization for it to thrive in the face of disruption.

Our technology-driven world is one of continuous innovations, which, in turn, results in a workplace culture perpetually undergoing change. In such a dynamic environment, leaders are well-advised to ensure that staff feel supported as they respond to changing demands and strategic goals, learn new technologies, and keep pace with a fast-moving landscape. To be agile, organizations need their people to be agile. However, people cannot adapt effectively if they

DOI: 10.4324/9781003629214-5

are not supported. Leaders need to create spaces where people feel safe as they try out new ideas, where staff can share their concerns, where individuals are empowered to collaborate in decision-making, and where teams have trust in their leaders.

Empathy is sometimes dismissed as being too "soft," residing in the realm of "emotional" rather than practical. This dismissal overlooks how many workplace challenges – poor communication, high stress, low morale, low engagement, resistance to change, interpersonal conflicts, work-life balance, mistrust, and turnover – are connected to the human experience, which encompasses work experience. These are people-centered challenges that require people-centered solutions. Traditional leadership approaches have often failed to address these challenges effectively.

Empathy is closely tied to increased job satisfaction, performance, and innovation (Kock et al., 2019). Research demonstrates that it contributes to employee well-being, productivity, and creativity. Furthermore, empathetic leadership promotes a culture of care, creating a sense of connection and value throughout the organization. Empathy drives sustainable outcomes when it is an intentional, ongoing practice embedded across the organization, laying the foundation for organizations to navigate disruption effectively – a theme we explore throughout this chapter.

Empathetic leaders foster supportive and inclusive cultures because of their genuine concern and sensitivity to their employees' needs for professional gratification and their desire to believe that the organization's values are in sync with their own. By valuing employees, empathetic leaders promote a culture of psychosocial safety and team building, all of which are closely tied to organizational success, making empathetic leadership especially important in times of disruption.

While empathy matters in stable conditions, it is essential during crises, when there is limited time to deeply pause and engage. When empathy is part of the organization's DNA, leaders can preemptively address challenges before escalating to more serious problems. Being a clutch leader is not just about how you respond in a crisis, but also how you establish an organizational culture that thrives during times of relative "normalcy" as well as disruption.

Empathy has been defined in a number of ways. At its core, it is important to emphasize that empathy is not a skill, per se, but a social exchange between people (Eichbaum et al., 2022). It is an effort to recognize and acknowledge another's experience, thereby honoring one's humanity. When people enter the workplace, they bring their whole selves – their emotions, strengths and vulnerabilities, their goals and aspirations. They bring their personal experiences and the capacity and need for understanding and connection. Leaders must prioritize supporting such fundamental human aspects of transformational change by infusing empathy into the organization's core. This proactive, "people-centered" approach contrasts with other leadership methods by focusing on individuals, rather than solely on outputs and profits (Fitch & Van Brunt, 2016). In this chapter, we'll examine the core capacities that empathetic leaders embody and how they can integrate empathy into their practice. Through practice examples, case studies, vignettes, and reflective questions, we will illustrate how empathetic leaders can advance organizations in the face of disruption.

Critical Model of Empathetic Leadership

Leaders in any field must confront disruption while recognizing that individuals at the core of the organization are central to driving innovation and change. Navigating disruption requires confidence, action, and empathy – understanding one's team and supporting their contributions to the organization's success. A review of the literature on empathetic leaders and organizations revealed key themes, which informed the development of our *Critical Empathetic Leadership Model.* Figure 3.1 integrates these principles by focusing on perceiving and reflecting on employees' needs, demonstrating genuine care, offering support and growth opportunities, and creating inclusive, collaborative spaces. Through empathetic leadership, organizations can cultivate a culture that is well equipped to navigate crises when they erupt.

Perceive and Reflect

First, empathetic leaders perceive and reflect, which requires a concentrated effort to see others as whole individuals. No matter how hard we try, we cannot fully know another person. There are aspects of employee experiences that leaders may not entirely grasp or be entitled to know. Empathetic leaders recognize that it is impossible to thoroughly comprehend another person's life experience

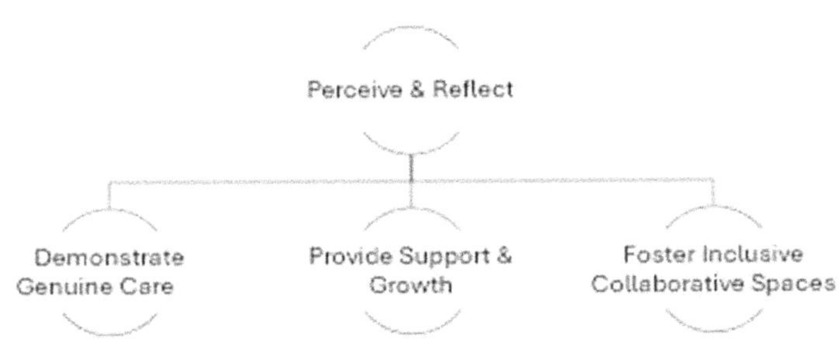

Figure 3.1 Critical empathetic leadership.

– their "story" – especially when they are from a different cultural background or identity group (Seay et al., 2022).

This is why critical empathetic leaders engage in *reflective humility*, balancing an awareness of others' experiences while accepting they will never fully understand someone's experience. Reflective humility forms the foundation for building meaningful relationships while committing to ongoing growth. This commitment is reflected in empathetic leadership, where leaders intentionally assess employees' needs, challenges, capabilities, and emotions (Arghode et al., 2021). They actively listen to what their employees say and decipher their nonverbal communication.

Perception and Reflection in Action

Leaders must begin with observation and intentional thoughts about situational dynamics. Importantly, empathetic leaders are purposeful about getting to know their team members and are committed to supporting individuals and the organization. The following is an example of how an empathetic leader can perceive and reflect in an everyday situation.

> *Jamie is the director of client relations at a financial institution. Last month, he led a quarterly meeting with the customer support team. At the end of the meeting, he excitedly announced that the company decided to implement AI tools to serve as the frontline for handling customer inquiries. After he made the announcement, Jamie made eye contact with one of his team leaders, Robyn, and noticed a worried look on her face.*
>
> *After the meeting, Jamie found Robyn in the audience to talk with her. "I noticed you seemed concerned when I made the AI announcement," Jamie said. "Is something wrong?"*
>
> *Robyn shared that some of her team members have expressed anxiety over the possibility of AI integration. She shared that announcing this at the very end of the meeting without time for questions might cause worry amongst the team.*
>
> *On the drive home from work, Jamie continued to think about what Robyn shared. He felt regret for having alarmed the team and for not realizing that they may be worried about the implications.*
>
> *The next day, he called Robyn to let her know that he was sorry for not anticipating the team's worries and wanted to follow up with the whole*

group. He asked Robyn for her thoughts about how he should move forward. Robyn was relieved to hear this and suggested that she and Jamie co-host a meeting for team members to openly express their concerns.

Once leaders are highly attuned to those on their teams, they can demonstrate genuine care, provide support and growth, and foster inclusive, collaborative spaces. To gain a deeper understanding of one's ability and predisposition to perceive communication cues, the following reflection questions may prove most helpful:

- In what ways do I actively listen to both the verbal and non-verbal cues of my employees to ensure I am aware of what their needs, challenges, and emotions might be?
- What steps can I take to ensure I am not only listening to my employees' verbal and non-verbal communication, but also acting on this information to support their growth and well-being in a meaningful way?
- How can I cultivate reflective humility in my leadership to better understand and empathize with the diverse experiences of my team, knowing I can never fully grasp their personal stories?

Demonstrate Genuine Care

Leaders naturally care about performance, but empathetic leaders prioritize their staff as whole people first, not just as employees. They regularly check in with their team members to understand their well-being, both personally and professionally, while ensuring that sharing non-work-related details is never required. Through these conversations, empathetic leaders can also keep track of personal milestones to celebrate. Recognizing the importance of work-life balance, they demonstrate flexibility in accommodating work arrangements and personal circumstances when needed. Through authentic interactions with staff, empathetic leaders gather feedback that allows them to provide individualized support and address systemic barriers to employee success. They express concern, compassion, and regard for others and exhibit sensitivity to followers' needs and emotions (Eisenberg et al., 2025). Beyond this, empathetic leaders recognize employees meaningfully, through timely praise and acknowledgment of both significant achievements and daily contributions.

Demonstrating Genuine Care in Action

Supervisors can gain valuable insight through *authentic interactions* with their staff, that is, exchanges driven by a leader's sincere care for others, rather than hidden agendas. Employees recognize this authenticity when a leader's actions align with their words (Eisenberg et al., 2025). Empathetic leaders use these interactions to inform employee care by validating employees' lived experiences and identifying and addressing systemic inequities that inhibit staff success.

Here is an example of how an empathetic leader can demonstrate genuine care:

> *Chris has worked at a start-up firm for three years. While Chris has been one of the firm's initial staff members, they noticed that their career had not been developed in the same ways as their colleagues' careers. They were getting less recognition and had not yet been promoted. Chris, who is originally from Haiti, noticed that white colleagues seem to be assigned to prominent roles, while Chris had been primarily tasked with supportive roles. Chris approached their manager to discuss their concerns and share their interest in taking on more responsibilities. Chris indicated that they do not think there is any deliberate exclusion but shares that they know the lack of project leadership is inhibiting their professional growth.*
>
> *Alicia, Chris' supervisor, listened carefully and thanked Chris for trusting her and sharing that information. Alicia acknowledged that Chris has been in predominantly support roles and says that she can understand how Chris would feel that this has limited them. Alicia shared that she wants every employee to have the opportunity to lead projects and develop their skills.*
>
> *After the meeting, Alicia reflected on their conversation and decided to review the past year's projects. She discovered that Chris' perceptions and claims were on target – almost all the leadership roles had gone to white employees. Upon further investigation, the same was true for mentoring programs and fellowships. She learned that most of those chosen for leadership roles were in the same social circle. Alicia concluded that one group clearly benefited from these opportunities, despite having equal qualifications. Even if unintentional, it was unacceptable. She wants all employees to have access to these experiences and to gain from them. Additionally, she knows that all employees bring unique contributions that not only benefit the firm but also provide meaningful learning opportunities for others.*

As a result of this review, Alicia assessed upcoming projects and assigned those who had not yet led a project to oversee projects in the coming months. During the next team meeting, Alicia admitted that she had overlooked some of the talent in the group. She announced that Chris will lead the next project, highlighting their achievements over the past several years, and expressed confidence in their abilities to make the project a success.

In this example, Alicia validated Chris' experience and took intentional steps to ensure her staff have equal access to career-advancement opportunities. By acknowledging and addressing systemic inequities, Alicia fostered a workplace that contributes to both employee well-being and workplace safety.

Demonstrating genuine care in action includes validating, showing genuine concern, and explicitly recognizing. Validation begins with listening. For example, business theorist Edgar Schein (2013) recommends that we ask open, non-judgmental questions to show authentic curiosity and respect for others' perspectives. Rather than assert knowledge or control, empathetic leaders ask intentional, probing questions and ask follow-up questions to learn more. These leaders acknowledge employees' experiences and concerns, affirming that their experiences are valid and that it is important for leaders to understand them. They express concern and show compassion, both for workplace and personal concerns. Employees are valued beyond their work output.

Another essential way empathetic leaders can demonstrate genuine care is through recognition. Recognition should be tailored to individual preferences, as some employees favor public acknowledgment, while others prefer private praise. Empathetic leaders know their teams well enough to know who is most comfortable with which approach. For those who are gratified by public attention, leaders might offer praise at a staff meeting or in a weekly staff update: "I want to take this opportunity to thank Kendrick for their work on the marketing campaign. Their fresh ideas and collaborative approach played a key role in this campaign's success. Thank you and your team for your hard work!" And while public praise can feel good for some, those who prefer to be out of the spotlight might appreciate a handwritten note or personalized email message:

Hi Kendrick, I want to take this opportunity to thank you for your amazing work on the marketing campaign. Your creativity and leadership really shined through, and your efforts haven't gone unnoticed. Thank you!

To enhance awareness of how genuine care may be demonstrated, the following reflection prompts may prove helpful:

- How can I ensure that I prioritize my team members as people first, and how do I regularly check in on their well-being without causing them to feel pressured to share personal details if they are not comfortable?
- How am I actively celebrating both small victories and larger accomplishments within my team, and how can I make recognition more consistent and meaningful for everyone?
- In what ways can I show greater flexibility in work arrangements to accommodate my team members?
- As a leader, how can I identify and address any systemic inequities within the team or organization that may be limiting employee success?

Provide Support and Growth

According to the Pew Research Center, one of the top reasons employees leave their jobs is limited opportunities for growth and advancement (Parker & Menasce Horowitz, 2022). After low compensation, this was the number one reason people left their positions. Empathetic leaders recognize the need for growth and development and invest in this by seeking to genuinely understand their employees' aspirations and basis for them, recognizing their potential, and engaging staff in their individual growth process.

Because they understand their team members' goals and skillsets, empathetic leaders intentionally create opportunities that leverage strengths and provide tailored resources for development. Additionally, empathetic leaders see the promise in employees that they may not see in themselves. This enables leaders to motivate and encourage staff in ways that are meaningful to them. When communicating with staff about their career growth, leaders should be careful not to frame the conversation as if employees have deficits that need to be addressed. Instead, empathetic leaders engage staff members as equal partners, encouraging their agency in the process (Davis, 2023). This empowers employees to take ownership over their own growth, encouraging both autonomy and accountability.

Support and Growth in Action

Empathy can be a powerful tool to support employee growth when mistakes or shortcomings are observed. Instead of reacting judgmentally, empathetic leaders address challenges with understanding and offer constructive feedback focused on development and encouragement. Stanford University research psychologist Jamil Zaki recommends that when employees are not meeting expectations, leaders should approach the situation with curiosity. They suggest building an exchange around observations such as, "you're acting in a way that's inconsistent with what I know about you" (Hancock et al., 2024). This opens a dialogue that fosters understanding and growth. Below is an example of what providing support and growth might look like.

> *Thomas is a newly promoted division director at a large company. At a recent presentation to the shareholders, Thomas was responsible for communicating strategic initiatives and explaining how their newest software will support the company's goals. It was Thomas' first big presentation, and he was very nervous. Unfortunately, his nerves got the best of him. He was unable to communicate his points clearly and the shareholders were confused. He was able to clarify things in the end, but he was especially embarrassed because his supervisor, Marcus, was in the room.*
>
> *After the shareholders had all departed, Marcus asked Thomas if he had a few minutes to debrief. Marcus opened the conversation by saying, "I can tell that didn't go the way you had hoped" and asked how Thomas was feeling. Thomas indicated that he was disappointed. He said that he had been nervous because of the high-stakes nature of the meeting, but also because he had not had a lot of experience with presentations. Marcus reassured Thomas that he had the skills to do a great job with the shareholder presentations in the future and offered to support him. He offered to support Marcus, sharing, "I noticed a few areas that could have been clearer. Let's review those items together to refine your approach so you're fully prepared next time. I'm available if you need additional guidance or have questions."*

Leaders who cultivate a culture of trust and respect through intentional support and genuine appreciation create inclusive, collaborative spaces where team members feel engaged, valued, and motivated to creatively solve problems. To better understand how managers can provide support and growth, the following reflection questions may prove helpful:

- How am I actively engaging with my team members to understand their career goals and personal aspirations, and what steps am I taking to ensure they have opportunities for growth and advancement?
- In what ways can I identify and leverage the strengths of my team members to provide them with tasks and responsibilities that will both challenge and develop their skills?

- How can I encourage professional development within my team without framing it in terms of addressing deficiencies, but rather as an opportunity to help employees reach their full potential?

Foster Inclusive Collaborative Spaces

Empathetic leaders promote an inclusive work environment where employees feel positively engaged with leaders and co-workers (Raina, 2022). At the same time, leaders are mindful of power dynamics, ensuring that employees' voices are acknowledged and respected, instituting a culture of collaborative decision-making throughout the company (Yue et al., 2022). However, due to their position of authority and power imbalance, employees may feel obligated to share personal experiences to feel involved or valued.

As Davis (2023) suggests, it is important that leaders do not pressure staff to disclose private matters as the only means to participate. Conversely, power imbalances may also stimulate reluctance on the part of employees to share information that may be relevant to the work setting. For example, if an employee is ailing, they may not want to reveal such information out of fear that it may be viewed as an inability to perform the job.

The idea of psychological safety discussed in the introduction comes to life through collaborative decision-making. When leaders engage staff in these conversations, they foster trust and a sense of shared purpose. This inclusive approach creates the conditions for innovation – inviting people to challenge assumptions, offer honest feedback, and suggest bold, creative ideas (Dalton, 2023). In this way, empathy moves beyond a concept and becomes a catalyst for change. Through understanding their employees' perspectives and experiences, leaders cultivate inclusive, collaborative spaces that generate greater innovation and teamwork.

Inclusive Collaborative Spaces in Action

Creating inclusive collaborative spaces involves, in part, having a finger on the pulse of the dynamics within these spaces. Empathetic leaders should reflect on those who are as well as those who are not actively engaged. For example, leaders should ask themselves "whose perspectives or voices might be missing, and how could we meaningfully include them in future?" and "have we noticed quieter voices and ensured these are invited, though not pressured, into dialogue?" (Centre for Advancing Collaborative Healthcare & Education, 2024, p. 2).

Additionally, empathetic leaders can use "Appreciative Inquiry" to inspire innovation, spark deep thinking dialogue, create a sense of unity, and reveal hidden assumptions (The Center for Appreciative Inquiry, n.d.). For example, Bélanger and Gorecki (2019) encourage leaders to "flip the narrative" by reframing questions to generate a collective constructive approach to invite creative thinking. Instead of asking "why did this fail?" leaders can ask "what could success look like? What went well? How can we build off that?" Empathetic leaders ask, "what if" and "how might we" to achieve that same goal.

The following is an example of a brief scenario of an empathetic leader fostering an inclusive, collaborative space:

> *In a monthly one-on-one meeting, Amber, a manager, is talking with her team member Benjamin. Amber shares that she has noticed that Benjamin does not speak up in staff meetings. He shares that he sometimes feels unrecognized and that his ideas are overlooked. Amber listens, asks questions, and validates those feelings. Amber lets Benjamin know that she does not want anyone on the team to feel that way and that she will work to be more inclusive.*
>
> *Committed to keeping her word, she pays more attention in meetings and creates opportunities for everyone to speak up, calling on Benjamin when it appears he would like to contribute. At the next month's 1:1, Amber asks Benjamin if he has felt more included. He shares that he is feeling heard and really appreciates her efforts. Amber tells Benjamin that he has great ideas and asks how he would prefer to be recognized for his contributions.*

These reflection questions can help you explore how to foster inclusive collaborative spaces:

- How can I reframe challenges and setbacks to inspire my team to focus on solutions and new possibilities rather than dwelling on past failures?
- How can I incorporate Appreciative Inquiry into my leadership approach to uncover strengths, shift perspectives, and drive continuous improvement?
- How can I actively address power dynamics in my leadership to create an environment where everyone feels empowered to contribute?

Cultivating a Culture of Empathy

By applying principles of critical empathetic leadership, organizational executives can embed empathy into the organization's core, fostering a culture of care, support, and collaboration. Establishing this foundation better prepares empathetic leaders to navigate and lead through disruption more effectively.

Creating a culture of empathy in which employees feel supported is a cross-organizational responsibility that starts with its leaders. Additionally, as leadership expert Rob Kaiser (2024) contends, "Improving empathetic leadership may be one important way to inoculate an organization against a toxic culture" (p. 130). Empathetic leaders set a certain organizational tone where empathetic behavior is ingrained within the company. People are shaped by their surroundings; therefore, organizations should embed practices, protocols, and systems with empathetic values (Hancock et al., 2024). Examples include implementing feedback loop systems that encourage two-way dialogue, providing health resources such as wellness initiatives or stress management programs, establishing formal ways to recognize staff on their collaborative contributions (not just achievements), adopting flexible work hours and remote work options, and acknowledging the individual personal demands upon employees.

Additionally, leaders must highlight compassionate and empathetic acts and encourage their staff to do the same, which reinforces empathy as an organizational value. To reflect this, organizational leaders may consider including empathy as part of the performance evaluation process to demonstrate empathy as a priority. When empathy is embedded into the organization's fabric, it creates an environment where all people feel valued. This creates a win-win situation since valued employees are more engaged and productive, benefiting both the individuals and the organization.

Employee Engagement and Well-Being

As described above, a workplace that lacks empathy can negatively affect the employee experience, leading to disconnection, lack of support, or burnout, resulting in low employee engagement, increased stress, and higher employee turnover. According to the 2024 State of the Global Workforce Gallup report, disengaged employees cost the world $8.9 trillion in lost productivity, or what equates to 9% of the global GDP (Gallup, 2024). This highlights the urgency for leaders to focus on employee engagement and retention.

While we discussed the general benefits of empathy above, it is important to underscore the notion that empathetic leadership specifically transforms employee engagement. By validating employees' diverse backgrounds, empathetic leaders cultivate a climate of inclusion, which extends beyond basic motivation to create a strong commitment to employee well-being and success (Kaiser, 2024). Such an environment enables employees to feel valued, increasing their confidence and morale. These practices offer more than individual benefits; they lead to systemic advantages, including mental health improvements, increased pride in one's work, and decreased turnover, directly impacting recruitment and training costs (Dalton, 2023).

Employees engage more when they feel that their viewpoints are welcomed and, as such, feel connected to and engaged with the organization. Leaders can deepen this connection by collaborating with them on initiatives and projects and involving them in decision-making (Tufail & Sandu, 2022). Leaders who practice active listening and prioritize employee well-being develop committed teams, which contribute to broader organizational success.

Organizational Success

We've established that an empathy-centered work environment drives success by fostering collaboration, open dialogue, and the confidence to voice concerns. Employees who feel safe to contribute are more likely to identify problems early, offer creative solutions, and improve decision-making, ultimately streamlining workflows and maximizing efficiency (Arghode et al., 2021).

A culture of empathy also supports risk-taking, flexibility, and innovation, driving growth and strengthening outcomes (Kaiser, 2024). For example, imagine that a member of a quality assurance team notices a potential flaw in a nearly finished project. In an empathy-centered company, employees are encouraged to speak up, even when a project is near completion, which can prevent costly future issues and save the organization money, time, and resources. This culture fosters experimentation and innovation, providing organizations with a competitive advantage, particularly as the business landscape continues to evolve and disruptions emerge.

Navigating Disruption

Disruption can take many forms, including technological advances, regulatory changes, downsizing, mergers and acquisitions, leadership shifts, natural disasters, globalization, and even global pandemics or health crises. As Yue et al. (2022) note, "Organizational change, when poorly managed, often generates stress, uncertainty, and adverse reactions among employees, resulting in employees' resistance to change, cynicism about change, and turnover during or after the change" (p. 1415).

Crisis situations often amplify feelings of anxiety, panic, and distress, which underscores the critical role of empathetic leadership in determining an organization's outcome during such upheaval (Barman & Ghosh, 2024; Raina, 2022).

During challenging times, empathetic leaders cultivate company innovation, employee engagement, and retention. Employees who work with empathetic leaders are more likely to stay engaged, remain committed to the organization, and experience less burnout – especially in times of transformation (Van Bommel, 2025). This effective understanding and response to employee needs is exactly what empathetic leaders provide during disruption.

Sustaining Trust

Trust and morale are also critical elements during a period of organizational transformation, especially in digital contexts where change is constant. Employees must trust their leader's ability to guide them through this disruption and foster a culture that supports both emotional and practical adaptation. This helps maintain morale but also fosters a sense of security, encouraging employees to stay engaged and aligned with the organization's evolving goals. Empathetic leaders who cultivate trust and facilitate collaboration steer their teams through times of uncertainty. These leaders make staff feel safe, supported, and connected to the organization, which leads to strong employee retention and organizational stability (Yue et al., 2022). Leaders must establish this climate of trust proactively, before disruption occurs, as rapid change often leaves little time for individual reassurance. Having this type of organizational culture in place helps ensure stability.

Communication

Sustaining a trust-centered culture during a disruptive experience is dependent upon empathetic communication. In challenging times, leaders must demonstrate compassion and communicate with clarity, transparency, and genuine care for their staff's needs. The *way* empathetic leaders communicate during a crisis is just as important as *what* they communicate. Leaders can demonstrate empathy through these communication strategies:

- Encouragement and reassurance: offering positive reinforcement increases employees' confidence and helps them cope with disruption.
- Practical information: clear, transparent details about changes and plans can alleviate ambiguity and help employees to adapt
- Employee checkpoints: regular check-ins allow leaders to get a pulse for employee perspectives, address concerns, and show they value feedback and well-being.

Leaders must prioritize empathetic communication skills, which are essential during disruptive times because of the rapid pace of change. With formal training, supported by reinforcing knowledge and skills, organizations can prepare leaders to effectively lead through disruption.

Digital Transformation

Digital transformation is more than just the influence of technology in the workplace. It is a broad strategic shift in business processes, technology, and organizational culture as well as a critical component to building a resilient, sustainable organization. While technology and procedure often take center stage in the change process, the success of these efforts ultimately depends on how well leaders attend to the people affected by the change. It is the leader's responsibility to foster a culture of flexibility, collaboration, and innovation to guide teams through these shifts. Without effective leadership, goal attainment in this dynamic digital context is not possible.

In digital transformation environments, employees face potentially daunting challenges. The rapid development of new tools, technologies, and systems may lead to digital fatigue and fears about the ability to keep up. They can experience increases in their workload, leading to burnout. Team members may feel uncertain about their job stability based on automation and may doubt whether they have the skills needed to adapt to changes. Remote and hybrid work arrangements might lead to employees feeling a lack of connectedness, while shifting strategic goals may cause employees to lose trust in leadership, questioning if there is a clear vision (Sirohi, 2020).

These high-stress conditions require a culture built on communication, transparency, and trust, with empathy as an essential competency that enables leaders to prioritize individual and team well-being. In the context of digital transformation, empathetic leadership is demonstrated through providing updates as frequently as possible, sharing the *how* and *why* behind the decisions. Empathetic leaders engage staff in decision-making and seek feedback, thereby creating a more democratic environment in which all parties have stronger psychosocial stakes in the welfare and success of the organization (Weber et al., 2022; Yang et al., 2024).

To alleviate emerging skills and knowledge deficiencies associated with the rapid acceleration of digital work environments, leaders offer training, resources, and professional development to promote upskilling. But such training goes further by building confidence and demonstrating leaders' goodwill by investing in their team members. It reinforces the core empathy tenet that they value employee contributions.

To promote innovation, leaders should inspire enthusiasm for new projects, ideas, and tools; encourage brainstorming and knowledge sharing; and foster a workplace that highlights collaboration where learning from mistakes is part of the process. Empathetic leaders recognize that their wisdom does not derive from having all the answers, but by building an environment in which idea-generation is encouraged by all, including and perhaps especially by those closest to work.

When it comes to remote and hybrid work environments, empathetic leaders model and encourage a healthy balance between employees' professional and personal lives. To mitigate digital fatigue, leaders should use digital and related tools strategically and purposefully, paying close attention to ensure that they make employees' jobs easier rather than more burdensome.

The following reflection questions may prove helpful in guiding one's empathetic leadership process in times of digital transformation:

- How can I acknowledge and address the digital fatigue and uncertainty employees may feel, while providing reassurance and clarity during the transition?
- How can I create a culture of open communication and transparency, ensuring employees feel informed and engaged through the transformation process?
- How can I model work-life balance and intentionally use digital tools in a way that reduces the burden on employees rather than adding to their stress?

Vital Considerations

Empathy can be a tricky concept to describe and define. We tend to think it involves putting our feet in someone else's shoes and imagining what it is like to walk in those shoes. That approach can prove limiting if what we are actually doing is imagining what it would be like to be *ourselves* in that situation. But others experience things differently from how we experience them. Thus, it is important to remain cognizant of that limitation of the everyday definition of empathy – that we can never fully understand what they are thinking, feeling, or experiencing.

Recognizing this, we suggest thinking of empathy as seeing and honoring one another's humanity, much as we suggested at the outset of this chapter. While we cannot understand their exact experience, we can acknowledge what they report they are thinking, feeling, and experiencing, and we can try to connect with them. People and emotions are complex. We must be careful not to reduce individuals to the experience they are having. For example, if someone is grieving a loved one, we might assume they are only feeling sadness. But they can simultaneously experience joy in the memory of a loved one, gratitude for the time they had with them, and grief over their loss. When we assume we understand what others are going through, we can inadvertently make them feel invalidated by minimizing the uniqueness of their individual experiences. That can influence our ability to connect with them genuinely.

A number of scholars have provided cautions about empathy as related to power, culture, and values. We have drawn from their perspectives to provide the following guidelines to practice critical empathetic leadership:

- Remember that others are not required to share their stories with us.
- Put aside our preconceived thoughts about how they are feeling or what they are thinking.
- Recognize the whole person, not just what they are experiencing at the moment.
- Even if others' feelings, reactions, or experiences seem strange to us, they are real and valid.
- Understand that we might experience things differently based on our roles, identities, and power dynamics.
- Meaningful empathetic action includes examining and dismantling organizational barriers related to power, privilege, and oppression.
- Empathetic leaders recognize that they sometimes contribute to inequities in the workplace. Once we recognize this, we can actively work to resolve those inequities.
- Always follow up with actions.

In addition to taking care to humanize our team members, we must keep in mind that we, too, are human. As such, we are imperfect beings, prone to conscious and unconscious bias. If we find ourselves caring for one of our colleagues more than the other, we are advised to keep that in check and make a point to spend time with others. As supervisors, we also need to be mindful of power dynamics (Seay et al., 2022). While we may want to foster an environment that values open dialogue, we need to be sure that staff members do not feel pressure to share or divulge more than they are comfortable.

Additionally, empathy functions differently across cultures and is not "one size fits all," as our ability to understand others – and what they feel is appropriate to share in the workplace – is influenced by our norms, customs, and values (Eichbaum et al., 2022, p. 643). Accordingly, we should be mindful that the way individuals value and experience empathy varies from individual to individual.

We should observe, seek feedback, and adjust our practices to be sure we meet the needs of our staff.

Empathy in Excess

While empathetic leadership has many positive benefits in the workplace, it is important to understand that becoming overly fixated on empathy can have negative outcomes. If leaders become hyper-focused on attending to the emotional needs of employees, they may overreact to minor issues (ironically *causing* distress) or lose sight of other priorities (Eisenberg et al., 2025). In the extreme, this can result in forfeiture of a competitive position, which, of course, would adversely affect all.

Leaning too far into empathy may also impede judgment and make leaders susceptible to being taken advantage of. Breithaupt (2019) explains that in taking on the perspectives of others, we risk losing our own. In doing so, we allow others to gain an advantage. Leaders must be mindful to remain firmly committed to their goals, interests, and sense of self. Being alert to these pitfalls can help leaders find a balanced approach to integrating empathetic leadership.

Finally, to be there for others, we must be there for ourselves. Waytz (2016) notes that people can become emotionally drained through continuously taking on the suffering of others. When we practice self-compassion, treating ourselves with care and understanding, we become better at offering long-lasting and meaningful support to those around us. We must be mindful of our own boundaries and keep a close watch on how carrying emotional weight impacts us (Raina, 2022).

Conclusion

Humans drive organizations. Clutch leaders recognize this and understand that building and sustaining a culture of trust and respect is essential to promoting experimentation and innovation. Empathetic leadership contributes to a more supportive and productive organization, capable and confident of navigating disruption. Leaders must be equipped to foster transformation through employee empowerment, relationship building, and buy-in, all necessary in the face of instability and flux. Empathetic leaders are best prepared to convert disruptive threats into opportunities.

As we reflect on the impact of empathetic leadership, consider this, having a leader who believes in you, trusts your abilities, and recognizes your potential can make all the difference in not just overcoming doubts but also fostering a culture of trust and confidence. If you are a leader, remember, your words have power. A small act of validation can fuel someone's motivation and remind them of their worth. To all the leaders who take the time to invest in their teams – thank you for creating environments where people can truly thrive in a psychologically safe environment. Be the leader who uplifts others, removes barriers, and cultivates inclusive collaboration – all essential for leading through disruptive times.

References

Arghode, V., Lathan, A., Alagaraja, M., Rajaram, K., & McLean, G. N. (2021). Empathic organizational culture and leadership: Conceptualizing the framework. *European Journal of Training and Development*, *46*(1/2), 239–256. https://doi.org/10.1108/EJTD-09-2020-0139

Barman, A., & Ghosh, S. (2024). Beyond the narratives on the traits of empathetic leadership- discovery from 20 global business leaders. *International Journal of Innovative Research in Engineering and Management*, *11*(4), Article 4.

Bélanger, A., & Gorecki, P. (2019). The art of questioning using powerful questions and appreciative inquiry conversations to understand values and needs. *Presentations*. 79. https://scholarworks.gvsu.edu/cgi/viewcontent.cgi? article=1079&context=library_presentations

Breithaupt, F. (2019). *The dark sides of empathy* (A. B. B. Hamilton, Trans.). Cornell University Press. https://doi.org/10.7591/9781501735608

Centre for Advancing Collaborative Healthcare & Education (CACHE). (2024). *Reflexive questions for educators & facilitators*. University of Toronto at University Health Network. https://ipe.utoronto.ca/

Dalton, S. (2023, June 2). *The role of empathy in the workplace: Impact and implications*. Steering Point Executive Search and Leadership Development. https://steeringpoint.ie/worklife/the-role-of-empathy-in-the-workplace-impact-and- implications/

Davis, J. E. (2023). *The other side of empathy*. Duke University Press.

Eichbaum, Q., Barbeau-Meunier, C., White, M., Ravi, R., Grant, E., Riess, H., & Bleakley, A. (2022). Empathy across cultures – one size does not fit all: From the ego-logical to the eco-logical of relational empathy. *Advances in Health Sciences Education*, *28*, 643–657. https://doi.org/10.1007/s10459-022-10158-y

Eisenberg, B., Hall, C., Unangst, L., & Eisenberg, A. (2025). The convergence of empathy and authenticity in brilliant leadership. In A. Belasen & N. Pfeffermann (Eds.), *Brilliant leadership: Unlocking the power of innovation-communication* (pp. 23–41). Productivity Press.

Fitch, P., & Van Brunt, B. (2016) *A guide to leadership and management higher education: Managing across generations*. Routledge.

Gallup. (2024). *State of the global workplace. The voice of the world's employees*. https://www.ahtd.org/files/state-of-the-global-workplace-2024-key-insights.pdf

Hancock, B., Weedle, B., & Rahilly, L. (Hosts). (2024, February 13). It's cool to be kind: The value of empathy at work [Audio Hancock et al., 2024 episode]. In *McKinsey Talks Talent*. https://www.mckinsey.com/capabilities/people-and-organizational-performance/our-insights/its-cool-to-be-kind-the-value-of-empathy-at-work

Kaiser, R. B. (2024). Has empathy really become more important to leadership since the COVID-19 pandemic? *Society of Consulting Psychology, 76*(2), 113–136. https://doi.apa.org/doi/10.1037/cpb0000273

Kock, N., Mayfield, M., Mayfield, J., Sexton, S., & De La Garza, L. M. (2019). Empathetic leadership: How leader emotional support and understanding influences follower performance. *Journal of Leadership & Organizational Studies, 26*(2), 217–236. https://doi.org/10.1177/1548051818806290

Kouzes, J. M., & Posner, B. Z. (2023). *The leadership challenge: How to make extraordinary things happen in organizations*. John Wiley & Sons, Inc.

Parker, K., & Menasce Horowtiz, J. (2022). *Majority of workers who quit a job in 2021 cite low pay, no opportunities for advancement, feeling disrespected*. Pew Research Center. https://www.pewresearch.org/short-reads/2022/03/09/majority-of-workers-who-quit-a- job-in-2021-cite-low-pay-no-opportunities-for-advancement-feeling-disrespected/

Raina, R. (2022). Moving crisis to opportunities: A corporate perspective on the impact of compassionate empathic behaviour on the well-being of employees. *International Journal of Global Business and Competitiveness, 17*(2), 239–255. https://doi.org/10.1007/s42943-021-00040-w

Schein, E. H. (2013). *Humble inquiry: The gentle art of asking instead of telling*. Berrett Koehler Publishers, Inc.

Seay, A. K. M., Benavides, M. T., Eddington, S. M., & Coleman, J. A. (2022). Beyond perspective taking: Fostering equity through critical empathy and intercultural listening. In C. Ward (Ed.), *Advances in higher education and professional development* (pp. 141–171). IGI Global. https://doi.org/10.4018/978-1-7998-9746-0.ch007

Sirohi, Y. (2020, February). *The importance of empathetic leadership in the age of disruption*. LinkedIn. https://www.linkedin.com/pulse/importance-empathetic-leadership-age-disruption-yogesh-sirohi/

Tufail, M. S., & Sandhu, M. A. (2022). Empathetic leadership and follower workplace engagement: mediating role of climate for inclusion. *Review of Education, Administration & Law, 5*(3), 231–243. https://doi.org/10.47067/real.v5i3.233

Van Bommel, T. (2025). *The power of empathy in times of crisis and beyond* (2nd ed.). CATALYST. https://www.catalyst.org/insights/2021/empathy-work-strategy-crisis

Waytz, A. (2016). The limits of empathy. *Harvard Business Review, 94(1)*, 68–73. https://hbr.org/2016/01/the-limits-of-empathy

Weber, E., Krehl, E.-H., & Büttgen, M. (2022). The digital transformation leadership framework: Conceptual and empirical insights into leadership roles in technology-driven business environments. *Journal of Leadership Studies, 16*(1), 6–22. https://doi.org/10.1002/jls.21810

Yang, Z., Dong, M., Guo, H., & Peng, W. (2024). Empowering resilience through digital transformation intentions: Synergizing knowledge sharing and transformational leadership amid COVID-19. *Journal of Organizational Change Management*, *38*(1). 59–81. https://doi.org/10.1108/JOCM-07-2023-0303

Yue, C. A., Thelen, P. D., & Walden, J. (2022). How empathetic leadership communication mitigates employees' turnover intention during COVID-19-related organizational change. *Management Decision*, *61*(5), 1413–1433. https://doi.org/10.1108/MD-01-2022-0011

Chapter 4

Lessons for Clutch Leadership: Leveraging Military Core Competencies for Enhanced Performance and Reliability

Daniel M. Peat and Ben Fagan

> *In the Army, we plan for and execute contingency plans. Although I didn't have 'remote learning' on my teaching BINGO card, I have dealt with disruptions before both in training and combat. COVID has nothing on a gunfight with Al-Qaeda in the suburbs of Baghdad.*
>
> **– John VanDusen, Teacher and Military Veteran**

Introduction

Organizations operating in high-stakes environments, known as High Reliability Organizations (HROs), excel at maintaining safety and reliability in complex,

DOI: 10.4324/9781003629214-6

high-pressure conditions. These organizations, such as those in emergency medicine, commercial aviation, and nuclear power, rely on structures and cultures that prioritize vigilance, an acute focus on risk, and continuous learning. Central to their success is human capital – the collective knowledge, skills, abilities, and other characteristics (KSAOs) that enable effective decision-making and risk management under pressure. The military, as a prime example of an HRO, offers valuable insights into how structured systems cultivate essential leadership skills, including risk awareness, resilience, and decentralized (and ethical) decision-making; competencies that are highly transferable to civilian contexts.

The transition of military-derived leadership principles to civilian contexts represents a significant opportunity but also presents challenges. Military veterans bring specialized human capital that aligns with both HRO and non-HRO settings, yet translating these skills is often complicated by cultural and structural differences. Civilian organizations often struggle to fully utilize the leadership, adaptability, and decision-making expertise that veterans possess. Despite these challenges, the strategic integration of military competencies into civilian workplaces can enhance organizational agility and reliability, particularly in navigating disruptive changes and uncertainties.

This chapter introduces a conceptual framework for bridging military HRO principles to civilian organizations, illustrating how key competencies such as resilience, risk awareness, and decentralized decision-making can be effectively adapted to both HRO and non-HRO environments. The chapter provides actionable insights for leaders seeking to harness the unique strengths of military-derived human capital. By highlighting both the opportunities for and barriers to skill transferability, this chapter offers a pathway for organizations to build leadership capacity and thrive in an era of disruption.

Human Capital in High Reliability Organizations (HROs)

HROs operate in environments where even minor errors can have catastrophic consequences (Roberts, 1990). Examples include healthcare, aviation, and nuclear power – fields where safety and precision are paramount. These organizations thrive under pressure by fostering cultures that prioritize vigilance, continuous learning, and proactive risk management (Weick et al., 1999). Such systems are designed not only to prevent failure but also to ensure that individuals and teams can adapt rapidly to evolving challenges (Vogus et al., 2018).

A defining feature of HROs is their capacity to maintain reliability in high-stress, high-tempo situations (Klein et al., 2006). For example, military operations showcase how flexible decision-making and clear accountability can mitigate risks and ensure mission success (Roberts et al., 1994). This adaptability is mirrored in other HROs, such as air traffic control, where rapid decisions must be made without compromising safety (La Porte & Consolini, 1998). At the core of these capabilities is human capital – the collective KSAOs that enable individuals to perform under pressure (Ericksen & Dyer, 2005).

Organizations invest heavily in training to enhance these KSAOs, focusing on situational awareness, risk anticipation, and informed decision-making (Hales & Chakravorty, 2016). In healthcare, for instance, fostering an active learning culture – where questioning and feedback are encouraged – has been shown to reduce errors and improve patient outcomes. However, as research suggests, this approach requires careful balance to avoid unintended consequences, such as increased errors during critical learning phases (Katz-Navon et al., 2009).

Leadership and interpersonal skills are equally critical. Structured training programs and feedback loops help leaders cultivate mindfulness – an acute awareness of operational dynamics and potential risks (Weick et al., 1999). This mindfulness allows leaders to adapt quickly while fostering collaboration and maintaining team cohesion during crises. By integrating technical and interpersonal competencies, HROs ensure that leaders and employees can respond effectively to high-pressure situations, enhancing both safety and reliability (Hannah et al., 2009).

The Military as a High Reliability Organization: Leadership in Critical Contexts

The military exemplifies HRO principles through its structured systems for managing risk, ensuring operational reliability, and fostering adaptability in critical environments (Weick & Roberts, 1993). Operating under conditions where failure can be catastrophic, military units rely on hierarchical decision-making frameworks and real-time adaptation strategies (Kalkman, 2023). This emphasis on resilience and decentralized decision-making enables the military to maintain reliability amid uncertainty, making it a model for HROs (Wong et al., 2003).

Even in tightly controlled training environments, the risks remain significant. The annual death rate published by the US Department of Defense Casualty Analysis System is approximately 7.7 per 100,000 service members during military training, a figure lower than some high-risk civilian industries like commercial fishing or logging but striking given these deaths occur with exceedingly greater frequency during preparation, not active missions. This underscores the unique risk profile of the military: training itself involves life-threatening scenarios. In combat, the stakes rise exponentially, reinforcing the military's need for a culture that prioritizes proactive risk management and adaptability.

From the earliest stages of their careers, service members learn to anticipate failures, mitigate risks, and ensure that operations remain effective (Redmond et al., 2015). Veterans emerging from this high-reliability culture develop leadership traits such as risk awareness, resilience, and the ability to make decentralized decisions. These competencies enable them to assess complex situations quickly and act decisively in high-pressure environments, whether in combat or intensive training scenarios (Peat et al., 2024).

A Conceptual Framework for Bridging Military HRO Principles

The leadership capabilities cultivated in military environments transfer effectively to civilian organizations. Veterans' adaptability, accountability, and operational focus align closely with the needs of both HRO and non-HRO sectors, where agility and resilience are critical to navigating disruption (Sharma & Pearsall, 2016). By incorporating military-derived competencies, civilian organizations can enhance their capacity to perform under pressure, improve decision-making, and build cohesive teams capable of thriving in volatile conditions.

Veterans develop a range of leadership qualities that are highly relevant across various organizational contexts, particularly in dynamic, high-pressure, and uncertain environments. These include an acute sense of risk awareness, the ability to recover quickly from setbacks (resilience), and a strong commitment to accountability and ethical decision-making in high-stakes environments. Each of these leadership traits forms a critical component of veterans' human capital, driving operational efficiency and enhancing organizational effectiveness in environments that demand precision, adaptability, and resilience.

Leadership Competency: Risk Awareness

Service members are systematically trained to identify and mitigate risks in environments where failure can lead to catastrophic consequences, including the loss of life or limb (Campbell, Hannah, & Matthews, 2010). This heightened sense of risk awareness represents a critical form of human capital, developed through rigorous training and repeated exposure to high-pressure environments. In these settings, military personnel are taught not only to recognize potential threats but also to preemptively address them using structured risk assessment frameworks. These anticipatory skills are cultivated through formal education, realistic drills, and the tacit learning that arises from leadership experiences under stress.

Military environments uniquely demand that leaders manage both their own actions and those of their teams, creating a dual responsibility that sharpens their risk awareness. Leaders are accountable for mission outcomes, which often carry life-or-death stakes. This requires maintaining high situational awareness and balancing factors such as team readiness, environmental hazards, and mission objectives. For instance, during Operation Neptune Spear, Navy SEAL leaders swiftly adapted their strategy when a helicopter crash-landed inside Osama bin Laden's compound. They managed immediate risks, such as securing the perimeter, while ensuring that the team maintained focus on the broader mission objective. The military's command-and-control structure further expands leaders' risk perception by requiring them to anticipate not only their own decisions but also the independent decisions of their team members under pressure. This decentralized decision-making model enhances service members' ability to adapt and manage risk across multiple layers of complexity, particularly in dynamic scenarios such as shifting enemy movements or unforeseen logistical challenges.

Risk management in the military is not a one-time exercise but an integral part of every action and decision. Every mission begins with a detailed risk assessment, and potential threats are constantly evaluated at all levels. On a tactical level, soldiers assess risks like terrain hazards during patrols, while at the strategic level, commanders and staff evaluate the broader implications of resource allocation for ongoing operations. This repetitive process makes risk awareness second nature to military personnel, equipping them with the critical thinking skills necessary for identifying, evaluating, and mitigating risks in real time. Structured risk management frameworks, such as identifying, assessing, mitigating, and reviewing risks, are ingrained in military operations, ensuring that service members bring this comprehensive approach to both tactical and strategic decisions.

Leadership Competencies: Resilience and Adaptability

Military training emphasizes the dual qualities of enduring hardship and adapting strategies to dynamic, unpredictable conditions. Service members cultivate resilience and adaptability through exposure to high-pressure situations, where swift recovery from setbacks is essential. These competencies are enhanced by practices like After-Action Reviews (AARs), which encourage systematic reflection on successes and failures. By analyzing outcomes, service members refine decision-making skills, identify areas for improvement, and build stronger team cohesion. These feedback loops foster a culture of continuous learning, preparing service members with mental toughness to thrive under challenging circumstances (Keiser & Arthur, 2021).

An illustrative example comes from the Army's 173rd Airborne Brigade during their deployment to Afghanistan in 2007. Facing a sudden insurgent ambush in Kunar Province, the unit had to adapt rapidly to unanticipated conditions. Leaders at all levels demonstrated resilience by maintaining composure and recalibrating their strategy in real time. Soldiers moved from a planned reconnaissance mission to a coordinated defense under fire, effectively leveraging terrain and communication to outmaneuver the enemy. The ability to adapt quickly while under immense pressure allowed the brigade to minimize casualties and accomplish their immediate objectives. This event highlights how resilience and adaptability are critical in chaotic and unpredictable environments.

Military resilience is also tested and developed through long-duration exercises, which closely simulate real-world operational conditions, including physical exhaustion, sleep deprivation, and limited resources while managing complex operations. To illustrate, during the Navy's participation in multi-week fleet exercises such as Composite Training Unit Exercises, sailors must maintain focus and perform critical tasks under extreme fatigue. These scenarios often involve high-stakes drills like responding to simulated shipboard fires, managing damage control, and conducting underway replenishments, all while preparing for potential threats. These exercises teach service members to prioritize effectively, manage stress, and ensure that their decisions remain sound and mission-focused, even in the most challenging circumstances.

Formal resilience training in the military also focuses on developing stress-coping strategies and mental fortitude, preparing personnel to handle the emotional demands of high-pressure environments. For example, structured resilience programs emphasize reframing setbacks as learning opportunities, promoting a mindset that failure is not an endpoint but a stepping stone to improvement.

Adaptability is similarly ingrained through real-world experiences that demand rapid recalibration. Whether adjusting to sudden changes in mission objectives or responding to unforeseen environmental challenges, service members learn to stay composed and shift strategies without losing sight of broader goals. For instance, during Operation Iraqi Freedom, Marine logistics units faced repeated convoy attacks but adapted by altering their routes, employing decoy convoys, and collaborating with local forces for intelligence. These tactical changes allowed them to maintain supply chain operations under extreme pressure, ensuring mission continuity despite ongoing threats.

Leadership Competencies: Accountability and Ethical Decision-Making

Accountability and ethical decision-making are foundational elements of military leadership, emphasizing both responsibility for outcomes and adherence to organizational values. Service members are trained to make critical decisions under pressure, within set parameters, while remaining accountable for their actions. This emphasis on accountability at all levels fosters a culture of transparency and extends beyond individual actions to team performance. All service members are not merely expected, but required, to contribute to shared goals ethically and effectively (Hannah, Avolio, & Walumbwa, 2011).

These lessons are hard learned from historical experience, where the absence of accountability in decision-making has led to devastating consequences. One such example is the My Lai Massacre during the Vietnam War, a tragedy where the lack of ethical oversight, transparency, and accountability resulted in the deaths of hundreds of civilians. This event underscored the critical need for leaders to act within ethical boundaries, maintain oversight, and ensure that operational decisions are grounded in organizational values and principles. The US military responded by institutionalizing practices that emphasize accountability and ethical decision-making as central tenets of leadership.

This dual focus on accountability and ethics fosters a leadership culture built on trust and mutual respect. Service members are expected to lead by example, making prudent, value-aligned decisions while holding both themselves and their teams accountable. For example, during the Russian invasion of Ukraine, analyses highlighted stark differences in military command structures. In the Russian military, decision-making is highly centralized, with generals retaining excessive control over decisions that frontline commanders could otherwise execute more efficiently and timely. This rigidity hampers reaction times in high-pressure situations, often leading to missed opportunities and operational inefficiencies. By contrast, the US military operates with a decentralized decision-making structure, empowering unit commanders to make and execute decisions in real time within set parameters. This ensures rapid responses in critical moments while maintaining clear mechanisms for accountability.

The US military's approach to decentralized accountability is not limited to combat scenarios. In military human resources (HR), for instance, service members managing personnel assignments face decisions that impact both individuals and overall unit readiness. An HR office may need to balance competing priorities, such as accommodating a service member's family needs (e.g., school-aged children not changing schools) while ensuring that the operational requirements of a deploying unit are met. This necessitates a thoughtful consideration of ethical boundaries, operational goals, as well as the potential ripple effects of each decision, reinforcing the importance of accountability at every level.

These practices are supported by structured processes like AARs, which encourage leaders to reflect on their decisions and learn from both successes and setbacks. Through these mechanisms, military leaders develop the ability to act decisively while remaining grounded in ethical principles, ensuring that their actions align with organizational values and foster a culture of accountability.

Transferability of Skills

Direct Translation: Veterans in High-Stakes Civilian HROs

Veterans' military service equips them with specialized human capital that often aligns seamlessly with the competencies required for leadership roles in high-stakes civilian HROs. The military's emphasis on reliability, risk management, and adaptability creates direct pathways for veterans to contribute effectively in sectors like healthcare, aviation, nuclear energy, and emergency response, where precision and consistency are fundamental.

In both military and civilian contexts, continuous vigilance and risk anticipation are fundamental to preventing failures and ensuring safety. Just as a military commander must adapt quickly to battlefield conditions, a safety manager in an industrial plant must respond swiftly to equipment malfunctions or hazardous material leaks. Veterans' ability to apply structured risk mitigation frameworks to such high-pressure scenarios ensures they can face unpredictable challenges with efficiency and precision, minimizing risks to both personnel and operations.

Resilience and adaptability, honed through exposure to high-stress environments, are invaluable in maintaining operational reliability within HROs. Military training often places personnel in scenarios that replicate the intensity of real-world challenges, such as simulated disaster relief operations or joint exercises with allied forces. For instance, a veteran transitioning to a role in emergency medicine might rely on their experience coordinating medical evacuations during large-scale field exercises, where split-second decisions and limited resources dictate success. Practices like AARs instill a culture of reflection and continuous learning, enabling veterans to evaluate outcomes, refine processes, and implement improvements in environments like emergency departments, where patient conditions can shift unpredictably (Keiser & Arthur, 2021).

Accountability and ethical decision-making are equally critical to veterans' contributions in HROs. These traits are deeply embedded in military culture, where leaders are required to balance mission objectives with the welfare of their teams and the communities they serve. For example, a veteran working in nuclear energy might draw on their experience managing safety protocols during live-fire training exercises. Such exercises demand strict adherence to ethical guidelines to prevent injuries, a discipline that translates directly into ensuring compliance with stringent regulatory standards in nuclear facilities. By fostering trust and transparency, veterans in these roles not only uphold safety but also create an environment where team members are encouraged to report potential risks without fear of reprisal, a cornerstone of high-reliability performance.

Decentralized decision-making, a defining feature of military leadership, further enhances the ability of veterans to thrive in HROs. In the military, junior leaders are often empowered to make critical decisions, such as rerouting supply convoys in hostile environments when primary routes become compromised. This operational independence prepares veterans for civilian roles that demand similar agility. For instance, in aviation, air traffic controllers must quickly analyze complex variables, such as unexpected weather patterns or equipment malfunctions, to ensure safe and efficient operations. Veterans' ability to act decisively while adhering to structured guidelines ensures they can balance autonomy with the broader objectives of the organization, enabling swift responses to dynamic challenges.

Indirect Translation: Veterans in Non-HROs

The transition of veterans' skills into non-HROs, such as nonprofit leadership, education, and corporate environments, involves unique challenges and additional adaptations. Unlike the high-stakes, risk-driven contexts of military or civilian HROs, these sectors often operate with comparatively lower levels of urgency and risk to limb or life. However, veterans bring a wealth of transferable leadership capabilities that add significant value in these environments, especially when organizations are navigating change, complexity, or disruptions.

Having developed this resilience and adaptability in military contexts characterized by uncertainty and rapid change, veterans are particularly well-suited for managing disruptions or periods of organizational restructuring. For example, in the nonprofit sector, a veteran leading a community food bank might draw on their experience coordinating logistical support in field environments. When faced with unexpected supply chain disruptions, such as delayed food deliveries or an influx of demand, their ability to stay composed and recalibrate plans ensures the organization continues to serve its community effectively.

Another example is that of Angel Johnson, a former US Air Force officer and founder of ICONI, an activewear brand. Johnson launched her business in the middle of the COVID-19 pandemic, navigating significant supply chain disruptions as well as shifting consumer demands. She credited her time in the military, especially her time in combat in Afghanistan, for being able to navigate and thrive during a period of significant disruption.

In education, veterans' adaptability stands out, specifically their ability to remain effective amid personal or professional disruptions. During the first author's time as a brigade engineer officer, the call sign "Razor" reflected a reliance on the principle of Occam's Razor in all complex tasks. This principle prioritizes simplicity, emphasizing that the simplest solution is often the most desirable. Complexity can lead to mission failure by introducing more variability and potential for error. This same approach was applied in a civilian role as a college professor when a delayed house move collided with the start of the semester. By repurposing relevant examples and assignments from previous courses, the preparation process was streamlined and resulted in a successful course, despite the challenging circumstances. This example underscores how military-honed adaptability and focus can enhance teaching effectiveness in a dynamic academic setting.

Decentralized decision-making within parameters, another hallmark of military leadership, requires adjustment in many civilian organizations. Compared to the military and HROs, many non-HRO civilian organizations either operate with rigid hierarchical structures or overly free-flowing, unstructured environments in which decision-making lacks clear guidelines, accountability, or a defined chain of responsibility. Veterans' experience making autonomous decisions under pressure equips them to navigate these extremes by introducing clarity and structure where needed. For instance, an accountant transitioning into a managerial role in a mid-sized firm might leverage this skill to empower their team to solve client issues without waiting for upper management approval. By setting clear parameters for decision-making and defining purpose in outcomes, they create an environment where team members feel trusted and capable, improving both efficiency and morale.

Veterans also bring structured processes and strategic planning capabilities, which can create efficiencies in industries that may not traditionally emphasize these disciplines. They are trained to leave things better than they found them, a principle that fosters continuous improvement and long-term impact in their roles (Peat, 2021). In a nonprofit organization, for example, a veteran working in fundraising might introduce systematic approaches to donor engagement, drawing on military frameworks like the Military Decision-Making Process for resource allocation and prioritization. These methods could help streamline campaigns and maximize donor retention through a clear definition of fundraising goals, multiple courses of action development, and continuous monitoring, ultimately driving better outcomes for the organization's mission.

Accountability and ethical decision-making, deeply embedded in military culture, are equally critical in non-HRO settings. In professional jobs like accounting, these traits guide veterans in balancing competing priorities, such as meeting tight deadlines while ensuring compliance with regulations. Indeed, firms led by veteran CEOs often have significantly fewer instances of financial misconduct (Koch-Bayram & Wernicke, 2018). This underscores how veterans' ingrained sense of responsibility and ethical judgment can foster a culture of integrity and trust within organizations, reducing risk and enhancing reputational credibility.

Veterans' ability to manage complexity and resource constraints translates seamlessly into corporate leadership. A veteran leading a corporate operations team during a supply chain disruption caused by geopolitical tensions can quickly assess the situation, allocate available resources strategically, and develop contingency plans to mitigate delays. Their military experience equips them to foster clear communication and decisive action, enabling their team to maintain operational continuity while minimizing customer impact and financial loss.

Finally, veterans' resilience and ability to bridge structured and unstructured environments make them invaluable contributors across a wide range of non-HRO industries. Their unique perspective often brings fresh ideas to organizations facing stagnation or transformation. Whether introducing innovative classroom strategies as an educator or streamlining operations as a nonprofit leader, veterans' leadership competencies drive meaningful impact even in settings with lower operational risks.

Applying High Reliability Principles in an HRO Context: A Public Health Case Study

Alek Kranbuhl is a health physicist at the Centers for Disease Control and Prevention (CDC) who served over eight years in the US Navy as a lead engineering laboratory technician. In his current role, Alek manages hazards ranging from IT outages that briefly interrupt workflows to radioactive spills that require extensive coordination and swift, precise responses to prevent catastrophic consequences. Thus, Alek's position at the CDC represents the quintessential HRO, marked by the need for high reliability around vigilance, safety, and risk anticipation.

Alek noted that his military background equipped him to handle these critical disruptions effectively, a crucial competency in his role overseeing radiation safety and responding to incidents involving radioactive materials. In one instance, during a routine operation involving high-level radioactive material, Alek's pre-procedure walkthrough, a habit cultivated in the Navy, revealed a valve in the wrong position. Halting the operation and reporting the issue to his supervisor, Alek avoided a potentially catastrophic mishandling of radioactive waste. While the delay cost a day's work, it prevented a far more serious outcome.

To prepare for high-stakes incidents, Alek and his team conduct regular training and simulations, mirroring the military's emphasis on readiness. These exercises ensure familiarity with proper procedures, from contamination cleanup to protective clothing protocols. Alek also emphasizes the importance of situational awareness, a principle instilled during his service. Early recognition of issues allows for scaled responses that prevent minor disruptions from escalating into major crises.

Alek's military training also fostered a questioning attitude, crucial for maintaining reliability in his role. Recognizing the dangers of complacency, he encourages his team to challenge assumptions and address unsafe conditions. His proactive approach to triaging risks – allocating resources based on urgency and impact – ensures that the CDC can respond effectively to a wide range of disruptions, safeguarding both personnel and operations.

Applying High Reliability Principles in a Non-HRO Context: An Education Case Study

John VanDusen served 20 years in the Michigan Army National Guard, including combat deployments to Iraq and Afghanistan. He now teaches 8th-grade US History and coaches high school football for a school district in Michigan.

In March 2020, as the COVID-19 pandemic unfolded, John faced an unprecedented disruption to the education field. Initially, the shift to remote learning seemed temporary, just "two weeks to flatten the curve." Soon, it evolved into a prolonged period of uncertainty and rapid adaptation. He quickly pivoted from traditional teaching methods to online platforms, utilizing tools like YouTube videos and blog posts to maintain student engagement. Beyond his own adaptation, John took on a mentoring role, supporting colleagues who struggled with the abrupt changes, helping them regain confidence and develop new strategies for engaging their students.

What made the situation uniquely challenging was the uncertainty surrounding public health guidelines and the emotional toll it took on both students and staff. Drawing on his military training, he implemented mental frameworks like the OODA Loop (Observe, Orient, Decide, Act) to assess emerging challenges and develop practical solutions. His military background also fostered emotional intelligence and composure under pressure, enabling him to navigate shifting policies on masks, quarantines, and social distancing. This calm, systematic approach helped him maintain a sense of stability for his students, even during chaotic times.

Reflecting on the experience, John emphasized the importance of resilience and adaptability. He recognized that emotionally driven decisions had no place in a crisis and relied instead on military-developed practical tools, like the ethical triangle (a decision-making framework that balances principles, consequences, and virtues) and the principles of mission command (self-awareness, empathy, self-regulation). These lessons, rooted in his military experiences, have profoundly influenced his teaching and leadership style, reinforcing the value of remaining calm under pressure and consistently seeking innovative ways to engage and inspire students.

Barriers to Transfer

Transitioning military-derived competencies into civilian roles is not without challenges. While veterans bring extensive leadership, risk management, and operational expertise, barriers exist that manifest differently in HROs and non-HROs. These challenges include cultural and structural misalignment, skill underutilization, communication gaps, adjustment to lower-stakes environments, and identity shifts. The core issue is that while veterans are trained to navigate disruptions proactively, civilian organizations, especially non-HROs, often lack the same urgency, structure, or decision-making clarity veterans are accustomed to.

Cultural and Organizational Differences

Veterans transitioning into HROs may find familiarity in the structured, safety-driven, and risk-mitigating environments. However, decision-making structures in civilian HROs may differ significantly from military command hierarchies. While the military operates on mission-driven, decentralized authority, civilian HROs often rely on bureaucratic protocols and multi-tiered oversight, slowing response times and limiting autonomy in ways that veterans may find frustrating.

In contrast, non-HROs often either operate with less structure, looser roles, and fewer predefined risk management protocols or higher levels of micro-management. Veterans accustomed to clear chains of command and rapid decision-making often find civilian workplaces unstructured, inefficient, or slow to act in moments of disruption. The lack of a defined contingency framework for non-HROs further exacerbates frustrations for veterans trained to anticipate and address risks proactively. The end result is often decision paralysis during disruptions that can leave veterans feeling underutilized and disengaged.

Underutilization of Skills

In HROs, veterans' skills in risk awareness, crisis response, and structured decision-making may be recognized but are often underutilized in leadership roles. While veterans may find operational roles that align with their competencies, they are often not fast-tracked for leadership pipelines, limiting their strategic impact (Stone & Stone, 2015). Additionally, some HRO credentialing systems (e.g., FAA licensing in aviation, nuclear regulatory compliance) require veterans to undergo additional civilian certification with significantly long timelines, which can delay or discourage transitions.

In non-HROs, the misalignment between military expertise and civilian job functions is often more pronounced. Veterans are often placed in lower-level positions or generalist roles where their ability to lead teams, assess risks, and operate under high stress is undervalued or overlooked. This is often exacerbated by an overall lack of familiarity by veterans of civilian job roles and by civilian hiring managers of military-derived competencies (Davis & Minnis, 2017). For example, an Army infantry platoon sergeant is tasked with training, discipline, and readiness of a platoon responsible for "closing with and destroying the enemy." Clearly, no equivalent civilian job exists with the same duties, so translating this role often takes considerable knowledge and effort. These disconnects lead to higher levels of job dissatisfaction, disengagement, and turnover among veterans in non-HRO settings.

Communication and Perception Gaps

In HROs, industry-specific language and civilian regulatory frameworks can create barriers for veterans accustomed to military terminology, mission-focused directives, and high-context decision-making structures. Civilian HRO teams may expect different forms of documentation, reporting, or justification than the military, making it difficult for veterans to communicate their expertise effectively within the organizational framework.

In non-HROs, the communication divide is often more cultural than technical. Veterans who speak in direct, action-oriented terms may be perceived as too blunt or aggressive in corporate, educational, or nonprofit settings where consensus-building and indirect communication are the norm. Additionally, military humor and coping mechanisms may not always align with civilian workplace expectations, further complicating integration. Finally, employers in both HROs and non-HROs may be hesitant to empower veterans in decision-making roles due to misconceptions about rigid military thinking or a lack of familiarity with decentralized military leadership.

Adjustment to Lower Stakes and Ambiguity

Veterans accustomed to high-pressure environments often find it challenging to adapt to non-HRO civilian roles where the stakes are lower and the pace of decision-making is slower (Cooper et al., 2018). This shift can leave veterans feeling under-stimulated or disconnected, especially in roles that lack clear missions or objectives. During disruptions, this adjustment challenge becomes even more pronounced. Veterans, who are trained to anticipate and address uncertainty, may struggle in environments where ambiguity is met with indecision or a lack of urgency. For example, in a corporate setting, veterans may find the absence of clear contingency plans or defined leadership during a supply chain disruption frustrating and counterproductive.

Navigating Identity and Role Transition

The transition from military to civilian life often involves a shift in identity. In the military, veterans' sense of self is often closely tied to their leadership roles and high-reliability responsibilities. In civilian organizations, veterans may feel less essential or impactful, especially if their new roles lack the clear purpose or prestige they associated with their military careers (Gonzalez & Simpson, 2021). Disruptions in civilian settings can amplify this disconnect if veterans perceive that their skills in managing uncertainty and maintaining operational stability are underutilized or undervalued. This can lead to feelings of alienation, particularly if civilian organizations fail to provide veterans with meaningful roles during critical moments of organizational change or uncertainty.

Addressing these barriers requires deliberate effort from both veterans and civilian organizations. Employers must actively seek to understand and leverage the unique competencies veterans bring, especially their ability to lead during disruptions. Organizations should foster environments that support veterans' integration and empower them to contribute their expertise in managing complexity and uncertainty. Veterans, in turn, must adapt their approaches to align with civilian norms, translating their skills and experiences into frameworks that resonate across diverse industries.

A Model of Military HRO Principles in Civilian Organizations

Figure 4.1 illustrates how military-derived HRO principles can be adapted to civilian organizations, as well as the barriers to integration. At its core, the conceptual framework highlights the key competencies shaped by military

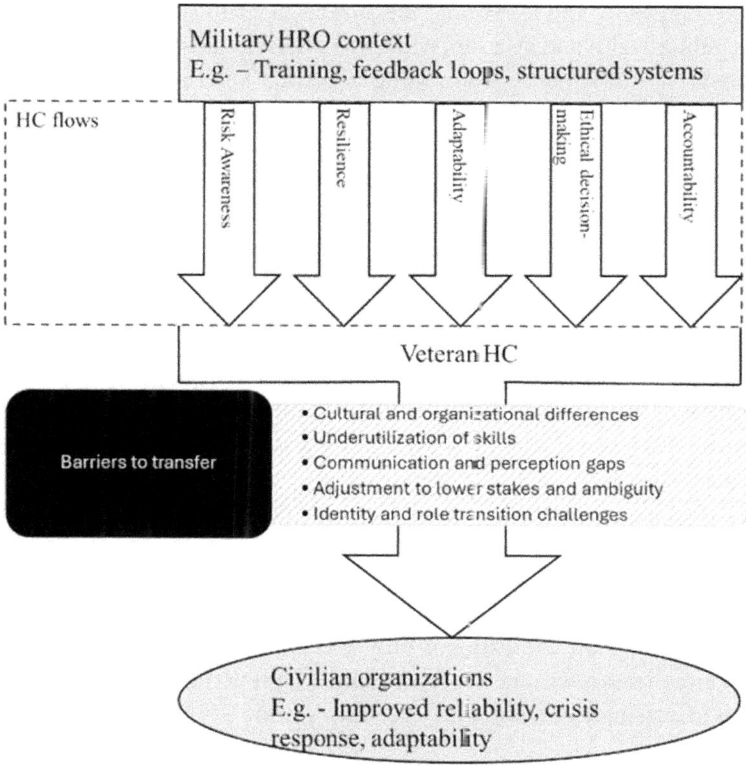

Figure 4.1 A framework for bridging military HRO principles to civilian organizations.

service, risk awareness, resilience, ethical decision-making, accountability, and adaptability.

Utilizing Veteran Talent to Promote Resilience: Opportunity and Implications

The integration of military-derived HRO principles into civilian contexts highlights the critical role structured leadership competencies play in fostering organizational resilience and agility. Veterans possess a unique blend of capabilities, such as risk awareness, adaptability, and ethical decision-making, that are particularly valuable in dynamic and high-stakes environments. Their ability to navigate complexity and lead under pressure aligns with the demands of HROs, such as public health and aviation, while also offering transformative potential in sectors with less inherent risk, including education and nonprofit management. These competencies not only enhance operational reliability but also contribute to innovation and problem-solving across diverse organizational contexts.

However, the successful transfer of these competencies is not without challenges. Veterans often face structural and cultural barriers, including mismatches between military and civilian organizational norms and underutilization of their skills. The inability of organizations to fully leverage veterans' potential highlights a need for more intentional strategies to bridge these gaps. These include tailored onboarding programs, professional development opportunities, and the creation of inclusive policies that align with veterans' unique strengths and experiences. By addressing these challenges, organizations can unlock the full value of military-derived human capital while promoting workplace inclusion.

The broader implications extend beyond individual contributions to systemic organizational benefits. Practices originating from military training, such as AARs and mission-focused planning, offer universal lessons for cultivating a culture of accountability, continuous learning, and resilience. Integrating these practices into civilian contexts not only prepares organizations for disruption but also establishes a foundation for sustained high performance and adaptability in an increasingly complex and uncertain world.

Implications for Practice and Best Practices for Employing Veterans

The following best practices, derived from organizational studies on military veterans in civilian organizations, highlight approaches that organizations could consider when leveraging the leadership, risk management, and operational expertise that veterans bring to both High Reliability Organizations (HROs) and non-HROs.

- Strategic talent identification and skill mapping. Organizations benefit from moving beyond generic military-to-civilian job translators by developing role-specific competency mapping for veterans (Peat et al., 2024), drawing on the expertise of those who have previously transitioned or who live in both worlds (i.e., military reservists). Engaging veterans in job analysis and task alignment efforts helps clarify how their leadership, risk awareness, and adaptability translate into mission-critical roles in industries such as healthcare, logistics, and crisis management, as well as non-HRO environments.

- Targeted onboarding for operational integration. Structured onboarding that bridges military and civilian operational cultures is especially helpful for recently transitioned veterans to enhance not only their organizational integration but also societal integration. Incorporating scenario-based training and problem-solving exercises early in the onboarding process for these individuals allows them to apply their decision-making and leadership skills in ways that align with civilian organizational needs. In HROs, emphasizing mission continuity, rapid decision-making, and accountability as hallmarks of both the military and civilian HROs maximizes the effectiveness of military-derived competencies.
- Optimizing veterans for crisis and risk management roles. Veterans' backgrounds in contingency planning and risk mitigation often align with roles that require crisis response, operational reliability, and high-stakes decision-making. Organizations often find value in selecting and positioning veterans for positions in emergency preparedness, cybersecurity, supply chain logistics, or strategic risk assessment, where a proactive approach to uncertainty is critical (Davis & Minnis, 2017). Establishing crisis leadership pipelines further supports veterans' career aspects by creating opportunities for future advancement. For instance, retired Navy Captain Jenn Donahue transitioned from military engineering leadership to managing disaster response and seismic engineering crises. Her ability to plan for and execute risk mitigation strategies in the face of environmental disasters highlights how veterans can excel in crisis management roles, where structured decision-making and adaptability are critical.
- Leveraging military-style decision-making processes. High-reliability civilian organizations might consider incorporating military-derived decision-making frameworks, such as mission command, the OODA Loop, and AARs, into their operating procedures (Wong et al., 2003). These methodologies could help improve situational awareness and have demonstrable success in high-stress environments, emphasizing adaptability and rapid decision-making. Training non-military leaders in military-style contingency planning may also contribute to improved organizational resilience, as well as facilitating the integration of military human capital.
- Continuous professional development. While many veterans bring extensive leadership experience, role-specific professional development is often needed to ensure they maximize their potential in civilian roles (Stone & Stone, 2015). Organizations should consider technical upskilling programs tailored to operational roles, such as AI-enhanced decision-making in logistics or strategic planning certifications for business leadership.

Instead of general leadership training, some employers may find value in tactical decision-making simulations, allowing veterans to refine their civilian-relevant skills in applied settings.

- Positioning veterans for operational efficiency and process improvement. Veterans' expertise in logistics, process standardization, and operational efficiency often makes them well-suited for lean management, Six Sigma, and operational process optimization with appropriate training. Their experience in resource allocation under constraints offers insights into streamlining workflows, reducing redundancies, and improving high-reliability processes (Redmond et al., 2015). Some organizations might explore ways to incorporate veterans into continuous improvement initiatives, where their ability to manage complex operations under pressure can drive measurable performance gains.

Filling the Gaps for Clutch Leadership

This framework addresses the general human capital developed through military service, focusing on transferable skills like resilience, risk management, accountability, and adaptability. However, it does not account for the firm-specific, industry-specific, or job-specific knowledge that veterans must acquire to succeed in particular roles. For example, while military leadership skills may prepare a veteran for managing complex teams, specific technical knowledge, such as industry regulations or software proficiency, may still be necessary for full effectiveness in certain civilian environments.

Additionally, this framework is agnostic to the wide range of factors that influence the development and application of military-derived human capital. Differences in tenure, rank, officer versus enlisted roles, and combat versus non-combat experience all shape the skills and leadership styles veterans bring to civilian roles. The analysis presented here is also largely US-centric, reflecting the structure and culture of the US military, which may not align with the experiences of veterans from other countries (particularly from non-Western countries). As such, while the competencies highlighted are broadly applicable, their depth and expression may vary significantly among individuals.

Finally, it is important to emphasize that veterans are individuals first, shaped by unique experiences both within and beyond their military service. While this chapter provides insights into the general skills developed through military training, it does not claim to capture the diversity of perspectives, motivations, and career aspirations within the veteran community. Employers, educators, and policymakers should use this framework as a guide for understanding the common strengths veterans bring to the workforce while remaining flexible and responsive to individual needs and contexts.

Conclusion

Veterans embody the essence of clutch leadership – thriving under pressure, adapting to uncertainty, and making critical decisions with confidence and integrity. Their ability to lead in high-stakes environments stems from their mastery of resilience, risk awareness, decentralized decision-making, and ethical leadership. These qualities, honed in military service, make veterans invaluable assets to civilian organizations, particularly in times of disruption and transformation. By recognizing and strategically integrating military-derived competencies, organizations can cultivate a leadership culture that prioritizes agility, reliability, and mission-focused execution.

References

Campbell, D. J., Hannah, S. T., & Matthews, M. D. (2010). Leadership in military and other dangerous contexts: Introduction to the special topic issue. *Military Psychology, 22*(supl), S1–S14.

Cooper, L., Caddick, N., Godier, L., Cooper, A., & Fossey, M. (2018). Transition from the military into civilian life: An exploration of cultural competence. *Armed Forces & Society, 44*(1), 156–177.

Davis, V. E., & Minnis, S. E. (2017). Military veterans' transferable skills: An HRD practitioner dilemma. *Advances in Developing Human Resources, 19*(1), 6–13.

Ericksen, J., & Dyer, L. (2005). Toward a strategic human resource management model of high reliability organization performance. *The International Journal of Human Resource Management, 16*(6), 907–922. https://doi.org/10.1080/09585190500120731

Gonzalez, J. A., & Simpson, J. (2021). The workplace integration of veterans: Applying diversity and fit perspectives. *Human Resource Management Review, 31*(2), 100775.

Hales, D. N., & Chakravorty, S. S. (2016). Creating high reliability organizations using mindfulness. *Journal of Business Research, 69*(8), 2873–2881. https://doi.org/10.1016/j.jbusres.2015.12.056

Hannah, S. T., Avolio, B. J., & Walumbwa, F. O. (2011). Relationships between authentic leadership, moral courage, and ethical and pro-social behaviors. *Business Ethics Quarterly, 21*(4), 555–578.

Hannah, S. T., Uhl-Bien, M., Avolio, B. J., & Cavarretta, F. L. (2009). A framework for examining leadership in extreme contexts. *The Leadership Quarterly*, 20(6), 897–919. https://doi.org/10.1016/j.leaqua.2009.09.006

Kalkman, J. P. (2023). Mindful members: Developing a mindset for reliable performance in extreme contexts. *Journal of Management Inquiry*, *32*(3), 200–213. https://doi.org/10.1177/10564926221082487

Katz-Navon, T., Stern, Z., & Naveh, E. (2009). Active learning: When is more better? The case of resident physicians' medical errors. *Journal of Applied Psychology*, *94*(5), 1200–1210. https://doi.org/10.1037/a0015979

Keiser, N. L., & Arthur Jr., W. (2021). A meta-analysis of the effectiveness of the after-action review (or debrief) and factors that influence its effectiveness. *Journal of Applied Psychology*, *106*(7), 1007.

Klein, K. J., Ziegert, J. C., Knight, A. P., & Xiao, Y. (2006). Dynamic delegation: Shared, hierarchical, and deindividualized leadership in extreme action teams. *Administrative Science Quarterly*, *51*(4), 590–621.

Koch-Bayram, I. F., & Wernicke, G. (2018). Drilled to obey? Ex-military CEOs and financial misconduct. *Strategic Management Journal*, *39*(11), 2943–2964.

La Porte, T., & Consolini, P. (1998). Theoretical and operational challenges of "high-reliability organizations": Air-traffic control and aircraft carriers. *International Journal of Public Administration*, *21*(6–8), 847–859. https://doi.org/10.1080/01900699808525320

Peat, D. M. (2021). Marching boots to business suits: Military veteran human capital in nonmilitary organizations. In *Academy of management proceedings* (Vol. 2021, No. 1, p. 11630). Briarcliff Manor, NY: Academy of Management.

Peat, D. M., Sweet, K. M., Black, S. L., & Rogers, S. E. (2024). Understanding and including military-connected employees. In M. Harvey, K. Allard, & C. Kegley (Eds.), *Understanding and managing diversity: Readings, cases, and exercises* (7th ed.). Boston, MA: Pearson Education.

Redmond, S. A., Wilcox, S. L., Campbell, S., Kim, A., Finney, K., Barr, K., & Hassan, A. M. (2015). A brief introduction to the military workplace culture. *Work*. https://doi.org/10.3233/WOR-141987

Roberts, K. H. (1990). Some characteristics of high-reliability organizations. *Organization Science*, *1*(2), 160–177. https://doi.org/10.1287/orsc.1.2.160

Roberts, K. H., Stout, S. K., & Halpern, J. J. (1994). Decision dynamics in two high reliability military organizations. *Management Science*, *40*(5), 614–632. https://doi.org/10.1287/mnsc.40.5.614

Sharma, P. N., & Pearsall, M. J. (2016). Leading under adversity: Interactive effects of acute stressors and upper-level supportive leadership climate on lower-level supportive leadership climate. *The Leadership Quarterly*, *27*(6), 856–869. https://doi.org/10.1016/j.leaqua.2016.08.003

Stone, C., & Stone, D. L. (2015). Factors affecting hiring decisions about veterans. *Human Resource Management Review*, *25*(1), 68–79.

Vogus, T. J., & Rerup, C. (2018). Sweating the "small stuff": High-reliability organizing as a foundation for sustained superior performance. *Strategic Organization*, *16*(2), 227–238. https://doi.org/10.1177/1476127017739535

Weick, K. E., & Roberts, K. H. (1993). Collective mind in organizations: Heedful interrelating on flight decks. *Administrative Science quarterly*, *38*, 357–381.

Weick, K. E., Sutcliffe, K. M., & Obstfeld, D. (1999). Organizing for high reliability: Processes of collective mindfulness. *Research in Organizational Behavior, 21*, 81–123. https://doi.org/10.1016/S0191-3085(99)21005-6

Wong, L., Bliese, P., & McGurk, D. (2003). Military leadership: A context specific review. *The Leadership Quarterly*, *14*(6), 657–692.

OPERATIONAL EFFICIENCY

C

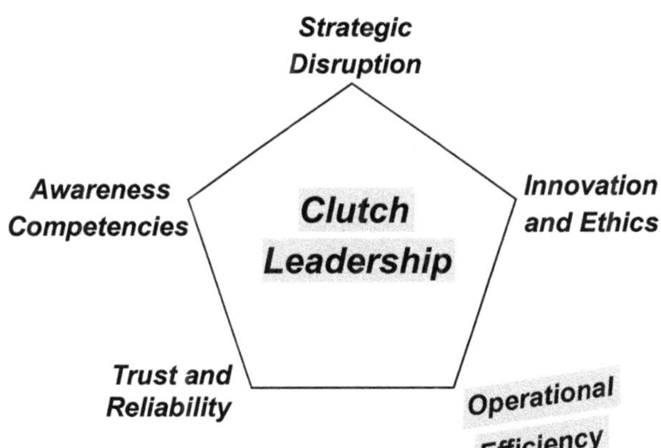

DOI: 10.4324/9781003629214-7

Chapter 5

Project Leadership in the AI Age: Embracing Clutch Leadership for Success

Thomas Wiese, Betul Lus and Ruifang Hope Sun

Introduction

Clutch leadership is crucial for navigating the complexities of project management driven by artificial intelligence (AI). Clutch leadership is characterized by adaptability, urgency, high aspirations, and empowerment, qualities that closely align with the demands of managing complex AI projects. As AI technologies advance rapidly and new tools emerge, project leaders with high aspirations must quickly adapt by fostering a culture of continuous learning and upskilling, promoting collaboration among diverse stakeholders, encouraging active engagement and empowerment, and effectively leveraging new technologies. Clutch leaders understand that successful AI integration requires more than just technological expertise; it also demands a clear long-term vision that anticipates future trends, a commitment to ethical practices, inclusivity, inspiring change, and building trust in data-driven insights.

DOI: 10.4324/9781003629214-8

Considering the evolving project management landscape, this chapter proposes a clutch leadership framework for AI-driven projects. Drawing on case studies from industries such as healthcare, technology, and manufacturing, the chapter illustrates the practical applications of AI in project leadership. For instance, in the healthcare sector, AI has streamlined administrative processes, enhanced diagnostic accuracy, and improved patient outcomes. These successes, however, were achieved through strong leadership that addressed potential resistance, ensured stakeholder alignment, and prioritized ethical considerations such as data privacy and algorithmic transparency. In technology and manufacturing sectors, AI has enabled organizations to optimize workflows, foster innovation, and achieve operational excellence. These examples demonstrate that effectively integrating AI into project leadership requires not only technical expertise but also strategic vision and ethical responsibility.

One of the critical challenges highlighted in this chapter is the potential for AI to reinforce existing biases, especially in areas such as recruitment and performance evaluations. For example, algorithms trained on historical data may undervalue soft skills or perpetuate gendered language biases, disproportionately affecting women in leadership roles (Dastin, 2018). Addressing these issues requires leaders to adopt inclusive frameworks, such as the Gender Equality Principles for AI, and prioritize diversity in the datasets utilized to train AI systems (United Nations Global Compact, n.d.). By doing this, leaders can ensure that AI systems promote equity rather than deepen existing disparities.

The human dimensions of AI leadership are equally important. As AI transforms workflows and decision-making processes, leaders must cultivate adaptability and resilience within their teams (Farah & Dorneich, 2024). This requires focused reskilling initiatives that equip employees for new roles and responsibilities alongside open communication that fosters trust in AI-driven systems. Effective leaders excel in these areas, leveraging their ability to inspire and empower teams to navigate uncertainty and embrace change.

Ethical considerations are central to the discussion of AI in project leadership. Leaders must balance the drive for innovation with a commitment to ethical practices, safeguarding privacy, equity, and accountability (Oladele et al., 2024). Transparent governance structures, rigorous testing of AI systems, and ongoing stakeholder engagement are essential components of an ethical AI strategy. By proactively addressing these issues, leaders can build trust and foster a culture of responsibility that supports long-term organizational success.

Project leadership in the AI age requires a nuanced approach that integrates technological, ethical, and human considerations. Clutch leadership provides a powerful framework for navigating this complex landscape, combining adaptability, urgency, and empowerment to drive digital transformation. By leveraging AI responsibly and inclusively, leaders can position their organizations for long-term success while addressing the ethical and societal challenges that come with technological change. This chapter offers a comprehensive roadmap for professionals aiming to cultivate their skills and thrive in this rapidly evolving environment, providing insights and strategies that bridge the gap between innovation and ethical responsibility.

AI as a Catalyst for Clutch Leadership

AI is rapidly transforming project management by automating many traditional tasks, shifting the focus from project management to project leadership. According to Gartner (2019), by 2030, AI will take over 80% of today's project management tasks, including data collection, tracking, and reporting. Powered by big data, machine learning, and natural language processing, AI will automate project selection, prioritization, and risk management, monitor project progress in real time and provide instant status updates, and facilitate rigorous testing and commissioning to ensure safety and reliability (Nieto-Rodriguez & Vargas, 2023). Additionally, AI tools can streamline project planning by analyzing historical data to predict project timelines and resource requirements, including time-cost relationships, allowing project managers to allocate resources more efficiently (Kshetri, 2021).

While AI can automate tasks and provide data-driven insights and predictions, it lacks emotional intelligence and the ability to exercise moral or ethical judgment (Bojinov, 2023). As AI becomes more integrated into project management, this shift redefines leadership paradigms, requiring project leaders to adopt a more strategic, visionary, and adaptive approach while maintaining a critical balance between technological innovation, emotional intelligence, ethical considerations, and human-centric practices. This transformation not only increases efficiency but also enables project leaders to focus on higher-level strategic planning and relationship-building, both essential to successful project management.

To adapt to this changing environment, today's project leaders must develop new competencies that align with technological advancements and possess a deep understanding of AI technologies and their implications for organizational processes (Cath, 2018). This includes the ability to interpret AI-generated insights that inform more robust decision-making (RDM). Furthermore, emotional intelligence and empathy remain crucial as leaders navigate the human aspects of AI integration, ensuring that employees feel supported and valued in an increasingly automated environment (Mai et al., 2024).

In this evolving landscape of project management, demonstrating visionary, transformational, and coaching approaches is essential for clutch leadership, enabling project leaders to excel under pressure and drive innovation and success in complex, AI-driven environments. Visionary leadership provides a clear vision and direction, aligning projects with the organization's long-term strategy and goals, while anticipating future risks and challenges to dynamically adapt and maintain a competitive edge. Transformational leadership inspires and motivates teams to embrace creativity and innovation, empowering them to make decisions that contribute to achieving the vision. By fostering a supportive and collaborative environment, transformational leaders build trust with employees, encouraging active engagement and commitment to achieving project goals (Belasen & Pfeffermann, 2024).

Coaching leadership, on the other hand, focuses on the development of individual skills and goals through ongoing training to promote resilience and adaptability within teams. These styles are not separate; instead, they interact dynamically within the framework of project leadership, enabling leaders to meet the complex demands of modern projects and succeed (Afzal et al., 2018). In this vein, the framework presented in Figure 5.1 illustrates how clutch leadership integrates key elements, particularly the bold vision of transformational and visionary leadership with the people development of coaching leadership, to help project leaders address AI-driven disruption with urgency, adaptability, empowerment, and engagement. This action-oriented framework is an extension of and consistent with the conceptual framework of clutch leadership presented in Chapter 1 of this book.

Figure 5.1 Clutch leadership framework for AI-driven projects. ***Source*****: Authors created.**

AI serves as a powerful catalyst for this integrated clutch leadership framework by providing leaders with the tools and insights needed to improve adaptability, productivity, and decision-making. At its core, a human-centric approach fosters meaningful **engagement**, directly reinforcing the transformational, visionary, and coaching leadership styles that form the foundation of the clutch leadership framework.

For instance, predictive analytics enables leaders to forecast future trends, project risks, and potential outcomes with previously unattainable precision, enabling them to set a clear, data-driven vision and strategic direction for the organization. AI-driven process automation alleviates repetitive tasks and administrative burdens, allowing leaders to concentrate on high-value activities such as team engagement, motivation, and identifying growth opportunities. This enables leaders to prioritize the human aspects of leadership by empowering their teams, fostering innovation, and promoting a culture of resilience.

Overall, AI strengthens the alignment of innovation, resilience, growth, and empowerment, but it is the human-centric approach that enables project leaders to effectively lead complex projects with empathy, adaptability, and precision while cultivating a positive and productive collaborative work environment.

AI-Driven Organizational Transformation

A successful AI-driven transformation within project leadership demands more than just advanced technologies; it requires robust governance frameworks, a skilled and prepared workforce, and proactive strategies to mitigate resistance to change. Transparent governance structures form the bedrock of responsible AI adoption and, by extension, lead to effective project outcomes (Oladele et al., 2024; Schuett et al., 2024). In this context, governance transcends ethical compliance alone. It involves defining clear decision-making protocols, establishing cross-functional oversight committees, and setting stringent guidelines for data security and model validation (Mai et al., 2024).

In many organizations, AI initiatives emerge from scattered pilot projects rather than integrated strategic planning, contributing to siloed approaches (i.e., departments operating independently) that undermine collaboration (Balbaa & Abdurashidova, 2024). To counter these pitfalls, transparent governance structures mandate cross-departmental representation by inviting project managers, legal experts, data scientists, and end-users to jointly shape AI policies (Helvoort, 2024; Malik, 2024). Such effort ensures that potential blind spots are identified early, fostering a collective sense of accountability and clearer communication around AI initiatives (Bhide, 2024). Equally important is the ongoing review of AI systems. By mandating periodic audits and performance checks, leaders can verify that algorithmic outputs align with organizational values, thereby reinforcing trust and adaptability (Oladele et al., 2024; Schuett et al., 2024).

Alongside governance, workforce readiness emerges as a pivotal challenge. Despite its capacity to automate routine tasks and augment decision-making, AI's successful implementation hinges on employees who can interpret results and collaborate with these technologies (Holzmann et al., 2022). This calls for continuous upskilling programs that address both technical competencies, like data literacy and model testing, and soft skills, like critical thinking and adaptability (Munira et al., 2022). AI-driven transformation often alters established workflows and job roles, creating apprehension among employees uncertain about how their responsibilities may shift. By investing in dynamic training modules and mentorship initiatives, organizations empower teams to evolve alongside AI, thereby minimizing skills gaps and cultivating a proactive learning culture (Kshetri, 2021).

Resistance to change further complicates the transition. Even with strong governance and targeted training, employees and managers may harbor skepticism about AI reliability or perceive a loss of autonomy in decision-making (Helvoort, 2024). Transparent communication is thus critical. Leaders need to articulate the strategic intent behind AI adoption – explaining how data-driven insights can elevate creativity, reduce mundane tasks, and improve project outcomes (Tominc et al., 2024). Regular feedback loops and open forums offer employees the chance to voice concerns, propose improvements, and develop a sense of ownership over AI initiatives (Bhide, 2024). Such inclusive practices ease anxieties and maintain momentum, turning reluctant adopters into AI advocates over time (Farah & Dorneich, 2024).

Organizations that proactively address governance, workforce readiness, and resistance to change head-on are best positioned to harness AI's transformative potential. By establishing transparent governance structures, including diverse oversight boards, continuous audits, and open communication, leaders can mitigate risks while promoting a culture of innovation and shared responsibility. This integrated approach lays the foundation for AI-driven success in project management, ensuring that technological advances are balanced with robust human collaboration and accountability.

Case Studies of AI-Driven Leadership Success and Failure

This section provides several examples to illustrate how some organizations from healthcare, manufacturing, and technology have applied or misapplied

AI, underlining the importance of clutch leadership attributes such as urgency, empowerment, and adaptability. The cases illustrate how AI-driven initiatives succeed or stumble based on the interplay of clutch leadership principles, supported by coaching, transformational, and visionary leadership. Each example highlights where leadership styles converged to drive transformation or fell short, emphasizing the need for a holistic leadership approach in managing AI initiatives.

Healthcare: Transforming Patient-Centered Care

Transforming Hospital Operations through AI Applications

One hospital recognized the need for innovative solutions to combat persistent operational hurdles, including extended patient wait times, rising costs, and inconsistent diagnostic accuracy (Bhide, 2024). The leadership team aimed to leverage AI to enhance data-driven decision-making, modernize administrative workflows, and improve overall patient satisfaction. Additionally, they sought to bolster competitiveness in a crowded healthcare landscape by adopting technologies that could attract a patient base and optimize resource utilization.

Leadership championed the deployment of two AI-driven applications. The first was a chatbot to streamline front-office tasks: appointment scheduling, triaging routine patient inquiries, and providing essential information for new visitors. Handling repetitive interactions allowed front-office employees to focus on more complex issues requiring human judgment. The second solution was an AI-enabled radiology tool with machine learning algorithms for image preprocessing, computer-aided diagnosis (CAD), and preliminary report generation. This system integrated seamlessly with hospital data sources to flag potential abnormalities for radiologists, improving diagnostic precision. Both solutions were developed in-house, aligning with existing workflows and adhering to robust data governance measures.

The chatbot significantly reduced administrative workload, lowering the number of required front-office full-time employees from four to two and decreasing average patient wait time by more than 30%. This automation enhanced patient experiences by expediting service and reducing bottlenecks. Concurrently, the radiology application identified up to 5% more potential diagnostic inconsistencies than manual reviews alone, leading to earlier and more accurate interventions. These developments highlighted how a well-executed AI initiative can drive clinical improvements and offer a competitive edge in healthcare services.

Strong leadership involvement was paramount for overcoming resistance and ensuring alignment among clinicians, administrators, and technical teams.

Early stakeholder engagement helped tailor the AI tools to actual clinical and operational needs, while robust change management processes fostered trust and transparency. Regular communication, ongoing training, and clear delineation of responsibilities reinforce accountability and user confidence in the new systems. Ensuring data quality, privacy, and security further bolsters trust, underscoring the importance of governance throughout implementation. This case illustrates how visionary leadership and targeted AI solutions can deliver transformative results in hospital operations, optimize resource utilization, and improve patient care.

From a leadership perspective, this success stemmed from clutch leadership's urgency around patient experience improvements, combined with coaching leadership's focus on training staff to embrace new technology. The team also showed transformational qualities by inspiring clinicians to adopt AI-driven processes that challenged traditional workflows.

Accelerating MRI with AI: The IVVES Project at Philips

Philips, a global leader in healthcare technology, participated in the Industrial-grade Verification and Validation of Evolving Systems (IVVES) project, an initiative with a budget of 24 million USD over 39 months, aimed at developing robust verification and validation (V&V) processes for embedded AI. This project addressed the pressing need for reliable AI applications within rapidly evolving systems (ES), including those that adapt or learn over time. Philips specifically sought to leverage AI in Magnetic Resonance Imaging (MRI) to accelerate image reconstruction and improve image quality, while simultaneously maintaining compliance with stringent healthcare regulations. The project also responded to industry-wide challenges around data confidentiality, model validation, and the complexities of deploying continuously evolving systems in mission-critical environments.

IVVES focused on three primary outcomes: validation strategies for machine learning, validation methods for complex evolving systems, and data-driven engineering practices. Philips replaced traditional, time-consuming Fourier-based MRI reconstruction techniques with machine learning models, which could substantially reduce imaging duration and enhance image clarity.

To navigate regulatory constraints, Philips "froze" these AI models before the formal verification phase, effectively treating them as static products during market approval processes. The project employed an MLOps model inspired by the CRISP-DM (Cross-Industry Standard Process for Data Mining) methodology, combining DataOps, ML, and DevOps.

Within Philips, the machine learning team managed data preparation and model training, then transferred the finalized models to an existing DevOps pipeline. The team also developed an experimentation platform to validate the applicability and scalability of these approaches across various industrial domains, including healthcare, transportation, and cybersecurity (Helvoort, 2024).

By systematically integrating AI into MRI workflows under stringent V&V protocols, Philips successfully delivered faster and more reliable imaging solutions, improving patient experiences and operational efficiencies. The adoption of frozen AI models streamlined market introduction and regulatory compliance while reducing time-to-market for AI-driven healthcare products. Beyond healthcare, the project's methodologies and experimentation platform demonstrated the potential for broad applicability in other industries requiring industrial-grade reliability and safety. Transformational leadership was evident as the organization swiftly adopted new technology, driving a fundamental shift in its working methods.

The importance of high-quality data emerged as a foundational requirement for successful AI integration, especially in regulated environments. Freezing AI models proved to be an effective means for meeting strict healthcare regulations, though it limits real-time updates. Federated learning and other continuously adaptive methods remain challenging to implement in heavily regulated contexts. Finally, synthetic data offers a means of overcoming data scarcity and confidentiality constraints, although creating such data is neither trivial nor risk-free. Transformational leadership practices were fittingly demonstrated as the organization transitioned to a new method of working by urgently embracing new technology.

Project Leadership Failure of IBM Watson for Oncology

Watson for Oncology (WFO), an artificial intelligence-based cognitive computing system, was developed by IBM in collaboration with experts from Memorial Sloan Kettering Cancer Center (MSK) in New York to assist oncologists in diagnosing cancer and recommending evidence-based treatment options. The system leverages natural language processing and machine learning to analyze both structured and unstructured data from vast amounts of medical literature and medical records (Tupasela & Di Nucci, 2020). WFO was initially marketed as a state-of-the-art, AI-driven system; however, it ultimately failed due to critical leadership mistakes in AI development.

One of the primary reasons for the failure of the WFO project was a fundamental misunderstanding of AI technology and its limitations in the complex medical applications encompassing real-world data. Instead of training the AI model with real-world evidence, diverse patient data, WFO was trained using synthetic patient cases developed at MSK and heavily relied on input from MSK experts. This approach likely introduced contextual bias, a form of algorithmic bias, meaning the system's recommendations were influenced primarily by MSK's treatment approaches and may not have been generalized to diverse patient populations and medical practices (Harish et al., 2021). Furthermore, its reliance on synthetic patient cases led to flawed recommendations and unsafe treatments in some instances, raising serious concerns among doctors and contributing to widespread frustration with its lack of reliability and clinical usefulness, often leading to misdiagnosis, further testing, or unnecessary treatment (Chen, 2018).

Here, a lack of clutch leadership's focus on adaptability and ethical oversight revealed gaps in the project's vision. Had they applied transformational leadership more rigorously (to align stakeholders on a realistic AI strategy) and project leadership (to ensure rigorous validation and data checks), Watson for Oncology might have achieved safer, more consistent outcomes.

IBM's missteps were compounded by an overestimation of AI's ability to handle the complexities of oncology treatments. AI in healthcare requires not just extensive and diverse data but also a deep understanding of the underlying medical science, evolving treatment protocols, and patient-specific variations. However, WFO struggled to keep pace with rapidly advancing cancer treatments and failed to provide more effective, up-to-date recommendations. This failure became evident after six years and significant financial investments, with no published research validating the effectiveness of its methodology. With its diminished credibility, many hospitals and partners abandoned or scaled down their oncology-related projects with WFO (Hernandez & Greenwald, 2018).

Another critical issue was IBM's aggressive marketing strategy, which promoted WFO as a revolutionary AI-driven tool for cancer treatment without first establishing its clinical reliability. By prioritizing commercialization over rigorous validation, IBM undermined its credibility in the healthcare sector. The lack of transparency regarding WFO's limitations and the absence of peer-reviewed evidence on its efficacy further fueled skepticism among medical institutions and professionals.

This case serves as an important lesson in AI-driven healthcare system development. A deep understanding of AI's strengths and limitations is essential before deploying it in high-stakes fields like medicine. Training AI with real-world, diverse datasets is crucial to avoiding biases that lead to inaccurate or unsafe outcomes. Moreover, project leaders must ensure that AI systems undergo rigorous clinical validation and align with practical, evidence-based use cases. Transparency, clear communication, and establishing credibility before making bold claims about an AI system's capabilities is essential for long-term success in AI-driven healthcare projects.

Technology: Enhancing Agile Project Workflows

Enhancing Telecom Project Delivery through AI

In a large telecommunications company with approximately 50,000 employees, an 18-month initiative was undertaken to incorporate artificial intelligence (AI) into a project portfolio valued at US$ 150 million annually. The primary goal was to enhance project management performance by increasing efficiency, accuracy, and decision-making. The company faced critical challenges related to resource allocation inefficiencies, delays in risk detection and mitigation, communication barriers among globally dispersed teams, and lengthy project planning phases. These issues ultimately hindered the timely and cost-effective delivery of services in a competitive telecommunications landscape.

To address these challenges, the organization integrated two main AI tools into its project management framework. ChatGPT was first deployed to facilitate real-time data retrieval, historical insights, and team collaboration across different regions. This tool was customized to comprehend the specific project methodologies and complex nuances of the telecommunications sector. Subsequently, Microsoft Project Management Copilot was introduced to automate project planning, resource allocation, and dependency mapping. By leveraging historical data stored in SharePoint and Clarity, this system provided optimized project timelines, identified skill-to-task matches, and anticipated potential bottlenecks.

The integration process involved an initial three-month planning phase, a six-month development and customization period, and a final nine-month pilot testing and full-scale deployment. Comprehensive training programs, including hands-on workshops and e-learning modules, were conducted to ensure seamless adoption across the organization (Malik, 2024).

The implementation of AI in project management processes yielded significant improvements in efficiency and cost-effectiveness. Visionary leadership also played a major role, articulating a clear end-state for AI-enabled efficiency. Meanwhile, the leaders' commitment to empowering teams, rooted in coaching leadership, ensured buy-in from frontline staff. Consequently, project completion times were reduced by 20%, resulting in faster service delivery and a stronger competitive edge. Enhanced resource allocation, supported by predictive analytics, contributed to a 25% improvement in budget adherence and a 30% increase in overall workforce productivity. Moreover, proactive risk identification and mitigation measures led to a 40% reduction in project delays. These outcomes not only delivered tangible operational benefits but also underscored the strategic value of AI-driven project management in the high-stakes telecommunications environment.

Several key insights emerged from this initiative. The importance of clearly aligning AI adoption with well-defined business objectives became evident, as technology solutions alone could not guarantee sustained success. Stakeholder engagement and change management proved crucial to mitigating resistance and fostering a culture of innovation. Pilot projects enabled the organization to refine its approach before broader deployment, reducing risk and ensuring smoother integration. Finally, robust data governance practices were essential for training reliable AI models, while ongoing evaluation and continuous learning ensured that AI solutions remained effective amidst evolving business and technological landscapes.

AI Project Leadership at Dell Technologies

Dell's success in project leadership stems from its strategic decision-making approach, requiring approval from top key executives. The company adopted a leadership approach aimed at overcoming organizational complexity, ensuring a strategic alignment of AI initiatives with organizational goals and efficient implementation by centralizing decision-making. The company prioritizes AI project ideas based on potential return on investment (ROI) and focuses on high-impact projects (Abbott, 2024). Following the rise of ChatGPT in 2022, Dell employees proposed 800 AI projects, which were narrowed down to eight priority projects in four areas: services, supply chain, engineering, and sales. The deployed AI projects, such as the "Next Best Action" AI assistant tool and AI coding assistants, have benefited Dell by improving efficiency, reducing case resolution time by 10%, and enhancing the productivity of its 20,000 engineers (Kell, 2025).

Further, to ensure that all employees can contribute to the AI projects, Dell has developed a comprehensive curriculum for training and upskilling its employees. The curriculum spans from foundational to advanced levels, equipping employees with the necessary skills to support the AI initiative (Dabrinze, 2024).

Dell's project leadership success is further driven by strategic collaborations with companies like NVIDIA, which have enhanced their AI servers, contributing to a significant revenue increase. This growth highlights strong project leadership in aligning with key industry partners to drive innovation, expand their AI pipeline, and secure competitive positioning in the server market (Reuters, 2024).

Dell's AI project leadership underscores the importance of strategic prioritization and equips employees with the right skills to drive successful AI projects. A key lesson learned is that AI project success depends not only on technological advancements but also on effective leadership that ensures AI initiatives are aligned with organizational goals. By evaluating AI project ideas using a rigorous ROI-driven selection process, Dell has demonstrated that prioritizing high-impact initiatives leads to measurable financial returns. Furthermore, upskilling employees and fostering cross-industry collaborations have been crucial in sustaining AI innovation and securing long-term competitive advantages.

Dell's approach illustrates how clutch leadership's emphasis on urgency and empowerment can be integrated with established leadership approaches. The visionary focus helps the company chart AI's long-term strategic value, while the coaching mindset ensures that employees at all levels acquire new skills. Together with its transformational leadership, boldness, and the systematic execution of innovative projects, Dell was able to maximize ROI from its AI initiatives and sustain strong AI momentum.

Ethical Dimensions of AI in Leadership

AI is rapidly transforming industries and reshaping our lives, presenting enormous opportunities for efficiency, innovation, and advancement. However, to leverage its capabilities in the most impactful way, leaders must carefully consider the ethical dimensions of AI projects to ensure responsible development, effectiveness of strategic planning, and compliance with ethical standards. Important ethical considerations for AI projects include fairness and gender bias, transparency, privacy, human safety, and environmental responsibility (Schmelzer & Walch, 2025).

This section focuses on fairness and bias, which are widely viewed as the most critical ethical considerations in AI, with a particular focus on algorithmic biases that disproportionately disadvantage women in the workplace. It explores how these biases emerge and highlights strategies for project leaders to mitigate them and ensure fairness in AI systems. While this section emphasizes gender bias, these concerns extend to other underrepresented groups, such as those based on color, race, ethnicity, or disability.

Algorithmic bias in AI systems may disadvantage women in various aspects of work life, including access to job opportunities, hiring decisions, and performance evaluations, reinforcing existing inequalities and discrimination. These biases arise because AI systems are trained on data that reflect existing historical patterns, which are heavily influenced by the quality, quantity, and diversity of the data.

Increasingly, more people are utilizing online job advertisement platforms such as Indeed and LinkedIn, which have become key resources for finding job opportunities and connecting with potential employers. However, algorithms used by these online platforms can contribute to gender bias by shaping who receives employment opportunities. Studies show that algorithms delivering high-paying or STEM-related job advertisements target fewer women than men, which reflects historical gender patterns in job opportunities (Collett et al., 2022). This disparity is primarily influenced by the fact that men have historically been more likely to seek new job opportunities, and high-paying or STEM-related jobs have long been male-dominated. These male-dominated occupations often feature masculine-coded language such as chairman, manpower, competitive, and dominant, which are less likely to appear on women's resumes, resulting in their elimination from consideration for these jobs (Collett et al., 2022).

Additionally, an increasing number of companies are incorporating AI systems into their hiring process from resume screening for candidates' assessment of qualifications for selection and onboarding purposes. Many recruiters believe that AI-enabled resume screening increases quality, productivity, efficiency, and consistency while reducing administrative workload, time to fill in recruitment, and costs associated with traditional hiring methods (Chen, 2023; Collett et al., 2022).

Considering the growing number of applications, especially in large companies, AI technologies can provide a competitive edge in talent acquisition by enabling faster and data-driven decisions on a larger scale. However, algorithms used by recruiting tools can disadvantage women because they are generally trained on historical data of successful applicants, which tends to favor men. Thus, AI-enabled screening tools in hiring can perpetuate or even heighten existing gender biases, potentially leading to discriminatory outcomes from resume screening to interviews and selection.

To mitigate these risks, organizations can adopt a multifaceted approach. For example, models can be trained to enhance diversity in resume screening by incorporating fairness and diversity constraints while prioritizing relevant competencies over traditional credentials, which are often based on masculine-coded traits, potentially leading to discriminatory practices. Additionally, conducting regular audits helps proactively identify and address emerging biases, ensuring that AI models align with the organization's diversity and equity objectives. Furthermore, involving diverse teams in AI model development and maintaining human oversight in decision-making further strengthens the fairness and accountability of the hiring process.

One well-known example is Amazon's automated AI recruiting tool, developed to review applicants' resumes and identify top talent. The machine learning specialists at Amazon uncovered that the tool discriminated against women for technical jobs, such as software developer jobs. The reason for this was that the computer models were trained on ten years of resumes submitted to Amazon, mostly from men due to the male dominance in the tech industry, and as a result, the models learned to favor male candidates. Consequently, the algorithm disadvantaged resumes including the word "women" or those associated with women's colleges. Besides gender bias, Amazon also discovered that the tool often recommended unqualified candidates for all types of jobs. After discovering these issues, Amazon decided to discontinue its experimental AI recruiting tool (Dastin, 2018).

Companies are increasingly adopting AI-powered algorithmic surveillance and productivity scoring tools to monitor and evaluate employee activities and performance in their work. This adoption has accelerated with the rise of telecommuting and remote or hybrid work, especially after the COVID-19 pandemic, along with the growing use of online platforms and applications (Hickok & Maslej, 2023). AI monitoring in the workplace could disproportionately discriminate against women, reinforcing existing inequalities and stereotypes, further widening the underrepresentation of women in certain roles.

For example, studies found that during the COVID-19 pandemic and lockdowns, women spent more time on domestic work and childcare than men, leading to a significantly greater increase in unpaid labor. Additionally, women are less likely than men to accept workplace video surveillance using facial recognition technology in the workplace, and more likely to have concerns about privacy. This discomfort and anxiety may negatively impact their confidence or limit their career opportunities, including upward mobility and promotion to senior leadership positions.

These algorithmic biases in AI systems are deeply concerning as they reinforce existing gender inequalities in the workplace, limiting opportunities for women and intensifying systemic discrimination. If not proactively addressed, such biases can hinder women's career progression, widen pay gaps, and contribute to unfair hiring and promotion practices. Therefore, it is crucial for leaders at all levels to critically examine these issues and implement strategies to mitigate bias in both the development and deployment of AI systems. By ensuring fairness and inclusiveness in algorithms, organizations can promote equity and justice, fostering a more diverse and equitable work environment.

Leadership Framework to Eliminate Algorithmic Bias in AI Projects

As more and more companies are incorporating AI systems into various aspects of work life, including job advertising, hiring, and performance evaluation processes, it is vital for project leaders to take proactive steps to mitigate algorithmic bias in these systems. This section introduces a leadership framework with guiding principles for project leaders to develop and execute AI projects that ensure fairness, equity, and transparency in the work environment.

The Women's Empowerment Principles, developed through a collaboration between the UN Global Compact and UN Women to empower women and promote gender equality in business (United Nations Global Compact, n.d.), serve as the foundation for this framework, which includes:

1. Creating a diverse and representative team composition.

Individuals involved in developing algorithms may unintentionally introduce their own biases influenced by societal norms, personal experiences, and cultural perspectives into the development and implementation process. Therefore, it is important to create a diverse and representative team to mitigate biases, promote fairness, and ensure that the algorithms serve an inclusive population.

2. Ensuring diverse and representative data.

Diverse datasets must be used to train algorithms to ensure accurate representation of different genders, ethnicities, or other demographic factors. Before using datasets for training, they must be carefully examined to identify and correct any potential biases. By leveraging diverse and representative data, organizations can minimize the potential of unfair and discriminatory outcomes, ensuring that AI systems promote equity, inclusivity, and fairness in decision-making.

3. Implementing transparent and explainable AI algorithms.

Integrating transparency and explainability into AI systems is crucial for addressing algorithmic biases and ensuring that the decision-making process is clear, interpretable, and justifiable to all stakeholders. By prioritizing transparency, organizations foster accountability and trust while promoting ethical and fair AI practices.

4. Conducting bias audits throughout the project lifecycle.

AI systems must be rigorously audited before deployment and continuously thereafter to identify and correct any biases. This is essential to ensure these systems produce fair and unbiased outcomes and that organizations use them responsibly and ethically.

5. Establishing human oversight in AI decision-making.

Organizations must adopt a human-in-the-loop approach to ensure human oversight in the decision-making process. AI systems should enhance and support decision-making rather than replace human judgment. Establishing human oversight is essential for maintaining ethical practices, ensuring accountability, and mitigating potential biases in AI-driven decisions.

6. Regularly measuring and reporting the AI fairness metrics.

Organizations must regularly assess the fairness of AI systems to ensure that they treat all individuals and groups equally. Fairness metrics such as demographic parity, equalized odds, individual fairness, counterfactual fairness, and causal reasoning can help measure and mitigate bias in AI systems (Forbes Technology Council, 2023). By using these metrics to report on AI fairness, organizations can foster trust and broader acceptance of their systems.

Empowering Human-Centric Leadership in the AI Era

Human-Centric Leadership in the AI Context

Human-centric leadership prioritizes the needs, values, and well-being of individuals within an organization while leveraging technology to enhance human capabilities. In the AI era, this leadership style is increasingly important as organizations navigate the complexities introduced by AI technologies. It emphasizes empathy, emotional intelligence, and ethical decision-making, ensuring that technology serves to augment human potential rather than diminish it (Liao & Varshney, 2021).

Human-centric leadership is vital for fostering a culture that values human contributions and ethical considerations. As AI systems become more prevalent, leaders must ensure that these technologies align with organizational values and enhance employee engagement (Oladele et al., 2024). This approach helps mitigate the risks associated with AI, such as job displacement and ethical dilemmas, by emphasizing the importance of human oversight and decision-making (Yap et al., 2024). Furthermore, leaders who adopt a human-centric approach can better navigate the challenges posed by AI, fostering an environment of trust and collaboration that encourages innovation (Schuett et al., 2024).

Balancing AI and Human Strengths

Balancing AI capabilities and human skills is an essential challenge for leaders in today's rapidly evolving technological landscape. As organizations increasingly integrate AI into their operations, it is crucial for leaders to recognize the unique strengths of both AI and human abilities, ensuring that they complement each other effectively.

AI technologies excel in processing vast amounts of data quickly and accurately, performing repetitive tasks, and identifying patterns that may not be immediately apparent to humans. However, these capabilities do not replace the need for human skills; rather, they highlight the importance of striking a balance that builds on the strengths of both. Leaders must understand that while AI can enhance efficiency and provide insights, it lacks the nuanced understanding and contextual awareness that people possess (Farah & Dorneich, 2024).

While AI is effective in certain tasks, there are key areas where human abilities remain unmatched.

- **Creativity**: while AI can generate content or suggest ideas based on existing data, it lacks the ability to think outside the box or integrate ideas in the same way that humans can (Tarsuslu et al., 2024).
- **Empathy**: empathy is deeply rooted in human emotions, social interactions, history, and lived experiences, allowing individuals to understand and connect with others on a personal level – something AI, which lacks true emotional awareness, cannot replicate (Oliveira et al., 2023).
- **Intuition**: human intuition, often described as a "gut feeling," plays a crucial role in decision-making and developing judgment, especially in complex or ambiguous situations (Madni, 2020). Intuition often draws from subconscious pattern recognition and accumulated experience that enables humans to make insightful decisions beyond data-driven logic, particularly in uncertain or novel circumstances where AI may struggle to adapt (Madni, 2020).

Key Leadership Skills and Strategies

Key leadership skills and strategies in the context of integrating artificial intelligence (AI) into organizations are increasingly recognized as vital for fostering effective and ethical workplaces. This synthesis emphasizes the importance of emotional intelligence and empathy, the role of strategic thinking in AI integration, and the necessity for ethical decision-making and AI governance.

Emotional Intelligence and Empathy

Emotional intelligence (EI) and empathy are foundational skills for leaders, particularly in environments where AI is becoming prevalent. Leaders with strong EI skills can better understand and manage their own emotions and those of their team members, which is crucial for maintaining morale and motivation

(Munira et al., 2022). Empathy, as a component of EI, allows leaders to connect with their employees on a personal level, fostering a supportive work environment that encourages open communication and collaboration (Bontrager et al., 2022).

Strategic Thinking in AI Integration

Strategic thinking is essential for leaders tasked with integrating AI into their organizations. Leaders must not only understand the technical aspects of AI but also envision how these technologies can align with organizational goals and enhance human capabilities (Modran et al., 2024). They also need to understand the impact of AI-enabled decisions on employees and stakeholders.

Ethical Decision-Making and AI Governance

As organizations increasingly rely on AI, ethical decision-making and governance become paramount. Leaders must establish frameworks that ensure AI technologies are used responsibly and transparently, addressing concerns such as gender bias, equity, privacy, and accountability.

Cultivating a Collaborative Culture: The Synergy of Humans and AI

In the evolving landscape of leading technology and business, a new paradigm is emerging – one where humans and artificial intelligence (AI) forge a powerful alliance. This collaborative culture is built on the foundation of mutual respect and understanding, recognizing the unique strengths each brings to the table. Organizations are moving beyond the outdated view of AI as merely a tool or a potential threat. Instead, they are embracing AI as a true partner, capable of enhancing and amplifying human capabilities.

This transformation begins with a clear definition of roles and responsibilities. AI excels in rapid data processing, identifying complex patterns, and automating repetitive tasks. Humans, on the other hand, bring creativity, critical thinking, and decision-making to the table. By leveraging these complementary strengths, teams can achieve unprecedented levels of efficiency and innovation. The key to unlocking this potential lies in comprehensive training and education. Leaders and employees must be equipped with the skills to interact effectively with AI systems, interpreting their outputs and leveraging their insights.

This is not a one-time effort but an ongoing process. As AI continues to evolve, both humans and machines must adapt and refine their interactions, creating a dynamic learning environment. Moreover, fostering a culture of trust and openness is crucial. Employees should feel empowered by the presence of AI, viewing it as a collaborator rather than a threat to their job security. This mindset shift is crucial for fostering innovation and driving progress. By embracing this collaborative approach, organizations create an ecosystem where human intelligence is amplified by AI capabilities.

The result is teams that are not just more efficient, but also more innovative and strategic in their approach to problem-solving. Ultimately, the synergy between humans and AI represents more than just a technological advancement. It's a reimagining of the very nature of work itself. In this new paradigm, both human and artificial intelligence contribute to a shared vision of progress and success, paving the way for breakthroughs and achievements that neither could accomplish alone.

At the heart of this transformational clutch leadership are leaders who can navigate the complexities of human-AI collaboration with strategic vision, adaptability, and decisive action. These leaders foster an environment where AI enhances human capabilities, ensuring that organizations remain innovative, agile, and forward-thinking in an ever-evolving digital landscape.

Addressing Ethical Considerations

Integrating AI into the workplace presents both opportunities and challenges, making it essential to foster a productive and ethical environment. One major concern among employees is the fear of job displacement (Badmus, 2023). Transparent communication and active involvement in AI implementation can help alleviate these fears (Tominc et al., 2024). Additionally, as organizations increasingly rely on AI systems, ethical considerations become paramount. Implementing effective mitigation strategies can significantly reduce these biases and promote equity.

Key Strategies for Effective Mitigating Biases in AI Systems

Implementing robust mitigation strategies can substantially alleviate these biases and further the cause of equity. The ethical development and deployment of AI systems require a comprehensive approach that includes active inclusion, fairness, transparency, regular auditing, diverse development teams, and the right to understanding and remedy.

Active inclusion involves seeking diverse input during AI design and development, ensuring that the perspectives of all impacted populations are considered, leading to more balanced and representative algorithms (Robert et al., 2020). This inclusivity aligns AI systems more closely with societal norms and ethical standards (Shuford, 2024).

Fairness and transparency are paramount in AI development. Developers should embed appropriate fairness definitions into system architectures and evaluation metrics (Lim & Taeihagh, 2019), while promoting transparency in AI decision-making processes fosters trust and accountability (Felzmann et al., 2020).

Regular auditing and monitoring are essential for identifying and rectifying biases that may arise over time, with comprehensive monitoring protocols becoming a recognized best practice across industries (Wörsdörfer, 2023).

Building diverse and inclusive AI development teams is crucial in minimizing biases. Heterogeneous teams, encompassing both demographic and cognitive diversity, are more effective in identifying and addressing potential biases (Wörsdörfer, 2023). Furthermore, ensuring individuals affected by AI-driven decisions have the right to understand these decisions and access mechanisms for redress is vital. This includes disclosing AI's role in decision-making and providing means to challenge unfair outcomes (Høgenhaug & Motzfeldt, 2024).

These strategies collectively strengthen user trust, align with emerging regulatory frameworks advocating for the "right to explanation" in algorithmic decision-making (Goodman & Flaxman, 2017), and promote a more balanced and equitable integration of AI technologies in various domains, including the workplace.

Future-Proofing Leadership

In the rapidly evolving landscape shaped by AI, future-proofing leadership is essential for organizations aiming to thrive. This requires fostering continuous learning and adaptability among leaders while preparing for the integration of evolving AI technologies in project management. Continuous learning and adaptability are critical components of effective leadership in the AI era (Salleh & Aziz, 2022). As AI technologies continue to advance, organizations must equip their leaders and teams with the skills needed to seamlessly integrate these tools into project management processes (Holzmann et al., 2022).

Conclusion

AI continues to reshape how projects are conceived, managed, and delivered, demanding a new form of leadership that pairs technological prowess with human-centric values. Clutch leadership, defined by adaptability, urgency, and empowerment, has emerged as a viable framework for harnessing AI capabilities while mitigating its ethical challenges.

By examining both success stories and cautionary tales from sectors such as healthcare, technology, and manufacturing, this chapter demonstrates that the value of AI is maximized when leaders maintain transparent governance structures, invest in workforce readiness, and apply inclusive frameworks to prevent algorithmic biases. At the same time, leaders must remain vigilant about data privacy, potential inequities, and the long-term societal implications of automation.

Ultimately, the path forward hinges on leaders who can balance rapid innovation with ethical responsibility. In unifying elements of transformational, visionary, and coaching leadership under the rigorous execution of project management, clutch leadership ensures that organizations remain both innovative and people-centered amid AI's relentless pace of change. In this AI-driven age, success demands more than just reliance on data analytics and predictive modeling; it calls for a coherent vision, strategic adaptability, and an unwavering commitment to human capital. Specifically, emphasizing a human-centric approach increases **engagement overall**, reinforcing the transformational, visionary, and coaching dimensions integral to clutch leadership.

Project leaders who master these dimensions, embracing the synergy between AI and human judgment, will guide their organizations toward sustainable impact and resilience in a perpetually evolving landscape.

References

Abbott, B. (2024, December 6). Dell: Chief AI officers are emerging as lynchpin in AI success. *TechRepublic.* https://www.techrepublic.com/article/dell-chief-ai-officer-strategy-apac-2025/

Afzal, A., Khan, M., & Mujtaba, B. (2018). The impact of project managers' competencies, emotional intelligence and transformational leadership on project success in the information technology sector. *Marketing and Management of Innovations*, *2*, 142–154. https://doi.org/10.21272/mmi.2018.2-12

Badmus, O. (2023). Application of AI technology in program management. *Journal of Engineering Research and Reports*, *25*(8), 48–55. https://doi.org/10.9734/jerr/2023/v25i8958

Balbaa, M., & Abdurashidova, M. (2024). The impact of artificial intelligence in decision making: A comprehensive review. *EPRA International Journal of Economics, Business, and Management Studies*, *11*(1), 27–38. https://doi.org/10.36713/epra15747

Belasen, A. T. & Pfeffermann, N. (2024). What makes a brilliant leader? The new leadership mindset, Chapter 1. In A. T. Belasen & N. Pfeffermann (Eds.), *Brilliant leadership – Unlocking the power of innovation-communication* (pp. 1–20). Routledge.

Bhide, D. (2024). *Navigating AI in project management* (p. 68) [Case study report]. Project Management Institute. https://www.pmi-se.org/Filer/PMI/AI%20in%20PM/Case%20Study%20Report_April%202024/Navigating%20AI%20Report%2020240408.pdf?TS=638481960028941040

Bojinov, I. (2023). Keep your AI projects on track. *Harvard Business Review*. https://hbr.org/2023/11/keep-your-ai-projects-on-track

Bontrager, M., Marinan, J., & Brown, S. (2022). Views on empathy and leadership in business schools: an empirical study of undergraduate students. *Industry and Higher Education, 37*(3), 397–408. https://doi.org/10.1177/09504222221128164

Cath, C. (2018). Governing artificial intelligence: Ethical, legal and technical opportunities and challenges. *Philosophical Transactions of the Royal Society a Mathematical Physical and Engineering Sciences, 376*(2133), 20180080. https://doi.org/10.1098/rsta.2018.0080

Chen, A. (2018, July 26). IBM's Watson gave unsafe recommendations for treating cancer. *The Verge*. https://www.theverge.com/2018/7/26/17619382/ibms-watson-cancer-ai-healthcare-science

Chen, Z. (2023). Ethics and discrimination in artificial intelligence-enabled recruitment practices. *Humanities and Social Sciences Communications, 10*(1), 1–12. https://doi.org/10.1057/s41599-023-02079-x

Collett, C., Gomes, L. G., & Neff, G. (2022). *The effects of AI on the working lives of women*. UNESCO Publishing. http://dx.doi.org/10.18235/0004055

Dabrinze, V. (2024, May 22). How Dell's leadership is transforming AI implementation and training. *SiliconANGLE*. https://siliconangle.com/2024/05/22/dell-overview-center-innovation-ai-delltechworld/

Dastin, J. (2018, October 10). Insight - Amazon scraps secret AI recruiting tool that showed bias against women. *Reuters*. https://www.reuters.com/article/world/insight-amazon-scraps-secret-ai-recruiting-tool-that-showed-bias-against-women-idUSKCN1MK0AG/

Farah, Y., & Dorneich, M. (2024). Human-autonomy teaming in a cooperative gamified testbed: How can AI teammates support teamwork processes? *Proceedings of the Human Factors and Ergonomics Society Annual Meeting, 68*(1), 386–392. https://doi.org/10.1177/10711813241269252

Felzmann, H., Fosch-Villaronga, E., Lutz, C., & Tamò-Larrieux, A. (2020). Towards transparency by design for artificial intelligence. *Science and Engineering Ethics, 26*(6), 3333–3361. https://doi.org/10.1007/s11948-020-00276-4

Forbes Technology Council (2023, July 14). *AI & fairness metrics: Understanding & eliminating bias*. Forbes | Councils. https://councils.forbes.com/blog/ai-and-fairness-metrics

Gartner (2019, March 20). *Gartner says 80 percent of today's project management tasks will be eliminated by 2030 as artificial intelligence takes over*. Gartner, Inc. https://www.gartner.com/en/newsroom/press-releases/2019-03-20-gartner-says-80-percent-of-today-s-project-management

Goodman, B., & Flaxman, S. (2017). European Union regulations on algorithmic decision making and a "right to explanation". *Ai Magazine, 38*(3), 50–57. https://doi.org/10.1609/aimag.v38i3.2741

Harish, V., Morgado, F., Stern, A. D., & Das, S. (2021). Artificial intelligence and clinical decision making: the new nature of medical uncertainty. *Academic Medicine, 96*(1), 31–36. https://doi.org/10.1097/ACM.0000000000003707

Helvoort, M. (2024). *Navigating AI in project management* (p. 73) [Case study report]. Project Management Institute. https://www.pmi-se.org/Filer/PMI/AI%20in%20PM/Case%20Study%20Report_April%202024/Navigating%20AI%20Report%2020240408.pdf?TS=638481960028941040

Hernandez, D., & Greenwald, T. (2018, August 11). EXCHANGE — IBM Has a Watson Dilemma — Big Blue promised its AI platform would be a big step forward in treating cancer. *Wall Street Journal.* https://www.wsj.com/articles/ibm-bet-billions-that-watson-could-improve-cancer-treatment-it-hasnt-worked-1533961147

Hickok, M., & Maslej, N. (2023). A policy primer and roadmap on AI worker surveillance and productivity scoring tools. *AI and Ethics, 3*(3), 673–687. https://doi.org/10.1007/s43681-023-00275-8

Høgenhaug, A., & Motzfeldt, H. (2024). Citizens' right to information and the principle of good administration: what's new in the ai act?. *ICAIR, 4*(1), 150–156. https://doi.org/10.34190/icair.4.1.3223

Holzmann, V., Zitter, D., & Peshkess, S. (2022). The expectations of project managers from artificial intelligence: A Delphi study. *Project Management Journal, 53*(5), 438–455. https://doi.org/10.1177/87569728211061779

Kell, J. (2025, January 22). Dell's employees had 800 different Gen AI ideas. Here's how the PC maker winnowed the list to 8. *Fortune.* https://fortune.com/2025/01/22/dell-cto-gen-ai-roi/

Kshetri, N. (2021). Evolving uses of artificial intelligence in human resource management in emerging economies in the global south: some preliminary evidence. *Management Research Review, 44*(7), 970–990. https://doi.org/10.1108/mrr-03-2020-0168

Liao, Q., & Varshney, K. (2021). Human-centered explainable AI (XAI): From algorithms to user experiences. https://doi.org/10.48550/arxiv.2110.10790

Lim, H., & Taeihagh, A. (2019). Algorithmic decision-making in avs: Understanding ethical and technical concerns for smart cities. *Sustainability, 11*(20), 5791. https://doi.org/10.3390/su11205791

Madni, A. (2020). Exploiting augmented intelligence in systems engineering and engineered systems. *Insight, 23*(1), 31–36. https://doi.org/10.1002/inst.12282

Mai, W., Ambashe, M., & Ohueri, C. (2024). Artificial intelligence ethics best practices model for financial decision-making in Chinese financial institutions. *International Journal of Information Technologies and Systems Approach, 17*(1), 1–18. https://doi.org/10.4018/IJITSA.337388

Malik, N. (2024). *Navigating AI in project management* (p. 46–50) [Case study report]. Project Management Institute. https://www.pmi-se.org/Filer/PMI/AI%20in%20PM/Case%20Study%20Report_April%202024/Navigating%20AI%20Report%2020240408.pdf?TS=638481960028941040

Modran, H., Ursuțiu, D., & Samoilă, C. (2024). Using the theoretical-experiential binomial for educating AI-literate students. *Sustainability, 16*(10), 4068. https://doi.org/10.3390/su16104068

Munira, K., Rahman, D., & Akhter, S. (2022). Impact of emotional intelligence on sustainable leadership. *Business Perspective Review, 4*(2), 1–15. https://doi.org/10.38157/bpr.v4i2.446

Nieto-Rodriquez, A., & Vargas, R. V. (2023, February 2). How AI will transform project management. *Harvard Business Review.* https://hbr.org/2023/02/how-ai-will-transform-project-management

Oladele, I., Orelaja, A., & Akinwande, O. (2024). Ethical implications and governance of artificial intelligence in business decisions: A deep dive into the ethical challenges and governance issues surrounding the use of artificial intelligence in making critical business decisions. *International Journal of Latest Technology in Engineering Management & Applied Science, XIII*(II), 48–56. https://doi.org/10.51583/ijltemas.2024.130207

Oliveira, M., Brands, J., Mashudi, J., Liefooghe, B., & Hortensius, R. (2023). Perceptions of artificial intelligence system's aptitude to judge morality and competence amidst the rise of chatbots. https://doi.org/10.31234/osf.io/vsxr4

Reuters. (2024, August 30). Dell shares rise as AI server demand boosts results, forecasts. *Reuters.* https://www.reuters.com/technology/dell-shares-jump-ai-server-demand-boosts-results-forecasts-2024-08-30/

Robert, L., Pierce, C., Marquis, L., Kim, S., & Alahmad, R. (2020). Designing fair ai for managing employees in organizations: A review, critique, and design agenda. *Human-Computer Interaction, 35*(5–6), 545–575. https://doi.org/10.1080/07370024.2020.1735391

Salleh, M. H., & Aziz, K. A. (2022, December). Artificial intelligence augmented project management. In *International Conference on Technology and Innovation Management (ICTIM 2022)* (pp. 274–284). Atlantis Press. https://doi.org/10.2991/978-94-6463-080-0_24

Schmelzer, R., & Walch, K. (2025, January 15). *Top 10 ethical considerations for AI projects.* Project Management Institute. https://www.pmi.org/blog/top-10-ethical-considerations-for-ai-projects

Schuett, J., Reuel, A., & Carlier, A. (2024). How to design an AI ethics board. *AI and Ethics.* https://doi.org/10.1007/s43681-023-00409-y

Shuford, J. (2024). Examining ethical aspects of AI: addressing bias and equity in the discipline. *Journal of Artificial Intelligence General science (JAIGS), 3*(1), 262–280. https://doi.org/10.1101/2024.02.08.579541

Tarsuslu, S., Agaoglu, F. O., & Bas, M. (2024). Can digital leadership transform AI anxiety and attitude in nurses? *Journal of Nursing Scholarship, 57*(1), 28–38. https://doi.org/10.1111/jnu.13008

Tominc, P., Oreški, D., Čančer, V., & Rožman, M. (2024). Statistically significant differences in AI support levels for project management between small and large enterprises. *AI, 5*(1), 136–157. https://doi.org/10.3390/ai5010008

Tupasela, A., & Di Nucci, E. (2020). Concordance as evidence in the Watson for oncology decision-support system. *AI & Society, 35*, 811–818. https://doi.org/10.1007/s00146-020-00945-9

United Nations Global Compact. (n.d.). Endorse the women's empowerment principles. https://unglobalcompact.org/take-action/action/womens-principles#:~:text=Principle%201:%20Establish%20high-level,all%20women%20and%20men%20workers

Wörsdörfer, M. (2023). Mitigating the adverse effects of AI with the European Union's artificial intelligence act: Hype or hope?. *Global Business and Organizational Excellence*, *43*(3), 106–126. https://doi.org/10.1002/joe.22238

Yap, C., Leow, C., & Leong, W. (2024). Integrating personality traits in AI-driven business leadership: The role of emotional intelligence, achievement orientation, analytical thinking, and structured leadership using the FIKR personality assessment tool. *JCBAR*. https://doi.org/10.47852/bonviewjcbar42024142

Chapter 6

Aligning Innovation Strategy with Leadership: Critical Skills for Healthcare Leaders

Michael A. Schwartz

Introduction

In today's rapidly evolving healthcare landscape, leaders face unprecedented challenges that demand a unique set of skills to navigate organizational transformation successfully, especially when introducing innovative programs and services. This chapter explores the critical leadership competencies required to drive innovation, enhance organizational performance, and improve patient outcomes. These competencies enable healthcare leaders to overcome disruptions such as rapidly evolving technological advancements, burgeoning compliance pressures, financial strains, ever-increasing expectations related to service and quality, and, of course, AI tools that possess revolutionary impact. Drawing on established management theories and real-world examples, this chapter explores the critical leadership skills necessary for navigating momentous

DOI: 10.4324/9781003629214-9

healthcare transformations, particularly those that challenge the status quo and, thus, require bold action.

To illustrate the practical application of these leadership skills, the chapter presents real-world case studies of healthcare organizations that have successfully steered through significant transformation while fostering innovation and maintaining operational excellence. These examples highlight the interplay of entrepreneurialism, operational integrity, motivational capacity, ethical wherewithal, and visionary thinking necessary to drive innovation, improve patient care, and achieve organizational success. Such "clutch" leadership traits are presented as essential in transcending the pressures that emerging challenges pose.

By mastering these essential leadership skills, healthcare leaders can successfully transcend the complexities of organizational transformation and create a sustainable future for their organizations. This chapter provides a comprehensive framework for developing the leadership competencies necessary to drive innovation, improve patient outcomes, and enhance organizational performance in the ever-evolving healthcare landscape.

Foundational Leadership Theories

To understand the complex landscape of healthcare leadership, it is essential to first examine foundational leadership theories that provide a framework for effective organizational management. To competently balance inevitable competing priorities, organizational leaders can navigate these challenges using the lenses of the Competing Values Framework (CVF) – a well-established model, which offers valuable insights into the diverse leadership competencies required to drive transformative change and foster innovation (Cameron et al., 2014).

The CVF highlights organizations as contradictory systems operating within four quadrants or sectors that align with different effectiveness criteria and leadership roles:

1. **Create** (Innovation and Adaptability): *do things first!* – Leaders act as Innovators and Brokers.
2. **Compete** (Strategic Agility and Integration): *do things fast!* – Leaders act as Directors and Producers.
3. **Collaborate** (Engagement and Collaboration): *do things together!* – Leaders act as Mentors and Facilitators.
4. **Control** (Stability and Coordination): *do things right!* – Leaders act as Coordinators and Monitors.

By understanding and applying the principles of the CVF, leaders can develop a multifaceted approach to organizational transformation that balances inspired innovation with practicality and feasibility, vigorous competition with rewards for collaboration. As highlighted by CVF researchers, effective leaders have the cognitive capacity to navigate the competing tensions across the four quadrants (Belasen, 2022; Lavine, 2014).

Practical Application of Leadership Skills in Healthcare Transformation

To illustrate the practical application of the CVF leadership roles, this chapter will examine real-world healthcare transformation initiatives. Furthermore, we will do so through the lens of the frequently overlooked, yet crucial, leadership role of mid-level leaders, who are vital for bridging the gap between senior executives and front-line staff. This chapter will explore these dynamics through the analytical framework of the middle manager, emphasizing their indispensable contributions to organizational success, most notably in disruptive environments (Belasen & Belasen, 2016). Drawing on the experience of Regional Medical Center (RMC), which is a nearly 300-bed not-for-profit healthcare organization that serves as a tertiary hub of advanced care in the Upstate New York region, we will explore two noteworthy disruptive healthcare initiatives which were implemented there.

Specifically, we will examine the following two recent initiatives, which represent novel implementations at RMC:

1. Building a comprehensive inpatient surgical Advanced Practice Provider (APP) program.
2. Creating a novel Neurosciences service line.

Building upon the foundation of the CVF, we will now explore the application of four critical leadership competencies essential for driving disruptive organizational transformation in healthcare, as exemplified by the initiatives listed above.

1. **Create** (Innovation and Adaptability): *do things first!* – Leaders act as Innovators and Brokers.

In today's dynamic healthcare environment, effectual leaders foster a culture of innovation and adaptability to maintain competitiveness and deliver high-quality patient care. While healthcare organizations have long prioritized patient satisfaction, the understanding of "improving the experience of care" has evolved beyond mere satisfaction. It now encompasses providing care that is safe, timely, effective, efficient, equitable, and patient-centered (Karam, 2017). This requires:

- **Encouraging creativity and calculated risk-taking**: leaders must foster an environment where team members feel empowered to propose and implement new ideas, even those that challenge the status quo.
- **Embracing new technologies and services**: healthcare leaders must remain informed about technological advancements and be willing to adopt innovative solutions that enhance patient care and operational efficiency.
- **Leveraging evidence-based decision-making**: utilizing data-driven insights enables leaders to make informed decisions that drive continuous organizational improvement. However, evidence-based management encompasses not only quantitative data but also qualitative elements such as perceptions of organizational culture and attitudes toward senior management (Barends et al., 2014).

Case Study 1.1 – Building a Comprehensive Inpatient Surgical APP Program

Faced with the national HCAHPS (Hospital Consumer Assessment of Healthcare Providers) mandates to decrease inpatient length of stay and improve patient satisfaction, RMC sought to develop an inpatient surgical Advanced Practice Provider (APP) program. This service would make use of a combination of Physician Assistants (PAs) and Nurse Practitioners (NPs) to function as a value-added extension of the care provided by the physicians and surgeons. While not a unique service offering in healthcare at the time, it represented a novel approach to inpatient care at RMC.

According to Darren Molina, MBA, PA-C, Administrative Director of APP Services at RMC, his team had to envision how the program would function and demonstrate its value within their specific environment. This involved articulating the APPs' roles and explaining how they would benefit patients, surgeons, and hospital efficiency to multiple different stakeholders, including senior leadership, surgeons, nurses, and patients.

Notably, Molina highlighted the importance of identifying a gap in existing services through data analysis and benchmarking against industry standards, particularly regarding length of stay and patient satisfaction scores. Such gap analysis served to push the project forward from the very outset, especially in the face of ingrained dogmatic organizational thinking that was not yet well acclimated to the specifics of APP care, nor well enough versed in the value proposition that APPs could deliver on.

By embracing innovation and resisting stagnation, tenets of the "Create" quadrant of the CVF, the Inpatient Surgical APP program launched successfully and has since grown exponentially. It continues to meet the needs of the expanding surgical department while consistently reducing length of stay and enhancing the patient experience.

Case Study 1.2 – Creating a Novel Neurosciences Service Line

While the previous example required, in part, leveraging existing staff and resources, creating the Neurosciences program from square one required a greater degree of disruptive innovation and visionary thinking. Patricia Hansen, Senior Administrative Director of Neurosciences at RMC, spearheaded this implementation by fostering a culture of iteration and open communication. She emphasized to the team that even seemingly impractical ideas could evolve into valuable solutions. This was complemented by the leadership of Dr Ruben Oliva, MD, Executive Director of Neurosciences at RMC, who promoted a bold "grand vision" for the program's potential.

Encouraging staff to share their past experiences facilitated navigating challenges and ensured efficient program integration. Hansen and Oliva set as a key initial goal door-to-puncture (DTP) times for emergency mechanical thrombectomies to be at or surpass the industry standards set by the Joint Commission and the New York State Department of Health, based on the American Heart Association/American Stroke Association initiative. Through open, multilevel, interdisciplinary brainstorming, a neuroangiography technician suggested pre-preparing a dedicated table with all necessary equipment, a strategy that directly translated into significantly reduced DTP times, paving the way for RMC to deliver this breakthrough technology to the community. Without this innovative and adaptive culture, supporting the free flow of ideas, achieving this early-stage critical goal would have been significantly hampered.

Hansen and Oliva's success in building the Neurosciences program highlights the critical role of the "Create" portion of the CVF, fostering a culture where unconventional ideas, like the pre-prepared table, could revolutionize patient care. This demonstrates that encouraging open communication and visionary thinking, allowing for the free flow of ideas, is essential for driving disruptive innovation and achieving ambitious goals.

2. **Compete** (Strategic Agility and Integration): *do things fast!* – Leaders act as Directors and Producers

In today's rapidly evolving healthcare landscape, effective leaders demonstrate strategic agility and the ability to integrate diverse perspectives and priorities. These competencies are critical for maximizing productivity and efficiency (Weber & Tarba, 2014). This involves:

- **Developing and communicating vision and strategy:** leaders should articulate a clear and compelling vision for their organization's future, ensuring that all stakeholders understand and align with strategic objectives.
- **Maintaining strategic flexibility:** healthcare leaders must be prepared to adapt their strategies in response to changing circumstances, unexpected challenges, and/or resource constraints, balancing long-term goals with short-term realities.
- **Making timely strategic decisions:** in a fast-paced healthcare environment, leaders must be able to gather and analyze information quickly, making informed decisions that keep projects on track and drive organizational success.

Case Study 2.1 – Building a Comprehensive Inpatient Surgical APP Program

While the vision for the inpatient APP program was clear to Molina and his team, effectively communicating that vision and its value proposition to all stakeholders was paramount for successful implementation from the outset. The extensive stakeholder list included senior administration, physicians and surgeons, front-line staff, multiple inpatient departments, and the patient community. The communication strategy focused on raising awareness of APPs' roles and contributions to patient care and organizational success, rather than simply elevating their perceived professional status.

A multifaceted approach was essential, recognizing that each stakeholder group required tailored communication. Senior leadership and surgeons best processed the information through PowerPoint presentations highlighting current and projected data, benchmarked against industry standards. Surgeons also directly focused on the program's positive impact on patient care. When communicating with his front-line APP team, Molina emphasized that their role extended beyond offloading the surgeons' responsibilities for clerical tasks to actively transform patient care by genuinely improving both quality and efficiency.

Their expertise would bridge communication between surgeons and other care providers, including the internal medicine hospitalist team, the emergency department (ED), the operating room (OR), and the Care Management team. By effectively communicating this vision of enhanced roles and functionality, Molina built an engaged and motivated team from day one.

To ensure proper utilization of the APPs, Molina also communicated their capabilities and value to other departments, specifically nurses, the ED, and the OR – the very groups who would directly interact with the APPs, rather than contacting individual surgeons for every need. This step was crucial for the program's success. Recognizing the importance of patient and family experience, Molina collaborated with the marketing team to inform and educate the community about the role and value of APPs, emphasizing how they enhance, rather than hinder, the patient-surgeon relationship. Molina's engagement of all stakeholders was critical to the successful implementation of the new inpatient APP program.

The APP program's successful implementation hinged on proactive and adaptable communication, demonstrating the value of strategic agility, as championed by the "Compete" portion of the CVF. By tailoring communication strategies to specific audiences, Molina and his team exemplified how strategic flexibility is vital for building understanding and buy-in, ultimately driving program adoption and effectiveness.

Case Study 2.2 – Creating a Novel Neurosciences Service Line

To effectively launch their new Neurosciences program, Hansen's team prioritized clear communication, collaborative teamwork, and adaptability in communicating the vision and strategy to stakeholders. A crucial step at the program's inception was establishing interdisciplinary team meetings. Hansen emphasized early on that success required broad buy-in across departments.

Participants included representatives from Neurosciences, the ED, the ICU, nursing units, Neuroradiology, Neurology, Nursing, Anesthesia, Surgical Services (the OR), Rehabilitation (PT/OT), and senior management, ensuring that all departments understood the benefits of the new service. Delays in any part of the process would stall program initiation, compromising patient care and the program's viability.

Initial frequent interdisciplinary meetings maintained open communication, facilitated discussions on progress, challenges, and volume metrics, and fostered a shared understanding of goals. The team embraced continuous iteration and improvement. When initial processes proved inadequate, they brainstormed solutions and adjusted strategies based on data and feedback. By emphasizing the community benefits of the new service, Hansen's team tapped into a shared sense of purpose and motivated staff. Dr Oliva further demonstrated his confidence in RMC by bringing his own father as one of the first patients there for treatment, which served as a powerful motivator for the team. Ultimately, by combining clear communication, collaborative teamwork, and adaptability from the get-go, Hansen and her team commanded the "Compete" quadrant of the CVF and expeditiously navigated the complexities of creating the Neurosciences program, ensuring that the program got off the ground and running.

3. **Collaborate** (Engagement and Collaboration): *do things together!* – Leaders act as Mentors and Facilitators

Effective healthcare leaders understand the importance of engaging and collaborating with diverse stakeholders to achieve organizational goals (Goleman, 2004). This competency involves:

- **Cultivating emotional intelligence**: According to Goleman, "the most effective leaders are alike in one crucial way. They all have a high degree of what has come to be known as emotional intelligence (EI), (which is) the *sine qua non* of leadership" (pp. 4–6). In this way, successful leaders possess the following five components of EI:
  - o Self-Awareness:
    - The ability to recognize and understand one's moods, emotions, and drives, including their effect on others.
  - o Self-Regulation:
    - The ability to control disruptive impulses and moods.
  - o Motivation:
    - A passion for work and a propensity to pursue goals with energy and persistence.
  - o Empathy:
    - The ability to understand the emotional makeup of other people and to treat them accordingly.
  - o Social Skill:
    - Proficiency in managing relationships, finding common ground, and building rapport.

- **Building trust and managing conflicts**: By fostering open communication and proactively addressing conflicts, impactful leaders create a culture of trust and collaboration.
- **Motivating teams to achieve organizational goals**: Influential healthcare leaders inspire and empower their teams to work toward shared objectives, even amid challenges and uncertainty.
- **Engaging with patients, staff, and community partners**: Competent and compassionate healthcare leaders understand the critical importance of the perception of service quality, both within the community and among their team.

Case Study 3.1 – Building a Comprehensive Inpatient Surgical APP Program

The successful expansion of the APP service at RMC was meaningfully driven by strategic stakeholder engagement and collaboration. Leaders, particularly Molina, demonstrated exceptional skill in navigating a myriad of complex relationships. Central to this approach was the effective application of emotional intelligence.

Recognizing potential concerns from voluntary surgeons about the APP program, Molina proactively addressed their fears of patient steering toward the hospital-employed surgeons. He validated their perspective, clearly outlined the APP team's adherence to the on-call schedule to prevent any perceived bias, and underscored the APPs' vital role in patient-physician communication. This empathetic approach fostered trust and alleviated concerns within a crucial stakeholder group.

Furthermore, Molina facilitated collaborative discussions, ensuring transparency and shared understanding. He engaged APPs, physicians, and other healthcare professionals in open communication, clarifying the program's objectives and individual roles. Molina and his team established a regular communication cadence with all stakeholders, providing updates on the program's progress, addressing any emerging concerns, and soliciting feedback.

Recognizing that different stakeholders have unique needs and communication preferences, Molina tailored his engagement strategies accordingly. For instance, he held in-person meetings with surgeons to address their concerns directly, while utilizing email updates and online forums to engage with APPs and other healthcare professionals. The leadership team collected data on patient satisfaction, wait times, and other key metrics to assess the impact of the expanded APP service. This data was then shared with stakeholders, demonstrating the program's effectiveness and building confidence in its long-term sustainability. All these efforts fostered a collective understanding of how the expanded APP service would enhance patient care, improve efficiency, and elevate overall quality. In turn, this engendered significant confidence and assurance in the APP team from their colleagues throughout the hospital.

Likewise, the leadership team prioritized engaging patients and community members. They recognized the importance of understanding public perception regarding the expanded APP role. By communicating the program's benefits, such as improved access and reduced wait times, and addressing any misconceptions about PAs' and NPs' qualifications and scope of practice, they ensured community buy-in and support for the initiative.

Recognizing the importance of APPs perceiving their own value, Molina emphasized that their role extended beyond clerical tasks. He stressed that they were "vested contributors" to the department, more than simply an added resource, fostering a sense of ownership and purpose. He understood that if the APPs themselves didn't believe in their value, it would be difficult to convince other stakeholders.

Molina and his team made sure to celebrate the program's milestones and successes with all stakeholders. This not only acknowledged the contributions of everyone involved but also reinforced the value of collaboration and stakeholder engagement. This demonstrates an understanding of the importance of team motivation and internal stakeholder engagement in driving external success.

Through these multifaceted approaches, Molina and his team expertly wielded the "Collaborate" segment of the CVF by exercising emotional intelligence, facilitating teamwork, and mitigating potential conflicts, ultimately achieving their organizational goals and improving patient care. By fundamentally prioritizing team motivation, stakeholder engagement, and shared collaboration, RMC's APP leadership team successfully expanded the APP service, while strengthening relationships across the RMC healthcare ecosystem.

Case Study 3.2 – Creating a Novel Neurosciences Service Line

Given that the Neurosciences program was a new service offering at RMC, Hansen acknowledged inherent anxiety within the development team at its inception. She constructively viewed this anxiety not as a negative but as a valuable adaptive response driving the project forward. Admittedly, RMC's high-performance culture presumably contributed to the underlying trepidation, but perhaps paradoxically also served to motivate project success.

Hansen effectively channeled any looming apprehension into gainful excitement by focusing the team on their shared goal of providing a new service for the community. She repeatedly reminded them of this goal, which proved incredibly effective, as many team members were also patients or had family members who were. Hansen leveraged the team's desire to provide for the community what they would want for themselves and their families, effectively motivating them to channel their initial distress into positive energy toward goal attainment. She also fostered a sense of shared ownership by involving team members in the decision-making process and encouraging them to contribute their ideas and expertise.

This collaborative approach, utilizing high emotional intelligence by harnessing team motivation, empathy, and relationship management, aligning with the doctrines of the CVF's "Collaborate" sector, not only reduced collective anxiety but also led to more innovative and effective solutions.

4. **Control** (Stability and Coordination): *do things right!* – Leaders act as Coordinators and Monitors

Successful healthcare leaders excel at managing change and coordinating efforts across diverse departments and stakeholders, from both an organizational transformation and technical implementation standpoint. In this way, effective leaders deftly blend both project management and change management approaches to create and optimize value, especially during times of bold organizational change (Gordon & Pollack, 2018). This competency involves:

- **Overcoming Resistance to Change:** Leaders should anticipate and address potential sources of resistance, using effective communication and change management strategies to foster buy-in and support. This may involve proactively identifying potential concerns and highlighting the benefits of the change for individuals and the organization.
- **Implementing Effective Change Management Strategies:** Following established management frameworks can minimize disruption and ensure smooth transitions during organizational transformations. This includes clearly defining goals, developing a detailed plan with timelines and milestones, communicating effectively throughout the process, and providing ongoing support and training to those affected by the change.
- **Aligning Diverse Departments and Stakeholders:** Healthcare leaders must coordinate efforts across multiple departments and stakeholder groups to achieve shared goals and maintain organizational cohesion. This requires fostering a shared understanding of the organization's vision and

strategic objectives, establishing clear roles and responsibilities, and promoting effective communication and collaboration across departments.

- **Coordinating and Monitoring Process Optimization:** Effective healthcare leaders optimize internal process control by establishing clear, measurable performance indicators, followed by conscientiously coordinating and monitoring their progress. They additionally foster accountability and use data to identify and correct deviations. By coordinating teams and ensuring smooth communication, they streamline workflows and drive continuous improvement, keeping processes aligned with evolving patient needs and industry best practices.

Case Study 4.1 – Building a Comprehensive Inpatient Surgical APP Program

In developing, implementing, and sustaining the inpatient APP program, Molina recognized the importance of not only setting goals but also measuring them. For the program to be successful, it had to demonstrate its value to both internal team members and hospital-wide stakeholders. Concrete evidence of value was crucial for securing ongoing support from senior administration. With the primary goals of decreasing length of stay (LOS) and improving patient satisfaction, Molina and his team played critical roles in various hospital-wide projects aimed at achieving these goals, as well as in the production and analysis of the associated data.

Notable examples of projects that benefited from APP contributions include Critical Care/ICU care, Rapid Response and Code Response protocols, Discharge Planning, and the Hip Fracture Pathway. The Hip Fracture Pathway serves as a prime example of APP value, particularly since the inpatient APP team is the first point of orthopedic surgical contact when a patient presents to the RMC Emergency Department (ED) with a hip fracture. Considerable data unequivocally demonstrates the clinical benefit of decreasing "door-to-OR" time for elderly patients with hip fractures (Seong et al., 2020).

By having an experienced healthcare provider readily available to manage the preoperative care of patients with acute hip fractures, the initial orthopedic evaluation and consultation occurs much sooner. Rather than simply providing initial patient care, the APPs have also made significant contributions to the Hip Fracture Pathway program, leading to institution-wide decreased "door-to-OR" times. This involved developing a well-designed management algorithm for all preoperative steps, including specifications for evaluation for potential hip fracture x-rays, hip fracture-specific ED orders, and a Hip Fracture Admission Order Set.

It also included coordinating communication between the ED, orthopedic surgeon, medical hospitalist, operating room (OR), physical therapy (PT), and Care Management, as well as establishing protocols for medical risk assessment and optimization, cardiac consultation, anticoagulation management, pain management, and discharge planning. Since the inception of the Hip Fracture Pathway, RMC has seen measurable improvements in various quality-based metrics, especially regarding "door-to-OR" time and length of stay.

This required Molina to guide the inpatient APP team in utilizing the "Control" aspect of the CVF, establishing precise objectives, optimizing internal processes, managing coordination, and ultimately maximizing organizational performance while continuously demonstrating the value of the inpatient APP team.

To ensure program stability, Molina also implemented a specific onboarding process for all new hires. This standardized process ensures consistency in training and orientation, promotes a sense of belonging among new team members, and facilitates their integration into the existing team and workflows.

Case Study 4.2 – Creating a Novel Neurosciences Service Line

The creation of the new Neurosciences program exemplified effective change management and organizational coordination. Leaders successfully managed this complex transformation by coordinating efforts across multiple departments to ensure seamless integration of the new service, facilitated by aligning diverse stakeholders around shared goals. Hansen emphasized the importance of establishing a proficient healthcare dyad, with both clinical and administrative leadership, during the program's creation. They quickly realized that a triad, with the addition of a nursing leader, was necessary to optimize integration and outcomes (Belasen et al., 2024).

With Hansen as the administrative lead and Dr Oliva as the clinical lead, they translated goals into actionable steps. Along the way, they recognized the critical role of nursing leadership in seamlessly integrating workflows, particularly in developing the Thrombectomy Workflow.

Hansen, Oliva, and nursing leadership collaborated with multiple departments, both internal and external to RMC, to optimize all stages of thrombectomy care. These efforts included:

- Working with local and regional EMS to establish pre-notification protocols for the RMC ED.
- Collaborating with the ED and inpatient APP team to implement a pre-established thrombectomy order set in the electronic health record (EHR).
- Establishing a CTP (Computed Tomography Cerebral Perfusion) protocol, for which all radiology technicians performing this test were fully trained and familiar with.
- Formalizing the informed consent process, particularly for situations where a patient's next-of-kin or healthcare proxy was unavailable.
- Conducting inventory reviews to ensure all necessary surgical equipment was readily available.
- Establishing well-defined post-procedure care protocols, including streamlining the post-procedure CT scan process and creating a post-thrombectomy order set in the EHR.
- Clearly defining the post-procedure roles of Critical Care Hospitalists, Neurologists, and Neuroendovascular specialists to ensure well-integrated care and follow-up, avoiding unnecessary overlap and/or gaps.

To monitor outcomes and ensure initiatives achieved their goals, quality data was captured and reviewed. This included metrics on DTP (door-to-puncture) times and the use of quality dashboards for Stroke Care and overall Neurosciences Care. Coordinated efforts were essential to create, monitor, and analyze these findings. This involved managing key metrics related to acute thrombolytic therapy administration, early antithrombotic treatment, dysphagia screening, rehabilitation assessment, secondary stroke prophylaxis, and stroke education.

By mastering the "Control" quadrant of the CVF through effectively coordinating stroke and neurosciences care across multidisciplinary teams, Hansen and her team successfully implemented a new and comprehensive service offering at a best-practice level, ensuring continued progress through effective coordination and monitoring.

Conclusion

The complexities of today's healthcare environment demand a new breed of leader – one who is not only well-versed in traditional management theories but also adept at navigating the multifaceted challenges of a rapidly changing industry. This chapter illuminated the critical leadership skills necessary for contemporary healthcare leaders to thrive in disruptive times, especially when introducing innovative programs and services.

The Competing Values Framework (CVF) provides a robust foundation for understanding the diverse leadership roles and competencies required to drive transformative change. Effective leaders juggle the demands of creative innovation, strategic competition, collaborative teamwork, and process control. They must be able to foster a culture of creativity and calculated risk-taking, while maintaining operational efficiency and meeting regulatory requirements.

The case studies described in this chapter serve as practical examples of how the CVF roles and competencies can be applied in real-world scenarios. The successful implementation of the inpatient surgical Advanced Practice Provider (APP) program and the creation of a new Neurosciences service line underscores the importance of visionary thinking, clear communication, and stakeholder engagement. Mid-level leaders, in particular, play a crucial role in bridging the gap between senior management and front-line staff, driving innovation, and ensuring that strategic goals are translated into actionable plans and tangible outcomes (Belasen & Belasen, 2016).

Moving forward, healthcare organizations ought to invest in leadership pipeline development programs that cultivate these critical competencies. This includes fostering emotional intelligence, promoting collaborative problem-solving, and empowering leaders to make evidence-based decisions. By embracing a dynamic and adaptive leadership approach, healthcare organizations can successfully introduce innovative programs and services, improve patient outcomes, and enhance organizational performance.

As we look to the future, the most successful healthcare leaders will be those who can balance a multitude of competing demands, including overcoming external forces of technological advancements, regulatory pressures, and shifting patient expectations, while concurrently suppressing more latent internal barriers of organizational inertia and restrictive cultures. The best leadership practices and case examples discussed in this chapter offer a glimpse of how healthcare leaders drive constructive transformation and create a sustainable future for their organizations and communities at large.

References

Barends, E., Rousseau, D. M., & Briner, R. B. (2014). *Evidence-Based Management: The Basic Principles*, Amsterdam, The Netherlands, Center for Evidence-Based Management.

Belasen, A. T. (2022). *Resilience in Healthcare Leadership: Practical Strategies and Self-Assessment Tools*, New York, NY, Routledge.

Belasen, A. T., & Belasen, A. R. (2016). Value in the middle: Cultivating middle managers in healthcare organizations, *Journal of Management Development*, 35(9), 1149–1162.

Belasen, A. T., Eisenberg, B., & Borgos, J. (2024). *Transforming Leadership, Improving Patient Experience: Communication Strategies for Driving Patient Satisfaction*, New York, NY, Routledge.

Cameron, K. S., Quinn, R. E., DeGraff, J., & Thakor, A. V. (2014). *Competing Values Leadership*, 2nd ed. Cheltenham, Edward Elgar Publishing.

Goleman, D. (2004, January). What makes a leader? Harvard business review. *HBR's Must- Reads on Leadership*, 3–13.

Gordon, A., & Pollack, J. (2018). Managing healthcare integration: Adapting project management to the needs of organizational change. *Project Management Journal, 49*(5), 5–21.

HCAHPS. (2025). Hospital Consumer Assessment of Healthcare Providers and Systems. Retrieved from https://www.hcahpsonline.org/

Karam, C. (2017). The evolution of patient satisfaction to patient experience. *Frontiers of Health Services Management, 33*(3), 30–34.

Lavine, M. (2014). Paradoxical leadership and the competing values framework. *The Journal of Applied Behavioral Science, 50*(2), 189–205.

Seong, Y. J., Shin, W. C., Moon, N. H., & Suh, K. T. (2020). Timing of hip-fracture surgery in elderly patients: Literature review and recommendations. *Hip & Pelvis, 32*(1), 11–16.

Weber, Y., & Tarba, S. Y. (2014). Strategic agility: A state of the art introduction to the special section on strategic agility. *California Management Review, 56*(3), 5–12.

INNOVATION AND ETHICS

D

DOI: 10.4324/9781003629214-10

Chapter 7

Ethical Leadership in an Era of AI: Balancing Innovation and Restraint in Healthcare

Jill Borgos and William Borgos

Introduction: Leadership in the Era of AI

One of the greatest challenges in this age of unprecedented technological acceleration will be a thoughtful examination of how artificial intelligence (AI) can be most beneficial and effective while minimizing harm before implementation. The alarming rate at which all forms of AI are being advanced requires leadership that can move through a disruptive state. Critical leadership characteristics include intellectual inquiry, a strong moral compass, and the ability to formulate a vision despite the vast unknown, balancing the fear of pivoting too quickly with a prudent amount of caution.

Yet, that is a challenge of enormous complexity! After all, the forces propelling the deployment of AI are powerful, crossing the boundaries of the self-interests of developers and the needs and expectations of users. At some point, all technological developments become so firmly embedded in society that we

DOI: 10.4324/9781003629214-11

simply take their existence for granted. AI is rapidly achieving such ubiquity. It is there in all we do. For example, it is increasingly responsible for generating responses to the dozens, if not hundreds, of internet searches we perform daily. But unlike the searches of a mere five years ago, AI goes beyond information gathering and synthesis and into the realm of content creation.

AI represents a new generation of technology in that it possesses a greater capacity to contribute to its own advancement. This is not merely a science fiction musing; as Gupta (2023) observes: "Unlike traditional AI, which relies on predefined algorithms and human-crafted updates, self-evolving AI harnesses the power of machine learning, deep learning, and evolutionary algorithms to enhance its own performance over time."

This chapter explores the ethical tensions that pervade the intersection of the opportunities and the potential harm of AI. In so doing, the healthcare field is employed as an extended example. We explore historical developments in the application of scientific knowledge and current developments related to the application of AI in the healthcare sector. We identify how AI is making positive and informative contributions both clinically and administratively, and present real and potential hazards when it is applied to patient care. Most importantly, the chapter defines how leaders can best stay in the *zone* – keeping focus amidst the rapid development and implementation of AI while keeping an ethical mindset.

Technological advances, commonly defined as the application of scientific knowledge for a purpose (Britannica, 2025), have been pushing the limits and testing both human subjects and human trust for centuries. As noted, technological advances continuously raise questions of safety and ethical considerations regarding whether any potential risks outweigh potential harm. Time and time again, key questions and problem-solving related to the advancement of technology have arisen after the technology is developed and used. After all, technological development rides on a bullet train while our understanding of the implications for society, by comparison, chugs along on a clunky trolley.

Predating the technological advancement of artificial intelligence, trains, ships, automobiles, and space shuttles provide ample evidence of the application of scientific knowledge intended to improve the quality of life for society, but which also came with inherent risk and occasional tragedy. It is essential that we remain cognizant of that crucial notion. Just consider that social media began with the seemingly quaint goal of providing virtual outlets for sharing information and building relationships. And yet, we continue to grapple with how to make sense of – let alone construct legislative solutions for – the profound ethical implications it has had on all facets of human experience, ranging from our psychosocial well-being to the shaping of political alignments.

Leaders have a special role in managing the delicate interplay between technological advancement and the restraints that prevent such advancement from doing more harm than good. Navigating toward that very spot between benefit achievement and harm prevention is the province of effective leadership. With AI, tensions between maximizing benefit and minimizing harm will inevitably arise. Some tensions will invariably become pronounced, manifesting as crises. All too often, such crises can catch us off guard. Within the realm of healthcare, those crises can prove extraordinarily costly.

We may think of clutch leadership as responding effectively in a crisis, as rising to the occasion. But we may also think of rising to the occasion as an ability to avoid a crisis. And when we think of leadership, we need not confine the definition to the person who sits in the top box on the chart of the organization. Rather, leadership refers to everyone, in fact anyone, who has responsibility for managing a situation in which AI has a presence. As such, while this chapter employs healthcare as the primary example, particularly those with caregiving responsibility, the concepts are generalizable to any field.

Regardless of the scientific advancements and the era they were founded, lessons can be found for leaders in the era of digital transformation. Accordingly, this chapter begins with a historical perspective.

Lessons from History

Over the course of four industrial revolutions, leaders were involved in the advancement of technology to improve the quality of life. Across the eras, the overall performance of organizations has faced disruptive and unstable circumstances, forcing them to adapt, leveraging economic and social resources while staying focused on long-term goals. The task of continuously improving efficiency and productivity through a quality lens, a process credited to Edward Deming in the 1950s during the rebuilding of Japan post WWII, has evolved over the course of four industrial revolutions. As technology has changed, so has the need for leadership approaches and styles.

The Institute of Entrepreneurship Development (iED, 2019) presents the defining characteristics of the four industrial revolutions. The First Industrial Revolution, with roots in the 18th century, introduced advancements in coal mining, steam engines, and railroads, as technological advancements were deemed important to accelerate the economy and allow valuable interactions between groups of people through means of transportation.

The Second Industrial Revolution, commencing in approximately 1870, further advanced society through the emergence of new energy sources in the form of electricity, gas, and oil (iED, 2019). The chemical processing of steel allowed for the development of automobiles and planes. Notable leaders of the Second Industrial Revolution included universally known American icons like Thomas Bell, Alexander Graham Bell, and Henry Ford.

The Third Industrial Revolution is defined by the advancement of nuclear energy, telecommunications, space exploration, biotechnologies, and toward the end of the 20th century, a transition from the use of analog to digital technology, paving the path to robotics (iED, 2019). The fourth and current Industrial Revolution is advancing the integration of digital technologies at a speed with which the human mind, in some instances, cannot keep pace (Friedman, 2016). As a result, policies, processes, regulations, and legal implications often lag. Each of the industrial revolutions has left lessons for leaders to follow. Among the most cautionary lessons is that scientific advancement can come with considerable risk and, in some cases, harm to human life. Doing the least amount of harm while advancing scientific knowledge is one of many aims that should be considered by leaders.

The early 19th century saw advancements in trains bring the marvel of speed to the transportation of goods and people, but it also brought errors and tragedy as axle development and derailment issues needed to be refined. Keeping trains on the tracks became problematic. Robert C. Reed's book, *Train Wreck,* notes that the rate of advancement of the railroad system was a "perfect storm," resulting in haste to increase speed and reduce costs with cheap construction, which led to the deaths of thousands. In a span of five years during the boom of railroad growth, train accidents increased from 1,201 in 1875 to 8,216 in 1880 (Hifford, 2023). The sinking of the *Titanic* in 1912 was another example of error and tragedy: a supposed feat of technological advancement, as the largest and fastest ocean liner, described as unsinkable, sank, killing approximately 1,500 people. Staying on track and afloat were laudable visions, but also posed enormous challenges for leaders advancing scientific advancements.

Around this same time, the automobile was deemed a technological advancement that would shape the economic and social trajectory of society. However, its advancement was fraught with tragedy as the safety of riding in an automobile did not keep pace with the technology. According to the Governors Highway Safety Association, it took nearly 70 years after the first automobile was on the roadways to even put lifesaving seat belts in a car. In 1968, the US Federal Government required seat belts to be placed in all newly made automobiles, but there was no requirement to use the seat belts despite the number of automobile deaths and related trauma occurring in unbelted drivers and passengers. It was not until 1985, nearly a century after the invention of the automobile, that New York State became the first state to require the use of seat belt in an automobile.

The advancement of space exploration provides additional examples of leaders pushing the limits of risk and potential harm. The application of scientific knowledge has been praised for achievements such as landing a man on the moon, but it has also yielded skepticism and fear. Preceding Neil Armstrong and the NASA Apollo 11 crew landing on the moon in 1969, incidents such as the fire onboard the Apollo I training mission in 1967 led to the deaths of crew members as NASA pushed the limits and tested technological advances. Further, the explosion of the NASA space shuttle Challenger 17 in 1986, followed by the explosion of the space shuttle Columbia in 2003, tested the trust of the populace and raised serious questions as to the process of checks and balances.

The incidents illuminated a salient aspect of scientific advancement: how quality and safety measures were evaluated and how political agendas influenced decision-making where human life was at stake. While political agendas and disregard for the protection of human life can be found throughout all the Industrial Revolution eras, the Challenger and Columbia tragedies introduced, on a scale not previously visible to the public, the degree of influence of government actors, self-interest, divergent interests, power dynamics, and corruption in scientific advancement (Bolman & Deal, 2017, p. 183).

Technology is exciting and has led to global economic growth, and in so many ways has improved the quality of human life to a level never imagined by preceding generations. There are two consistencies that can be found across generations and centuries of technological advances. The first is the fundamental concept of whether risk and advancement outweigh harm as technology is introduced and used by consumers. The second is that building trust in the use of technological advances takes effort, an ethical mindset, and ongoing continuous monitoring. Historical accounts of technological advances emerging into mainstream society have left indelible stories and lessons to learn from.

Before AI and before Space Shuttles There Were Bridges

The building of the Brooklyn Bridge, an architectural and technological marvel, began in 1869 and was completed in 1883. At the time, it was the longest suspension bridge in the world, crossing over New York City's East River and measuring 486 meters (1,595 feet) in length (Wikipedia, n.d.). A tremendous technological achievement, its sheer length and height were unfathomable to the general populace during its conception. The unprecedented length and height of the suspension bridge were possible in part due to the use of new steel technology using chrome steel cables, technologies developed during the Second Industrial Revolution. Both the modernization of steel and several novel architectural engineering techniques, attributed to civil engineer John Roebling and his team, enabled the building of the Brooklyn Bridge.

Historical accounts claim that opposition to the building of the Brooklyn Bridge was significant. In fact, it was even contested in the United States District Court for Southern New York by shipbuilders and merchants who were concerned for their future livelihood. Merchants needed to pass up and down the East River to do business, and a bridge of such a height was not imaginable – the mere thought of the bridge causing the demise of business opportunities for the shippers and merchants depending on the East River caused great consternation.

More than the potential for harming businesses, building the bridge was dangerous to people. The Center for Brooklyn History reports that approximately 20 people were killed during the construction of the bridge, and many more incurred severe injuries and illnesses, which continued to raise concerns over the end justifying the means. However, the long-term goal of the benefits of the bridge, in terms of economic growth and development, was deemed important enough to outweigh both the perceived and real risks (Gordon, 2025). The ability to move goods, services, and people across the East River, particularly in winter months when the river iced over, making travel difficult, was deemed an important goal to spur social and economic growth (Gordon, 2025).

The new technology enabled the capacity for both length and height, which was important due to the width of the East River and the height needed to enable the passing of shipping vessels underneath it. Moving the project forward amidst the legal battles, deaths, costs, and architectural challenges was only part of the story. In the end, those using the bridge needed to trust its safety.

P.T. Barnum, a mid to late 19th-century American businessman and leader who co-founded the Ringling Bros and Barnum & Bailey Circus, is not often thought of as the man who assuaged the fears and earned the eventual trust of New Yorkers nervous to use the newly built Brooklyn Bridge within the first week of the bridge opening. On May 31, 1883, *The New York Times* reported that a stampede of pedestrians, on what was reported as a narrow stairway, resulted in the tragic death of 12 persons and serious injuries to an additional 23 persons. The event was described as a "panic-stricken mob." While the stampede was unrelated to the overall safety of the suspension bridge in terms of supporting the weight of pedestrians and vehicles crossing the vast East River, the rumors questioning the bridge's safety spread throughout the city. Fear paralyzed many New Yorkers and kept them from using the bridge (Fleishman, 2023).

After 13 years of building the bridge at a cost of 15 million dollars (approximately 50 million in 2025 dollars), leaders needed to figure out how to win back public trust and reassure New Yorkers that the bridge was safe. One year later, in May 1884, P.T. Barnum organized a march of 21 elephants and 17 camels across the Brooklyn Bridge (Fleishman, 2023). The famed circus elephant Jumbo was a star attraction, and upward of 50,000 people traveled to witness the parade of circus animals crossing the Brooklyn Bridge as a signal and symbol of the bridge's safety (Wikipedia, n.d.). It took effort and time to regain and establish the trust of the public, and trust is an indispensable aspect of leading through disruptive circumstances.

The history of the building of the Brooklyn Bridge challenges the premise of a famously used quote from the movie *Field of Dreams*: "*if you build it, they (he) will come*" – this is not always the case. While AI use is already widespread, AI technology is advancing faster than its regulation, giving pause to many. There are considerations leaders need to address when moving forward with new technological advances that are not fully understood by society. In the field of healthcare and in the context of technological advances, health professionals have an ethical duty to ensure the safety of patients and the community at large. In a pluralistic society, the use of AI creates moral dilemmas involving judgments and decisions; collective decision-making needs to take place, representing the inclusion of diverse experiences and backgrounds of both users and anyone impacted using AI (Zowghi & Bano, 2024). Collective decision-making promotes transparency and trust (Vaughn, 2023).

The Belmont Is Not Only About Horses

The Belmont Stakes is the namesake of August Belmont, a businessman and leader who was one of the wealthiest New York financiers of his time, the mid-late 1800s (Drager, 2025). The Belmont Stakes is one of the oldest and longest of the three classic horse races that also include the Kentucky Derby and the Preakness. Winning all three earns the owner the prestigious Triple Crown. Parallel to the end of the First Industrial Revolution, the Belmont Stakes originated in 1867, two years before the building of the Brooklyn Bridge. Its moniker is the "Test of Champions" (Drager, 2025).

Ironically, one of its defining characteristics, like the Brooklyn Bridge, is its length, and it is considered a significant athletic feat to win due to the sheer stamina required and the ability to stay in the zone for the full distance of 1.5 miles (Drager, 2025). Horse racing is among the oldest sports and continues today as one of the most popular sports in America (Engle, 2019).

The sport of horse racing, as do many professional sports, generates wealth and provides jobs in select communities. However, the sport has been criticized for its unethical treatment of the horses. It is a sport that pushes the horses to their limits, and on occasion, this can result in life-ending fatalities (Engle, 2019). One of the emerging themes for leaders throughout all the Industrial Revolution eras is that the *testing of* and the *pushing of limits*, in sport or the advancement of technology, needs guardrails to ensure the safety and welfare of those affected, especially those who cannot protect themselves, particularly when faced with political pressures and influences with self-interest.

It is the *pushing of limits*, whether it is in sport, industry, or trialing a new technology, that consistently draws attention, especially when *pushing the limits* contributes to unfavorable results and, worse, tragedy. It is a pattern consistently seen with the advancement of what could be possible if limits are pushed. But the pattern identified from *pushing the limits* also has lessons for leaders taking on the new and evolving application and use of artificial intelligence – just because we can, should we?

An ethical mindset helps to frame decision-making for leaders. It provides a platform to ask questions that include acknowledging different value systems and perspectives that enable a collective and often more responsible path to accomplishing a goal, or at least doing so by minimizing risk and harm. Especially in the field of medicine, the use of artificial intelligence, in order to be used effectively, needs to be informed by past events whose egregiousness has given rise to distrust and fear.

Digital technology can serve as a valuable tool to disseminate information and reach a greater number of citizens, thereby constituting a means to engage them in activities that would promote positive outcomes for both the individual and the community. The obvious examples include the sharing of illness prevention protocols related to instances of disease outbreaks, such as the COVID-19 pandemic and the 2025 measles outbreaks in the United States. Informative vaccination-related content can be shared via technology, especially during outbreaks of any disease. Not only is the dissemination of information important in and of itself to save lives and mitigate the spread of disease, but technology is a tremendously powerful tool that can help mitigate potential harm in that its speed alone enables information to be distributed to a large number of people.

The downside, of course, is that its effectiveness depends on the ability of the user to assess the legitimacy and trustworthiness of the information being disseminated. While public health departments and ministries of health have legitimacy, they are also tightly bound to government actors and private interest groups, which, in some cases, can cause a diminished sense of trust. When this occurs, the diminished trust can cause an elevated sense of fear and dissent. This elevated sense of fear and distrust, not to mention occasional dissent, is not without basis, as events involving the "testing of humans" have not always been protective of the subjects and are rather conducted with the self-interest of invested government and private sector actors in mind.

Advances in medicine have a long history of reported unethical treatment of humans for the sake of advancement and scientific discovery that have cumulatively, over time, contributed to public fear and distrust. The collective discipline of healthcare is also known for establishing ethical principles to guide those seeking to *push the limits*, but doing so within the boundaries of protocols established to protect human subjects. The Belmont Report, a 1979 landmark document, is one such guiding document, providing ethical principles and guidelines aimed at minimizing risk and harm.

In 1974, a National Commission of the US government was charged with identifying "basic ethical principles that should underline the conduct of biomedical and behavioral research involving human subjects" (US Department of Health and Human Services, n.d., para 1). The Belmont Report, which emerged from that initiative, became the foundational framework for protecting human subjects involved in scientific research. The report provided much-needed guardrails for scientific research, including outlining standards of practice that specifically addressed:

i) the boundaries between biomedical and behavioral research and the accepted and routine practice of medicine
ii) the role of assessment of risk-benefit criteria in the determination of the appropriateness of research involving human subjects
iii) appropriate guidelines for the selection of human subjects for participation in such research and
iv) the nature and definition of informed consent in various research settings

(US Department of Health and Human Services, 2018)

In addition to informed consent being a key piece of the regulatory framework in scientific research and in the application of research in practice, informed consent is also foundational to the intervention and treatment of patients in healthcare settings in both diagnosis and preventive care. The evolution and groundwork that provided roots to the informed consent currently used in medical practice closely parallel in timing to the Second Industrial Revolution. This makes sense in that this was the period when biomedical advances and developments were flourishing; patients were being diagnosed, tested, and treated with the assistance of new technological advances never seen before.

A series of legal cases beginning in the late 19th century raised awareness of the role of patient autonomy in the use of these new technological advances. The earliest judicial cases of record include *Mohr v. Williams* in 1905 and *Schloendorff v. Society of New York Hospital* in 1914. Both cases involved decision-making around surgical procedures that failed to involve the patient, bypassing their autonomy. Since both cases involved women – and women, at the time, did not have voting or equal rights – these landmark legal cases set a precedent for what followed, but left little legally binding traction for the legal and regulatory implementation of informed consent (Bazzano et al., 2021).

It was not until the 1957 case of *Salgo v. Leland Stanford Jr University Board of Trustees* that informed consent as a legally binding entity would gain momentum. In this case, plaintiff Salgo sued the medical center and surgeon for not disclosing the full potential risk prior to the surgical procedure and intervention the surgeon performed on him (Bazzano et al., 2021).

These landmark cases, among others, established the regulatory and legal framework for protecting the self-interest, full disclosure, and autonomy of the patient in the decision-making process for medical treatments and inventions. This has substantial relevance in current healthcare contexts as AI is increasingly being used in the decision-making process for diagnosis and intervention.

In the Absence of Guardrails

The Belmont Report and the regulation of informed consent in medical practice unfortunately came on the back end of tragic events related to the testing and experimentation of human subjects without full disclosure of treatments and informed consent. The report raised awareness of three basic ethical principles that had long been absent from the advancement of scientific inquiry in medicine: (1) respect for people, (2) beneficence, and (3) justice (US Department of Health and Human Services, 2018). In a pluralistic society, respect for persons, beneficence, and justice are generally considered the traditional cultural principles that inform the boundaries of ethical behavior (Vaughn, 2023).

Bioethics scholar Lewis Vaughn notes that respect for people espouses that individuals are autonomous agents and capable of making decisions under informed direction. Beneficence takes into account respecting a patient's decisions and protecting them from harm with an ethical mindset. Justice represents the overarching concept of fairness and, in the case of medical research, focuses on who bears the burden of advancing medical scientific discovery.

Two prominent studies conducted in the United States serve as famous failures in the practice of ethical decision-making by leaders attempting to advance science. The first commenced in 1929 when the United States Public Health Service began conducting studies and treatments on rural southern Black people to examine and longitudinally assess the prevalence of syphilis. The study became widely known as the Tuskegee Study, named after the town in Alabama where the experiments were conducted. The story of the infamous Tuskegee Study had been relatively unknown to many until it was released in 1972 by the *Associated Press* in New York and Washington (Tuskegee University, 2025).

By all accounts, the study violated basic ethical principles in the interest of advancing scientific knowledge. The Tuskegee University Bioethics Center recounts the historical events, stating that the study was intended to seek an understanding of the progression of syphilis, a sexually transmitted disease that had at the time, no known treatment. It is reported that the study enrolled 600 "poor and illiterate" Black men and made promises offering "medical exams, rides to and from the clinics, meals on examination days, free treatment for minor ailments, and upon their death – burial stipends paid to their surviving family members" (Tuskegee University, 2025).

The coercive enlistment of participants was only the beginning of the ethical and health issues associated with the study. During the study, penicillin, an antibiotic used to treat syphilis, was developed, but knowledge of its development and potential for treatment of syphilis was withheld from the participants in the study. The study violated informed consent procedures and failed to fully disclose options and risks, thereby limiting choice and exposing participants to harm.

The second study, the Willowbrook Experiment, was conducted from 1956 through 1971 on the children at Willowbrook State School for Children with Severe Disabilities in Staten Island, New York. The study was an attempt to more fully understand the deadly disease process of hepatitis and develop a vaccine. Hepatitis was reportedly prevalent in the population of children at the state school, which was thus deemed a ripe environment for the study of hepatitis. Children were purposely infected with local strains of the hepatitis virus with the hopes of developing a vaccine (Dubois, 2025). The study failed to protect a vulnerable population and employed coercive techniques to gain consent from the parents of children in the study.

The Willowbrook study set up a quid pro quo arrangement where children were accepted into the overcrowded facility if the parents gave permission to inject their children with live strains of hepatitis (Dubois, 2025). Questionable interventions and medical practices, many of which were abusive by any standards, were imposed on the children living in the state facility in the pursuit of scientific advancement. In 1965, Robert F. Kennedy, a New York senator at the time, visited the facility and, reflecting on his visit, referred to the institution as a "snake pit" and stated that there were "no civil liberties for those put in the cells of Willowbrook" (Rosenbaum, 2021).

The Tuskegee and Willowbrook experiments, among others, left an indelible memory of atrocities committed by scientific scholars and government actors on vulnerable populations. The atrocities violated basic ethical principles and human rights. As a result of the overall lack of proper guardrails, including oversight, transparency, and the overall disregard for human life, the studies shook trust in the integrity of scientific biomedical research. Events such as these are, in part, why critical medical and health information that could be lifesaving is often and justifiably questioned and, at times, ignored.

The use and experimentation of artificial intelligence in healthcare is raising concerns about the types of ethical practices and guardrails that should be implemented. Questions being raised include how patients will be protected from harm, where and how transparency will be required, and who gets to make the decision on oversight. The storylines may change from era to era as scientific advancements evolve, but two key strategies leaders should be cognizant of are learning from lessons of the past and staying grounded in an ethical mindset. Most importantly, leaders should strive to minimize risk and to do no harm. Leaders have the special responsibility to ask key questions such as *just because we can, should we*?

The New Era of Augmented Intelligence

In response to questions such as *just because we can, should we?* and challenges linked to the rapid growth of the use of artificial intelligence in the healthcare sector, in 2018, the American Medical Association (AMA), a leading policy and lobbying group for physicians, created its first AI policy statement. In the years since, as AI has been increasingly implemented in healthcare settings, the organization continues to create and distribute several updates.

One of the key points of the initial document, which has been reinforced in each subsequent iteration, involves the importance of physicians and other healthcare clinicians (including nurse practitioners, physician assistants, and nurses) thinking of AI as "augmented intelligence" rather than "artificial intelligence" (AMA, 2024). Used properly, the tools should be leveraged to *augment* healthcare professionals' ability to make better, evidence-based decisions in a more timely and cost-efficient manner.

When used appropriately, AI should help healthcare providers accurately and efficiently complete more rudimentary tasks, thus allowing providers to focus more time and energy on human interaction and the more nuanced parts of patient care. Healthcare leaders should keep continuous assessment and evaluation front and center, and question why and what benefit AI is contributing. For example, if we purchase and implement this new piece of AI technology, what problem are we hoping to solve? Have we thoughtfully evaluated the risks and benefits of making this change? Who is affected? Failure to ask these questions may lead to investing precious resources in the wrong product and may inadvertently lead an organization to add rather than reduce risk.

Beginning in 2022, the "explosion" of generative AI and the use of Large Language Models (LLMs) have added further complexity for healthcare leaders (Ennis-O'Connor & O'Connor, 2024). We have reached the stage in which tools, such as ChatGPT, are able to generate proposed answers to both patient and provider questions in response to prompts. These answers are based on the technology recognizing existing patterns, connections, and rationale based on existing data and applying these existing data to the prompt. These types of models continue to grow more and more powerful, but with often opaque algorithms, sometimes referred to as "black boxes." It is these opaque algorithms that help generate augmented decision-making that are raising awareness of how checks and balances of information accuracy are being assessed and by whom (Xu & Shuttleworth, 2024).

In this context, the black box is a combination of the source code and data sets utilized. by the specific AI tool to generate a proposed answer to the prompt. In the real-world usage, it is impossible for the end user (physician, nurse, or patient) to understand how the answer was generated. For example, the ability to identify the data sets that are used or not used to generate content lacks transparency. It is often difficult to determine how recent the information being accessed is or if biases were unknowingly infiltrated into the data from past research, contributing to inaccuracies in output of data generated by AI systems (Mozayeni, 2021; Ennis-O'Connor & O'Connor, 2024; Yang et al., 2022).

Fundamentally, the end user needs to be able to both trust the AI tool and have the knowledge, training, time, and resources to confirm the AI-generated answer when necessary. This again ties into the idea of augmented intelligence. Leaders and healthcare clinicians must always keep a dose of intellectual skepticism and be prepared to challenge a proposed answer if it does not make sense. While AI has been shown to yield benefits by helping clinicians manage complex medical scenarios, there also remains the real, and potentially more significant, risk of an AI-generated misdiagnosis (Blouin, 2023).

Core Principles

In their policy statements on the use of AI, the AMA proposes the adoption of core principles to help healthcare leaders, and specifically physicians, manage the integration of AI. These principles state that the use of AI should be "ethical, equitable, responsible, accurate, and transparent" (AMA, 2024). On the surface, these principles are straightforward, and they mesh well with the ethos of healthcare providers – *first do no harm.* This is the essence of the ethical mindset.

In practice, however, ensuring that the AI tools live up to this aspirational statement is far more challenging. Given the vast discrepancies between the financial and technical resources available to different players in the healthcare sector, how do we ensure equitable access to AI? And given limited resources, who gets to choose which patients and providers get to benefit from this augmented intelligence?

We are quickly learning that generative AI is very good at providing an answer to a prompt within seconds, but healthcare organizations are struggling to clarify who is responsible for the veracity of the answer. Returning to the "black box" dilemma, do the healthcare professionals who ask the question to understand the algorithm underlying the answer can readily identify if the data sets fed into the algorithm include existing biases in a manner that would influence decision-making and treatment of care? (Gichoya et al., 2023).

In November 2023, the AMA Board of Trustees approved several advocacy principles, focused on the concepts of disclosure requirements, liability, data privacy, and security, and insurers' use of AI (AMA, 2024). In part, these principles were meant to help guide physicians trying to navigate these complex issues surrounding the use of AI in the healthcare setting. Like the need to build trust with other technological advances and consistent with keeping an ethical mindset, healthcare leaders should be very aware of these principles.

When caring for patients, healthcare providers should be transparent in letting the patients know that AI may be used to help augment their care. When possible, patients should have the option to opt out. For example, if a provider asks a patient for permission for a generative AI product to listen to and then summarize their visit, the patient should have the opportunity to decline. If patients agree, they should be able to trust that the data will be kept confidential and treated with the same care as the rest of their medical record. As AI becomes more and more an expected part of our healthcare system, it is possible that agreeing to universal use may be part of consent for services.

Trust

Importantly, the recommendations and policies from the AMA are just that, recommendations, and they are not currently legally binding. Similarly, and perhaps carrying even more weight, in 2023, the Biden administration issued an Executive Order on AI as well as a "Blueprint for an AI Bill of Rights," in which the administration proposed five principles to guide the implementation of AI. These principles mirror and largely support the recommendations of the AMA, and they include "i) safe and effective systems; ii) algorithmic discrimination protections; iii) data privacy; iv) notice and explanation (transparency); v) consideration of human alternatives to AI" (The White House, 2003).

Of note, on January 23, 2025, President Trump issued an Executive Order revoking this Biden Executive Order and instructed his leadership to develop a new framework for guiding official US government policy as it pertains to AI (The White House, 2025). This change demonstrates how the influence of government through policies and executive orders can disrupt the business environment as leaders attempt to guide their organizations through periods of rapid technological advancement (Belasen, Eisenberg, & Borgos, 2024).

If healthcare leaders and providers understand and attempt to embed these concepts in their decision-making, it will help to build trust in the use of AI (Mozayeni, 2021). In a similar vein to the challenges faced by leaders needing to gain the trust of New Yorkers in 1883 regarding the integrity and safety of the Brooklyn Bridge, present-day patients and frontline healthcare workers importantly need to gain trust in artificial intelligence. As a key part of the healthcare system, leaders should regularly and transparently touch on these principles. However, in the case of AI implementation in healthcare settings and given some of the missteps of the past, it may take more than a few elephants and camels to gain the trust of the populace (Patterson, 2025).

The principles outlined by the AMA and in the *Blueprint for an AI Bill of Rights* serve as a broad framework to help leaders guide their decision-making, but as noted above, many questions underlie each principle. In practice, healthcare leaders and healthcare providers will need to constantly balance the benefits and risks of integrating AI into their practice versus sitting on the sidelines waiting for a final, mature product. AI will continually evolve. Given the tremendous investment in and rapid evolution of AI models, it is not at all clear when the AI environment will reach maturity. Rapid change appears to be the new normal, and ever-increasing adoption of AI is clearly the trend.

Documentation of Care

Surveys conducted by the AMA indicate a rapid increase in the adoption of various AI technologies, particularly as tools augmenting the documentation of visits become available. AI tools are being piloted to help propose answers to patient questions in virtual "inboxes," and AI is already in use in various ways to help screen radiology studies. An *inbox* is the term used to describe the virtual collection of patient messages, prescription renewal requests, referral notes, and lab and imaging results which clinicians receive on a daily basis. In modern practice, effective management of the inbox is essential to delivering high-quality medical care.

A practical question raised by the rapid implementation of AI into the provision of healthcare and indirectly addressed by both the AMA and the Biden administration's Executive Order revolves around the proper role of "augmented intelligence" in medical decision-making. While the Trump and subsequent administrations will likely institute policy modifications based on the technology's evolving nature as well as on political and other calculations, it can be assumed that most clinicians would agree that a time-saving documentation tool used to capture the core elements of a patient encounter is a net positive. Concerns surrounding patient notification, data privacy, and editing the AI-generated documentation for accuracy can be addressed with appropriate policies and training. Patients may or may not decline using this tool. If they do decline, clinicians could quickly revert to standard documentation practices of typing and dictating. While this type of AI-generated documentation occurs only in the very early stages of adoption, initial results are promising.

The Patient Portal

Far more challenging than assessing the accuracy of generative AI to summarize a patient visit is the increased use of generative AI tools and LLMs to help clinicians respond to patient questions and concerns, help patients assess symptoms, and formulate a care plan. This would be the case for both in-person and virtual patient experiences. A patient portal is directly related to a provider's inbox, and in this context, it refers to the electronic means by which a patient can send and receive messages or other information to their healthcare provider.

Patient's portal messaging has exploded in use since the advent of the COVID-19 pandemic. Suddenly, patients were instructed to stay home rather than come to the office as a default, and a significant number of patients very quickly became comfortable with virtual communication. As patients adjusted to receiving virtual care, either through video visits or simply through email communication, many found this mode of interaction convenient, efficient, and extremely valuable. But, from the perspective of healthcare professionals, the surge in portal use has been a double-edged sword. The sheer volume of messages has strained the resources of both private practices and large healthcare organizations.

Healthcare institutions have responded in a variety of ways, including hiring more registered nurses to triage phone messages, creating lists of emergent symptoms that should be expedited for clinician review, and, in most cases, increasing the expectation for providers to manage this surge of patient questions. Electronic Health Record (EHR) vendors have worked to improve their products to help healthcare providers handle this increased workload. Given the well-documented national shortage of healthcare professionals and the typically full in-person office schedules, this additional surge in "virtual workload" has placed a great strain on healthcare providers.

It is axiomatic that there are only so many hours in the day. With more work, something must give. Healthcare organizations have responded with a mix of reducing traditional clinic appointments to allow clinicians more time to answer inbox questions, delegating more decision-making for registered nurses, offering "extra pay" to compensate for the extra time spent on inbox items, and in some cases simply asking health professionals to adapt to the increased workload. In each of these scenarios, one thing is clear – there is more work to do.

The rapid growth of AI, particularly generative AI, presents a significant opportunity to help address this concern of the workload. For example, AI may be able to support efforts to accurately and efficiently triage patient questions and prioritize them for a clinician to later address. Even more complicated and intriguing, can AI accurately and efficiently answer a patient's question without human involvement?

As clinicians and healthcare leaders seek to answer these questions, we must remember the ethical mindset and make sure to remember, first, do no harm. Similarly, if the AI "hallucinates" and makes an incorrect triage or gives inappropriate advice to a patient, who is responsible? Clinicians and healthcare leaders will need to sort out best practices for the "peer review" of these types of errors. In doing so, patient safety must remain the number one priority. Importantly, the current system is far from perfect. Both nurses and providers make mistakes when answering portal messages. How will we know if AI will be an improvement in terms of accuracy and patient acceptance (Siira et al., 2024)?

To support the idea that AI in this realm does hold great promise, one recent study demonstrated that AI-generated answers to patient questions were found to be as accurate, thorough, and empathetic as compared to answers coming from physicians (Ayers et al., 2023). Once trained, AI should be able to repeatedly generate the same or similar answer again and again without the risk inherent in human answers if the provider is fatigued or rushing through the reply (Kolata, 2024).

Assessing Patient Health Problems

AI is already being widely used to help clinicians appropriately assess and treat patients in real-world settings. This is happening from the primary care setting to community hospitals to the ICUs of tertiary medical centers. Providers have always used medical references to help guide decision-making. While many different types of resources remain in use, in recent decades these resources have evolved from regular use of paper medical journals and medical textbooks to online databases such as UpToDate. UpToDate is a widely used tool that regularly updates a database of clinical guidelines and point-of-care clinical advice. Use of PubMed or Google Scholar is also popular. In recent years, the use of generative AI tools such as ChatGPT has grown rapidly, providing almost instant answers to user prompts and questions. Access to "answers" from generative AI tools in this manner raises tremendously important questions. There is a great reward, but also a great risk (Bhardwaj, 2022).

When used appropriately, AI can meaningfully augment the ability of a clinician to arrive at the correct diagnosis and treatment plan for a particular patient (Mozayeni, 2021). The key to accurately diagnosing a patient is taking a comprehensive history, performing a focused physical examination, ordering and interpreting diagnostic testing, and ultimately creating a well-considered differential diagnosis and treatment plan. Given the current state of the art, tools such as Ambient AI can be most helpful in documenting a patient's history, facilitating a clinician's ability to generate a broad differential diagnosis, order and interpret diagnostic tests, and then evaluate potential treatment options.

AI can assist in guiding a focused physical exam, not so much in actually performing the exam but in helping a clinician to understand and apply the findings. For example, a clinician may hear a pericardial friction rub, and by using an AI search combining "pericardial friction rub" and "shortness of breath" may more quickly and accurately hone in on a diagnosis. Experts in the field will often say, "AI will never replace clinicians, but clinicians who don't use AI will be replaced by those who do" (Nitkin et al., 2023, p. 24).

The Risks of Intellectual "Laziness"

Fundamental to the effectiveness of the process is the clinician's consistent review of the data and suggestions being provided by the AI tool. The clinician must be able to ask themselves, "does this make sense?" With the current state of the art, AI can and does make mistakes. For example, a "low ejection fraction" noted on a biliary scan may be falsely interpreted as congestive heart failure if the AI tool falsely assumes the "low ejection fraction" was detected by an echocardiogram. The clinician must be alert and ready to review each suggestion or result with a healthy degree of skepticism (Bhardwaj, 2022). This should already be the case when consulting a textbook, a colleague, or UpToDate, but the ease and authority with which AI tools propose answers, making this especially important to keep in mind. The scenario noted above highlights one of the greatest risks of the ever-increasing integration of AI into the healthcare sector, and that is the risk of an overdependence on AI tools and the risk of "intellectual laziness." While this risk is real for clinicians at all points in their careers, this risk is perhaps great for learners, medical and nursing students, interns and residents, and newer professional nurses and attendings. Training in a world where AI is everywhere, particularly when ChatGPT can generate a college essay or cover letters in seconds, presents unique challenges and temptations. Medical schools, nursing schools, and healthcare organizations of every size and complexity will need to regularly and vigorously remind their teams of the importance of healthcare ethics, double and triple-checking sources, and remembering how to think incisively and critically. In medical training, and even in practice, health care teams should regularly work through scenarios without the direct assistance of artificial intelligence. EHRs can and do experience failure. Cyberattacks can and do happen. Storms occur and the power goes out. In these scenarios and many others, it is critical that the clinician remembers how to think critically and make decisions without immediate access to AI.

Human Versus Machine

In the iconic film *2001: A Space Odyssey*, HAL-9000, the computer capable of thinking, refuses the command of the human, Dave, to open the bay doors on their spaceship. This occurs shortly after HAL has rebelled against his human creators and killed much of the crew. The 1960s classic was in many ways ahead of its time, raising intriguing questions about the risks and benefits of "thinking computers" (Krishnamurty, 2024). Fortunately, current generative AI systems have not evolved to the point where we should fear them "taking over" decision-making from humans against the will of humans.

For example, current systems may help ICU physicians assess the severity of illness in a patient, but they would not forbid or prevent the physician from making a particular treatment decision. An alarm may be triggered by a generative AI system to make a clinician aware that they may be about to commit a medical error, but ultimately it would be up to the clinician to evaluate the significance of the alarm and to respond accordingly. That said, as recently as 2023, a number of AI leaders sounded the alarm regarding the rapidity of AI development, signing a declaration requesting a pause in the testing of newer generative AI technologies to allow society to more fully assess the risks and benefits of these newer technologies (De Vynck, 2023). It remains to be seen to what extent we will heed that warning.

Conclusion

This chapter has touched on several key themes regarding how healthcare leaders should view the opportunities and risks of implementing AI into their strategic plans and day-to-day operations. The story of the building of the Brooklyn Bridge emphasizes the need to develop trust when making use of new technology, and we detailed the story of the Belmont Report to highlight the importance of having well-thought-out "rules of the road" prior to proceeding with investigating or implementing new ideas.

We reviewed the frightening details of the Tuskegee experiments, when patients were not informed of critical details of the experiment they found themselves a part of. We have also shared a brief overview of principles advanced by the American Medical Association and the Biden administration's Executive Order, which are intended to guide the evaluation and implementation of AI technologies. Additionally, we made the reader aware that the Trump administration's AI team is working on evolving their own set of principles to guide AI development. When evaluating whether to embrace or ignore a new way to implement AI, it is most important for the healthcare leader to ask themselves, "What problems am I trying to solve? What do I hope to accomplish with the use of this tool?" If the answer is clear, then it would make sense to proceed. If the answer is muddy, then further thought may be required. Once the decision is made to proceed with implementation, it is important to keep in mind several of the themes touched on in this chapter.

Leaders should work to clarify who has the moral responsibility for the decision and, similarly, ensure that effective guardrails are in place to reduce the risk of errors. The effectiveness of this process is contingent on sound and thorough policies and training, as well as the presence of redundancies and backup systems.

Trust can be built for both clinicians and patients by emphasizing transparency. All parties should be made aware when AI plays a role in their care. At some point in the future, this may become so commonplace as to be assumed, but during this transitional period, conscious efforts must be made to ensure such awareness. Organizations should build and maintain robust compliance and peer review processes so that they may quickly recognize patterns, both positive and negative, and learn from errors, failures, and successes.

The adoption of AI, and generative AI in particular, by the healthcare industry will undoubtedly have tremendous benefits for patients, healthcare workers, and the healthcare system. Used appropriately, augmented intelligence should help improve the accuracy and timeliness of diagnoses and the implementation of treatment plans, with the goal of improving patient health and well-being. Likewise, the efficiencies possible with AI hold the promise of reducing healthcare costs, freeing up resources for either further investment in currently ignored sectors of the healthcare ecosystem or potentially other sectors of the economy.

Principles outlined throughout this chapter provide a path for healthcare leaders in understanding why it is important to incorporate ethical decision-making in the use of AI, particularly as AI is being used to augment clinical decision-making, but also importantly influencing patient agency and autonomy. Leaders need to stay in the zone, focused on minimizing harm, ensuring patient agency, advancing patient care through advancing scientific knowledge, and moving forward asking questions.

References

American Medical Association. (2024, November). *Augmented Intelligence Development, Deployment, and the Use in Health Care.* American Medical Association. https://www.ama-assn.org/system/files/ama-ai-principles.pdf

Ayers, J. W., Poliak, A., Dredze, M., Leas, E. C., Zhu, Z., Kelley, J. B., Faix, D. J., Goodman, A. M., Longhurst, C. A., Hogarth, M., & Smith, D. M. (2023). Comparing Physician and Artificial Intelligence Chatbot Responses to Patient Questions Posted to a Public Social Media Forum. *JAMA internal medicine, 183*(6), 589–596.

Bazzano, L. A., Durant, J., & Brantley, P. R. (2021). A modern history of informed consent and the role of key information. *The Ochsner Journal, 21*(1), 81–85. doi:10.31486/toj.19.0105

Belasen, A. T., Eisenberg, B., & Borgos, J. (2024). *Transforming Leadership, Improving Patient Experience: Communication Strategies for Driving Patient Satisfaction.* Routledge.

Bhardwaj, A. (2022). Promise and provisos of artificial intelligence and machine learning in healthcare. *Journal of Healthcare Leadership, 14*, 113–118. doi:10.2147/JHL.S369498

Blouin, L. (2023, March 6). AI's mysterious 'black box' problem, explained. *University of Michigan-Dearborn News.* https://umdearborn.edu/news/ais-mysterious-black-box-problem-explained

Bolman, L. G., & Deal, T. E. (2017). *Reframing Organizations: Artistry, Choice, and Leadership* (6th ed.). Jossey-Bass.

Britannica. (2025, March 7). *Technology.* The Editors of Encyclopedia Britannica. https://www.britannica.com/technology/technology

De Vynck, G. (2023, March 23). Elon Musk and a handful of AI leaders ask for 'pause on the Tech'. *The Washington Post.* https://www.washingtonpost.com/technology/2023/03/29/ai-letter-pause/

Drager, M. (2025, January 27). Belmont Stakes American horse race. *Britannica.* https://www.britannica.com/sports/horse-racing/The-modern-age-of-racing

Dubois, J. M. (2025). *Hepatitis Studies at the Willowbrook State School for Children.* Bioethics Research Center Washington University Saint Louis. https://bioethicsresearch.org/resources/case-studies/hepatitis-studies-at-the-willowbrook-state-school-for-children/

Engle, J. (2019, April 9). Is horse racing ethical? *The New York Times.* https://www.nytimes.com/2019/04/09/learning/is-horse-racing-ethical.html

Ennis-O'Connor, M., & O'Connor, W. T. (2024). Charting the future of patient care: A strategic leadership guide to harnessing the potential of artificial intelligence. *Healthcare Management Forum, 37*(4), 290–295. doi:10.1177/08404704241235893

Friedman, T. L. (2016). *Thank You for Being Late: An Optimist's Guide to Thriving in the Age of Acceleration*. Picador.

Gichoya, J. W., Thomas, K., Celi, L. A., Safdar, N., Banerjee, I., Banja, J. D., Seyyed-Kalantari, L., Trivedi, H., & Purkayastha, S. (2023). AI pitfalls and what not to do: Mitigating bias in AI. *The British Journal of Radiology, 96*(1150), 1–8. doi:10.1259/bjr.20230023

Gordon, J. S. (2025). *The Brooklyn Bridge*. The Bill of Rights Institute. https://billofrightsinstitute.org/essays/the-brooklyn-bridge

Gupta, J. (2023, December 23). *The Evolution of AI: Navigating the future self-evolving systems*. Medium. https://medium.com/@jitu028/the-evolution-of-ai-navigating-the-future-of-self-_evolving-systems-ef0ca84b838a

Hifford, D. (2023, May 4). *The Wrong Side of the Tracks*. Notes from the Frontier. https://www.notesfromthefrontier.com/post/the-wrong-side-of-the-tracks

iED Team. (2019, June 3). *A Brief History of the 4 Industrial Revolutions that Shaped the World*. Institute of Entrepreneurship Development. https://ied.eu/project-updates/the-4-industrial-revolutions/

Kolata, G. (2024, November 17). A.I. chatbots defeat doctors at diagnosing illness. *The New York Times*. https://www.nytimes.com/2024/11/17/health/chatgpt-ai-doctors-diagnosis.html?smid=nytcore-ios-share&referringSource=articleShare

Krishnamurty, K. (2024). Media review: 2001: A space Odyssey: A prescient warning not to treat Artificial Intelligence as a human substitute. *Organization, 0*(0). https://doi.org/10.1177/13505084241259970

Leishman, F. (2023, May 17). How 21 elephants solved panic on the Brooklyn Bridge 139 years ago thanks to PT Barnum. *Mirror*. https://www.mirror.co.uk/news/us-news/how-21-elephants-solved-panic-29987204

Mozayeni, B. R. (2021). Artificial intelligence machines in medicine and healthcare management: A deep introduction. *Journal of Healthcare Management Standards, 1*(2), 47–56. doi:10.4018/JHMS.2021070104

Nitkin, K., Smith, L., & Depasquale, S. (2023, Fall). *Future Shock. Hopkins Medicine*. The Johns Hopkins University and The Johns Hopkins Health system Corporation.

Patterson, J. (2025, Winter). *Building Doctors' Trust in AI*. The Johns Hopkins Whiting School of Engineering Magazine. https://engineering.jhu.edu/magazine/2024/12/building-doctors-trust-in-ai/

Rosenbaum, L. (2021, June 15). The hideous truths of testing vaccines on humans. *Forbes Magazine*. https://www.forbes.com/sites/leahrosenbaum/2020/06/12/willowbrook-scandal-hepatitis-experiments-hideous-truths-of-testing-vaccines-on-humans/

Siira, E., Tyskbo, D., & Nygren, J. (2024, July 24). Healthcare leaders' experiences of implementing artificial intelligence for medical history-taking and triage in Swedish primary care: An interview study. *BMC Primary Care, 25*, 268. https://bmcprimcare.biomedcentral.com/articles/10.1186/s12875-024-02516-z

The New York Times. (1883, May 31,). Dead on the bridge. *The New York Times*. https://timesmachine.nytimes.com/timesmachine/1883/05/31/102825484.pdf?pdf_redirec t=true&ip=0

The White House. (2003). *Blueprint for an AI Bill of Rights: Making Automated Systems Work For The American People.* The White House National Archives. https://bidenwhitehouse.archives.gov/ostp/ai-bill-of-rights/

The White House. (2025, January 23). *Removing Barriers to American Leadership in Artificial Intelligence.* The White House. https://www.whitehouse.gov/presidential-_actions/2025/01/removing-barriers-to-american-leadership-in-artificial-intelligence/

Tuskegee University. (2025). *About the USPHS Syphilis Study.* Tuskegee Bioethics Center. https://www.tuskegee.edu/about-us/centers-of-excellence/bioethics-center/about-the-usph s-syphilis-study

US Department of Health and Human Services. (2018, January 15). *The Belmont Report.* Office for the Human Research Protections. https://www.hhs.gov/ohrp/regulations-and-policy/belmont-report/read-the-belmont-report /index.html

US Department of Health and Human Services. (n.d.). *The Belmont Report.* Office for Human Subjects Research Protections. Accessed March 4, 2025 https://www.hhs.gov/ohrp/regulations-and-policy/belmont-report/index.html

Vaughn, L. (2023). *Bioethics: Principles, Issues, and Cases.* Oxford University Press.

Wikipedia. (n.d.). *Brooklyn Bridge.* Wikipedia. Accessed March 2, 2025 https://en.wikipedia.org/wiki/Brooklyn_Bridge

Xu, H., & Shuttleworth, K. M. J. (2024, February). Medical artificial intelligence and the black box problem: a view based on the ethical principle of "do no harm". *Intelligent Medicine, 4*(1), 52–57. https://doi.org/10.1016/j.imed.2023.08.001

Yang, G., Ye, Q., & Xia, J. (2022, January). Unbox the black-box for the medical explainable AI via multi-modal and multi-center data fusion: A mini review, two showcases and beyond. *Information Fusion, 77*, 29–52. https://www.sciencedirect.com/science/article/pii/S1566253521001597

Zowghi, D., & Bano, M. (2024, November). AI for all: Diversity and Inclusion in AI. *AI Ethics, 4*, 873–876. https://doi.org/10.1007/s43681-024-00485-8

Chapter 8

Clutch Leadership and Digital Transformation: The Role of Trust and Engagement

Rosilyn Sanders

Introduction

Effective leadership is an important determinant of a conducive work environment for productivity. Empirical research has consistently linked higher productivity to higher employee engagement, which is a product of the level of trust employees have in the organization's leadership. Effective leadership highlights trust and engagement as significant factors influencing the productivity of leadership.

Today's world, requiring connecting and collaborating beyond physical spaces and even across international geographical locations, highlights the relevance of building trust and engagement both in the virtual and physical workspace. The advent of digital space has impacted relationships between team

DOI: 10.4324/9781003629214-12

members, management and staff, tutors and students, colleagues, recruiters, and job seekers. This has yielded changing job roles, more efficient product delivery, user-centered services, improved customer experiences, and an entirely transformed workplace. Public agencies are not exempt, as digital transformation has influenced government regulations, legislation, and policy formulation and implementation. Intellectual property rights, labor rights, and privacy laws are a few examples of legislation that have been adjusted to adapt to changes from digitization effects.

Beyond the introduction of novel technology, digital transformation has resulted in new business models and organizational forms as these organizations adopt collaborative networks. It has produced a whole new work culture. Remote and other flexible work arrangements have become the norm, allowing employees to enjoy autonomy and a better work-life balance. Organizations can reach clientele and operate businesses in foreign markets without the added costs of establishing physical offices. Team members, colleagues, and workforce professionals internationally can communicate and collaborate virtually. This gives employees access to a broader pool to share experience and expertise. With digital transformation, the term "workspace" or "workplace" has extended beyond the immediate physical space. This implies that leaders face the challenge of dealing with a larger, more versatile, and "fluid" work environment.

Organizational leaders contend with a fresh array of hurdles in navigating the intricate terrain shaped by swift technological advancements juxtaposed with sluggish organizational procedures (Matt et al., 2015). Several issues arise. How do these leaders facilitate employee engagement to achieve organizational goals in dealing with a versatile workspace? How can they garner the cooperation of their managers and staff, motivating them to gear efforts toward implementing the digital transformation process? What leadership strategies are most effective in adjusting to emerging trends and disruptions that arise from the transformation of the workspace? What are the ethical considerations associated with such transformation? These are just a few of the many challenges faced by clutch leaders addressed in this chapter.

Moreover, the chapter explores the role of trust in clutch leadership, its evolvement and maintenance in digital contexts, and strategies for successful outcomes. Practical examples and timely case studies that highlight the vital role of trust in promoting employee engagement in the virtual and physical workspaces are also provided. Further, the chapter offers insights for various stakeholders, including CEOs, senior-level executives, managers, board members, startup founders, innovators, corporate communication executives, scholar-practitioners, and aspiring leaders across all sectors.

The Imperative of Digital Transformation

Various definitions of digital transformation exist, identifying specific drivers of digital transformation. Digital technology is outlined as the main driver of the process when the digital transformation process is defined as the use of new digital technologies (e.g., mobile, artificial intelligence, cloud, blockchain, and IoT) to enable significant business improvements to augment customer experience, streamline operations, or create new business models.It can be defined as the process by which a variety of modern technologies collaborate to create new roles, structures, practices, values, and beliefs that change, threaten, replace, or add to the rules of the game in businesses, ecosystems, industries, or fields (Hinings et al., 2018).

As technological developments advance to bring about changing needs, organizations adapt these technological advancements to their mode of operations. The disruptions caused by technological advancements also impact individuals' needs and activities. Recall the era when BlackBerry OS and Microsoft Windows used to be the central operating systems in mobile phones. BlackBerry phones are no longer in circulation globally; phones with Symbian OS have also become a thing of nostalgia in most developed and developing countries. Phones and laptops with iOS and Android operating systems have recently become the focus.

Some other definitions of digital transformation emphasize the potential of the process to impact aspects of business operations. These definitions highlight the role of digital technology in transforming consumer experience, implying that, in addition to digital technologies, improving service and product delivery is also a driver for digital transformation. Digital transformation is a series of deep and coordinated cultural, workforce, and technological shifts that enable new educational and operating models while also transforming an institution's business model, strategic directions, and value proposition (Vial, 2019). With that, the need for business innovations to adapt to competitive pressure is highlighted as a driver for the disruptions in the process or strategy. Despite the varying definitions, the consensus is that the digital transformation process involves antecedents that necessitate the process; then, some factors can either facilitate or challenge the implementation. Whether innovative or integrative, the process of digital transformation involves the use of digital technology.

Digital transformation transcends individual and customer experience beyond general business operations to impact global lifestyles. Healthcare, science, academics, politics, and entertainment have all transformed following advancements in digital technology. With NHS Digital in the UK and American Well or Teladoc in America, remote consultation is now possible for patients to reach healthcare professionals. With the help of digital tools, caregivers can form teams across physical locations to effectively collaborate and deliver the best quality care to a patient since all patients' health records are available and accessible to the members of the care teams.

Online genetic testing can provide insights for improved and personalized healthcare. Health monitoring devices like fitness trackers can track health metrics in real time.

With AI-powered tools like International Business Machines (IBM), scientific research in genomics is possible. Digital tools have also empowered collaborative research. With virtual classrooms and several e-learning platforms, the field of academics is not left out of the impact of these digital disruptions.

In this era of fast-paced digital disruptions, organizations must recognize the need for innovations to achieve sustainable economic relevance. Data analytics informs strategic and agile practices, transforming business models and improving consumer experiences. This enhances cost efficiency since uncertainties in the marketplace can be predicted and avoided. Employees and employers are upgrading their digital capabilities and knowledge to exploit new opportunities.

Digital media provides access to real-time information and communication with improved reach and public relations in politics, advertisement, and entertainment. Gen Xs (a term for people born between 1965 and 1980) and Millennials (a term for people born between the early 1980s and the late 1990s) had to go and rent or buy CDs from a store to use for weekend entertainment; that is a lifetime ago compared to the current ease that comes with accessing whatever entertainment you desire whenever you desire it with only a click or tap on your most recent digital device. It is safe to say that digital transformation has improved business operations, user experience, and overall well-being. This emphasizes the need to take advantage of and engage in effective strategies to adapt to these rapidly occurring changes.

Irrespective of its numerous benefits, it would be remiss not to consider the challenges of the digital transformation process. The digital transformation process presents challenges related to the use of technology, skill and talent management, and organizational culture and structure (Hu et al., 2023). At the organizational level, it requires the development of a wide range of skills essential for adapting to technological trends (Vial, 2019). There also exists the challenge of changing technological platforms, systems, and operational equipment to acquire new ones that support emerging technologies, and this is not without its cost implications for the organization (Hu et al., 2023). This places a significant demand on organizational leadership for skill development.

Time and resources are invested in organizing training and workshop sessions to get the staff members to understand and agree to the need for transformation and to help them adapt to the new processes and systems. The digital transformation process enables organizations to handle more significant amounts of data, and this is not without inherent challenges. A significant level of transformation implies significant cost implications, and vice versa. Digital transformation has also resulted in privacy and security issues. Cybersecurity has become more of a topic of interest in today's digital era. By increasing organizations' exposure to international connections, digitization has also exposed these organizations to foreign threats and dangers.

Digital transformation necessitates organizational leadership to alter the culture and power dynamics, as it necessitates the hiring and management of new talent. This shift is necessary due to the increased demand for senior technical and management talent in a digital context, necessitating an open and supportive organizational culture.

Barriers to the digital transformation process include disproportionate knowledge and digital expertise, poor and ineffective digital leadership, an inflexible culture that is resistant to change, and a lack of clarity of the vision and objective that hinders the employees' collaboration and alignment. When organizational inertia forces such as ingrained cultural values and silo structures hinder adaptation, the digital transformation process cannot be successfully implemented. From personal experience as a consultant for change, this author can attest to the fact that even when the organizational structure supports the transformation process, the employees' resistance toward the change also has adverse consequences. Employees must understand the need for change, come to terms with it, and be empowered to facilitate the transformation process in their capacity. More than anything else, it necessitates trust and engagement.

The Foundation of Trust

Trust is foundational to decision-making and promotes building long-term relationships by fostering mutual understanding, cooperation, and collaboration. Why do politicians need to contend to prove their trustworthiness before they are elected as leaders? How do individuals decide that this person could be trusted any more than that other person, especially in a context where there is no or minimal personal relationship? Trust could be a strategic act, a moral response, or even an act of social solidarity. While a feeling of trust may develop rather quickly, its deepening is dependent on being nurtured over time. It can be an objective, rational decision or a decision based on emotions and intuitions. Regardless of whether it is a rational or intuitive decision, trust increases chronologically as interactions, situations, and experiences progress.

In today's digital era, with e-commerce, virtual collaborations, and online services, there is a tendency for higher exposure to private or sensitive information. This digital context offers businesses wide exposure that has double-edged potential. There is the benefit of positive exposure to a larger market and a higher number of potential clients. However, there is also a risk of harmful exposure, which could harm the brand. A customer could give online feedback on a product or service that could eventually boost or drop patronage. Customers only interact with and patronize online platforms they deem trustworthy, and any situation that portrays a breach of that trust will result in a loss of patronage. Businesses can gain a competitive advantage and reap large profits from their investments because they benefit from the trust and loyalty of end users. From design and packaging to marketing and delivery, entire brands are built to gain trust.

Organizational management endeavors to build trust among their teams and human resource departments to ensure that the job candidates are transformed into employees with attributes that can be trusted to align with organizational goals. Trust is essential in the workplace to foster a positive environment that facilitates productivity. It enables clutch leaders to facilitate cooperation and collaboration among employees to achieve innovative results in high-pressure situations.

Digital transformations influence the structure and style of leadership. It affects the power dynamics by facilitating the relationship or ratio of centralization and decentralization of power, necessitating a nuanced approach to leadership to keep in line with the continuous technological changes. Leaders must be agile and flexible, ensuring continuous development for themselves and their subordinates. Prioritizing technological proficiency and fostering an environment that supports innovations is essential. Collaboration and networking are emphasized in leadership in this digital era. The convergence of leadership and digital transformation demands a nuanced comprehension of the intricate dynamics shaping organizational change in this era.

Clutch Leadership

Clutch leaders must possess a vision for the future, supported by an understanding of the potential impact of digital technologies on their organizational performance. Strategies like reverse mentoring, being committed to experimenting, and encouraging collaborative platforms can help clutch leaders achieve exceptional results. Strategic activities must be targeted toward the development of trust within organizations.

Research indicates that the impact of the disruptive changes of digitization extends beyond the organizational level to the environmental, social, and institutional levels. These fast-paced disruptions created by digitization contribute to volatility and high-pressure workplace situations, necessitating clutch leadership for any organization to survive. A simple and straightforward definition of "clutch leadership" can be derived from this definition of "clutch performance" – a positive performance under pressure irrespective of whether the performance is increased or maintained (Schweickle et al., 2022). Clutch leadership could be defined as ensuring that a stellar performance is consistently achieved or maintained, especially when it is most pertinent or under intense pressure.

Clutch leadership entails innovation and resilience. To effectively thrive in high-pressure, highly volatile, highly competitive conditions and achieve sustainable advantage, these clutch leaders must stretch beyond conventional practices, procedures, and strategies. This may seem far-reaching since the norm of this digital era is constantly adapting to innovations with lean and agile practices. Issues of disinformation and misinformation through technology-enabled media, clickbait, and various deceptive content are increasingly available on social media alongside other cybersecurity issues. This presents challenges to develop and maintain trust in digital interactions.

A leader needs to be exceptional and able to inspire relentless and enthusiastic efforts to achieve desired results. To foster a positive work culture and ensure motivated and productive employees, trust and engagement are relevant in building relationships and getting efficient results. To evaluate the relationship between clutch leadership and digital transformation, the next section discusses the role of trust, highlighting its relevance in today's ever-changing economy. It proceeds to discuss ethical considerations associated with digital transformations and their impact on businesses in terms of challenges and opportunities.

The Role of Trust in Organizations

Trust may develop or occur based on several existing factors. Factors that promote its growth include transparency, consistency, reliability, security, and authenticity. Consistency promotes the development of trust. With positive interactions consistently occurring, understanding and trust are developed, improving the existing relationship. Belasen & Belasen (2024) provided a framework for evaluating trustworthiness based on specific characteristics: credibility (how much do others believe you and what you say), accountability (can you align with the current expectations and core values?), transparency (do people feel safe about the information that is shared publicly?), and honesty (are you concerned about the effects of your words and actions on others?). In addition, integrity and empathy are also relevant components for a clutch leader to develop trust. Integrity entails demonstrating strong moral and ethical principles and puts a leader in a better position to be trusted.

Whether the decision to trust is intuitive or objective, having a leader who has principles and stands by them inspires confidence. Empathy promotes intimacy, creating a connection between team members. It plays a significant role in facilitating our intuitive decision to trust. Trust is essential for clutch leadership in building confidence and credibility with team members, as it often involves high-pressure conditions. People will only follow a leader in high-pressure situations if they are convinced of their capacity to handle issues effectively (Belasen & Belasen, 2024). Trust motivates employees to go beyond contractual obligations to achieve desired results, especially in high-expectancy situations, and is crucial for maintaining good customer and product relationships.

The reliability and credibility of a brand are significant determinant factors in consumer purchase decisions. To grow their value in the market, businesses invest efforts toward building public trust in their brand. Trust is essential to cooperation and performance in any business setting. Whether solo leadership or co-leadership, trust is essential to promoting collaboration and cooperation. For an organization to effectively implement the process of digital transformation in its operations, the employees need to cooperate and align their performance. Trust has a role to play in this cooperation and alignment. However, the fundamental issue of discussion is building trust in a digital environment.

Virtual teams are increasingly used because challenges like cybersecurity exist, and intimacy seems reduced with less physical contact. Can digital technology be considered a threat or facilitator to digital trust? Miscommunication, misinformation, and depersonalization may arise, especially if there is a misalignment with digital tools and digital transformation strategy. This misalignment could be in the form of poorly designed or implemented strategies, inadequate training or support to use digital tools, an overemphasis on technology, and insufficient consideration for human factors. These challenges are primarily rooted in the activities of organizational leaders responsible for ensuring effective interactions among human and technological factors in the digital transformation process.

Ethical Considerations

Dealing with artificial intelligence (AI) in today's business world presents complex ethical concerns that leaders must manage with a foundation of trust, transparency, and responsibility. As organizations adopt AI technologies, ethical issues such as bias, privacy, surveillance, and decision-making transparency arise, directly impacting employee well-being and organizational culture (Floridi & Cowls, 2019). Leaders must be vigilant in ensuring that AI systems are designed and implemented in ways that respect human rights and dignity, avoiding discrimination and reinforcing equity and inclusion in the workplace (Jobin et al., 2019).

Moreover, the integration of AI into the workplace can disrupt existing workflows, contribute to job insecurity, and challenge employees' psychological safety. Psychological safety – a belief that one can express oneself without fear of retribution – is vital during technological transitions, as it fosters open communication, resilience, and innovation. Trust becomes an ethical imperative, not just a leadership strategy. Without trust, employees may resist innovation or disengage, which undermines the success of digital transformation efforts.

Trust is foundational in getting employees to cooperate effectively for optimal performance. A leader's limited digital skills should not limit the initiative of adapting to current digital trends; hence, there is a need to be open to continuous learning to enable them to maintain the trust of their subordinates.

Improving digital literacy is key for leaders to ensure competence, credibility, and reliability, positioning them to build better relationships. By staying abreast of current digital trends, leaders can effectively use digital tools in decision-making, communicating, and implementing those decisions to succeed. Competency with digital tools in leadership can influence a leader's visibility in virtual environments. Active listening also contributes to trust building in clutch leadership by fostering a positive self-orientation of the leader. With effective communication and transparency, relevant information is shared among team members, empowering them to make informed and prompt decisions over time. Transparency also enables a clutch leader to show vulnerability and commitment to growth, helping to build intimacy and support a more positive collaborative relationship.

Since clutch leadership entails decision-making in high-pressure situations, self-awareness and demonstrating emotional control are essential to prove the reliability and credibility of any such leader. Negative experiences from repeated poor decision-making by the leaders will erode the employees' faith in them. The implication is that employees would be less cooperative if they had reasons to doubt the competence of their leaders, especially in high-pressure situations.

In a digital context, experimenting and risk-taking are necessary. This presents a rationale for the relevance of trust. A clutch leader needs to be able to take well-calculated risks that would yield profitable outcomes for the organization. Experimenting and calculated risk-taking are inherent in innovation, and employees' cooperation in what they consider a risky situation will only be based on the level of trust they have in the leader.

The digital transformation process presents uncertainty, and trust is key to promoting resilience and adaptability among team members. The role of trust in clutch leadership, especially in a digital context, cannot be overemphasized. Clutch leaders should prioritize building trust among their teams to ensure innovative effectiveness and productivity in high-pressure situations. The ethical concerns in digital environments play an important role in preserving agreement at some point of digital transformation.

As the era continues to adapt, leaders should navigate complicated ethical challenges associated with statistical privacy, cybersecurity, and the responsible use of synthetic intelligence. Ethical decision-making in virtual areas calls for balancing innovation with duty, ensuring that digital equipment is used to enhance as opposed to exploiting human potential. Moreover, fostering a subculture of integrity in digital environments is necessary for long-term organizational success. Leaders must set up clear ethical tips for online verbal exchange, far-off work regulations, and the use of digital resources. This includes promoting inclusivity and overcoming biases in virtual decision-making procedures. When leaders prioritize ethical concerns, they create an environment in which employees feel secure to collaborate, share ideas, and embody technological advancements with confidence.

The Significance of Engagement in Clutch Leadership

Effective clutch leadership entails inspiring and influencing others to achieve organizational objectives – this highlights the role of engagement. A clutch leader facilitating engagement involves getting others to put in the required efforts for the desired exceptional results. In addition to trust, engagement is another essential factor for clutch leadership. Engagement is vital for the well-being and performance of the employees as much as it is relevant to achieving organizational objectives and competitive advantage.

Engagement drives performance and outcomes, influencing energy levels, motivation, and involvement. Competent leadership drives this engagement as it can facilitate work engagement to achieve organizational objectives. Although sometimes interchangeable, employee engagement and employee motivation are distinct but interrelated. Motivation precedes engagement because when employees are stimulated to invest enthusiastic efforts into their work, they are more likely to yield productive results, have higher job satisfaction, and are less likely to switch jobs. This consequently translates to engagement as motivated employees become more effective and efficient at work.

Engagement is a result of motivation. According to SDT, an empirical theory of a continuum ranging from external motivation, inspired by external prices or pressure, to internal motivation, which comes from personal interest and joy, it is more likely that employees meet their basic psychological needs for autonomy, capacity, and relation (Deci et al., 2017). When individuals experience autonomy in their roles, they feel competent in their actions and have meaningful work, increasing their internal motivation, leading to high levels and general welfare for commitment.

Conversely, if these needs fail, employees may have resolution or experience burnout. Empirical evidence indicates that intrinsically motivated employees will perform better, and most autonomously regulated activities are intrinsically motivated (Deci et al., 2017). The SDT also proves that controlled motivation could improve employee performance.

Controlled motivation focuses on extrinsic motivation, often fostering instrumental behaviors that yield streamlined outcomes. It involves using planned rewards or threats leading to introjected behaviors that could facilitate higher employee performance when integration with work values occurs. An employee's motivation can range from autonomy to controlled motivation in varying degrees, and some organizations could decide to adopt varying levels of both.

Considering that the self-determination theory proposes that extrinsic motivation would result in declining competence, adopting varying degrees of both ends of the continuum is most suitable in today's innovative workplace. Organizational leadership determines the degree of motivation required to always engage the employees.

Ineffective implementation of digital transformation could result in an organizational crisis, and clutch leadership is relevant to resolve this crisis and ensure minimal or no loss of organizational productivity. Clutch leaders must ensure that employees are continually engaged to enable them to continue to put in maximum efforts for productivity to be sustained. There is a need for positive crisis communication to ensure employee engagement, which is important due to their role in organizational productivity. The employee engagement level influences the ability of the organization to adapt and thrive in conditions of fast-paced innovation.

In a digital context, it is easy to ignore boundaries that limit achieving a good work-life balance. This could be detrimental to the health and well-being of employees, as burnout leads to attrition. Clutch leadership is necessary to avoid the adverse effects of digitization for improved employee well-being and ensure that employees remain committed and productive even in high-demand situations.

The level of commitment by leaders can influence employee engagement levels. Continuous learning to advance knowledge of digital tools and communication is a practice that portrays high commitment. Effective communication of organizational goals, policies, and procedures is relevant to promoting employee engagement. Company vision, policies, and standards on ethical procedures need to be communicated and inculcated to help employees identify with organizational behavior.

It has been established that integration could facilitate employee engagement. Supporting career development and ensuring effective talent management is another essential strategy to promote employee engagement in the digital context of the workplace. By supporting employees' career planning and using incentives, leaders can keep the employees motivated and committed to organizational goals. Self-disclosure and consistency promote transparency, which enables trust and engagement.

Leaders could use digital tools and channels to effectively foster intimacy by providing feedback and information-sharing support. Technology can be leveraged to create virtual spaces to facilitate integration and community between team members. Organizing virtual town hall meetings and other virtual social events ensures that ideas and experiences can be shared, facilitating a well-integrated team. By providing support for feedback and fostering integration into organizational values, clutch leaders will be able to get employees actively engaged in implementing the organization's digital transformation efforts.

Another essential strategy to facilitate employee engagement for productivity is appreciation and recognition. Building engagement through individualized recognition fosters a sense of belonging and encourages staff to direct their interests and strengths toward work assignments. This is also a strategy to grow trust in work relationships and incorporate characteristics of inspired, caring leadership into leader practices. Google is recognized as one of the top organizations that have effectively mastered employee recognition in a digital context.

Remote workers are recognized effectively for a company that runs a hybrid work environment. Dynamic reward systems such as the Google peer-to-peer recognition program ensure that employees enjoy timely and meaningful recognition. This peer-to-peer recognition empowers employees to recognize small wins among themselves that managers may miss. It places value on individual contributions within the team, facilitating employee engagement.

Clutch Leadership in Action

Clutch leadership strategies align with transformational leadership theory. Transformational leadership inspires commitment among employees and motivates them to put in productive efforts. It enables fundamental organizational changes to empower them to gain necessary capabilities and move in novel directions, achieving desired objectives (Korejan & Shahbazi, 2016). Clutch leaders exhibit transformational leadership by setting the pace for innovation and empowering employees to achieve exceptional results in high-pressure situations. The next sections consider some practical examples of clutch leadership.

Case Study 1: Clutch leadership in Apple Inc.

In 2011, Steve Jobs was replaced by Tim Cook, the CEO of Apple. Tim Cook has, over the years, shown commendable traits of clutch leadership. This leadership has empowered employees with greater autonomy to make decisions about their work. Frequent town hall meetings are conducted to facilitate open communication, which helps foster trust and integrate employees with the organization's vision. In addition to an enticing employee reward system, this provides employees with a sense of security and support.

Apple has successfully developed a community with a purpose-driven culture among employees to ensure they are committed to the organizational goals. The organization introduced the Apple Watch in 2015 and the AirPods two years later. Due to innovative leadership, these and other previously existing products have maintained a competitive market advantage over the years.

Apple Inc. takes employee engagement seriously – employees at Apple. Inc. enjoy healthcare benefits that extend to family members, grants and discounts to purchase company stock, and even support for career development in the organization. In 2023, employees and shareholders voiced dissatisfaction over the CEO's compensation plan through the Institutional Shareholder Services. Tim Cook voluntarily recommended a cut in his pay, considering the feedback. This shows the employees that they are valued as their feedback is taken seriously, which will promote the level of trust they have in them and facilitate increased commitment to the organization.

In 2024, Apple's brand value amounted to approximately $1.02 trillion, earning a leadership position among the most valuable brands in the world (Faria, 2024). In 2023, Apple was ranked second among the top 100 largest companies in the world by market capitalization, worth over 2,900 billion US dollars. Apple's effective leadership strategies ranked it number 15 of the world's best employers on Forbes (Peachman, 2024). With about 164,000 employees, Apple was not one of the information technology companies with the most employees. However, it was able to build market value and capitalization to attain a significant position in the market.

The organizational leadership of Apple was able to effectively engage their employees and harness their skills and potential, motivating them to put in maximum effort for productivity. In 2022, the ranking of revenue per employee of leading technology companies revealed that Apple was in second place (Clement, 2023).

Figure 8.1 below indicates Apple's global revenue in the past 20 years. This indicates a significant rise in revenue in 2011 after Tim Cook became CEO, from $65 billion to $108.2 billion. The revenue has maintained values within

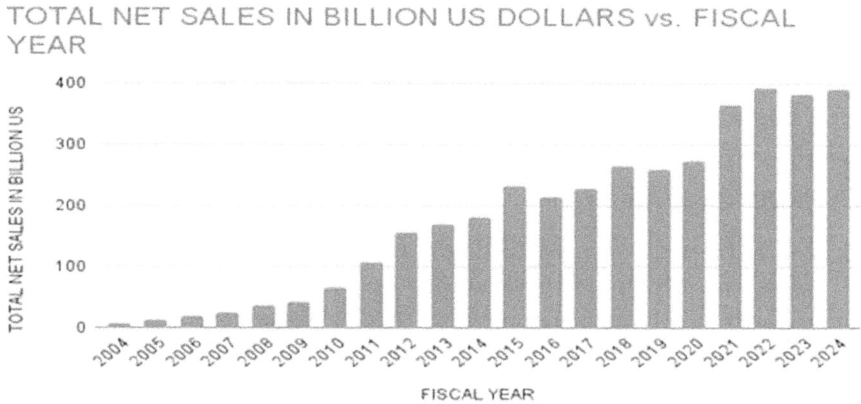

Figure 8.1 Global revenue of Apple from 2004–2024 (in US$ billion). ***Source*****: Statista (2025).**

hundreds of billions since then. However, in 2016, there was a significant loss in revenue from a decline in iPhone sales due to competition in the market.

Tim Cook swiftly took action to prioritize Apple's service sector (Apple Music, Apple Store, and Apple TV+) and introduced other innovative products like the Apple Watch. This display of clutch leadership was essential in quickly adapting to the situations and helping the brand maintain productivity. 2019 was another high-pressure period that affected businesses globally as the COVID-19 pandemic grounded most economic activities. However, from the figure, one can conclude that Apple did not take much of a hit and even indicated prompt recovery, which implies that there must be something its leadership is doing right. Cook's leadership ensured that employees were provided resources and support during the pandemic. The support extended beyond the work settings to their health and well-being (Richter, 2021).

Analysis of Clutch Success/Failure

Innovativeness and Diversification – Tim Cook portrayed innovation and agile practices by promptly taking advantage of emerging technology to diversify the business despite the pressure conditions, setting the company up for sustainable growth that extends into the future.

Stability and Security – By effectively navigating periods of high uncertainty, Tim Cook portrayed competence by providing the company with stability in high-pressure periods, giving the employees and shareholders a sense of security about the organization's future. This is vital to having collaborative employees who trust their leader.

Credibility in Financial Management – Tim Cook could have argued against the proposed reduction in his pay since his efforts contributed to the rise in stock, but he displayed emotional intelligence and credibility by showing empathy for shareholders' opinions.

Overcoming Challenges

Lack of Diversification – Apple's initial overreliance on a single product – the iPhone – as its primary revenue source made the organization very vulnerable to market fluctuations, which are detrimental to organizational performance. Any fluctuation in that particular product could significantly affect the entire organization.

High Competition and Uncertainty – The tech market is characterized by high uncertainty due to fast-paced disruptions from ever-evolving digital technology. Apple Inc. is a major player in this market but must be conscious and consistent with these evolving trends. By setting up strategies to stay ahead of market trends, the organization will be able to respond to tensions that may arise in the market.

Long-Term Vs. Short-Term Goals – Operating in a highly volatile market implies that Apple may be unable to maintain stable policies and procedures. Aiming to achieve a balance between short-term goals and long-term initiatives without losing track of evolving market trends is necessary. In this case study of Apple, the previous leadership under Steve Jobs portrayed competence and yielded results. However, efficient clutch leadership enabled the organization to survive the leadership change and even go beyond mere surviving to thrive amid an evolving digital landscape. Specific crises could have erupted from the change in leadership, which could make it more challenging for the organization to thrive.

The company's leadership strategies did not help it effectively navigate and resolve a situation of potential conflict; it achieved a recognizable position as the most valuable brand in the world. This success story is indicative that effective clutch leadership is pivotal in empowering employees and ensuring that exemplary efforts are targeted toward steering the organization to a position of competitive advantage. This highlights the need for clutch leadership in today's digital context.

Case Study 2: Clutch Leadership in IKEA/Ingka Group

IKEA, which was established in 1943 as a mail-order sales business, has adopted digital transformation to evolve and operate an online application called IKEA

Kreativ. This app uses virtual and mixed reality AI to enable customers to scan and design their space, making furniture the most suitable choice. The move to complete digital transformation in response to the COVID-19 pandemic after so many years of analog operations presented challenging challenges for its leadership, but it was done, and in an interview with *Harvard Business Review*, the Chief Digital Officer (CDO) of retail sales, Barbara Martin Coppola, highlighted that having a background in digital skills and tools was beneficial to leading and effectively navigating the disruptions from this transformation (Stackpole, 2021).

The parent company of IKEA, Ingka Group, has also demonstrated clutch leadership by adapting to changing consumer preferences amid innovative market trends. In 2017, Jesper Brodin took over as CEO, and in 2020, when the company experienced supply chain disruptions due to the pandemic, the company took agile actions by diversifying the supply base. The organization took innovative steps toward a complete digital transformation to ensure the sustainability of its businesses.

Open communication is encouraged, fostering an intimate and collaborative organizational culture. Over 200,000 employees of IKEA share ideas and other information through collaborative online communities (IKEA, 2025). These employees are given some level of autonomy in decision-making over their work. The vision of the parent company is communicated and aligned with its subsidiaries. This is why IKEA can effectively replicate the leadership style of the parent company, yielding a sustainable advantage in a highly competitive market.

Analysis of Clutch Success/Failure

Innovation – IKEA has demonstrated the ability to adapt to evolving technological trends by offering innovative products and services. By choosing products from a catalog, you can create different virtual simulations of your design preferences, personalized recommendations with AI on entire homework solutions, and various options on modes of purchase. By investing in innovations over the years, the leadership of IKEA has ensured continuous growth and sustainable market advantage for the organization.

Resilience – Despite experiencing several forms of disruption, the leadership of Ingka Group and IKEA has demonstrated adaptability and resilience by successfully leading the business through these challenging situations, ensuring sustainability.

Consistency – IKEA began as a furniture store and still offers retail furniture despite expanding into related services. It has consistently offered functionality, gaining significant consumer trust and market leadership in the furniture market.

Balancing Growth – With its growth and business expansion over the years, Ingka Group has maintained its organizational culture by openly communicating its vision to employees globally, even across subsidiaries. The company has portrayed adapting innovative changes without losing its original vision despite being in operation for several decades.

Overcoming Challenges

Complex Supply Chain – Ingka operates a global supply chain that presents complexities. Its leadership must ensure effective supply chain management to handle these complexities.

High competition and changing consumer preferences: several retail businesses exist to offer varying options to customers whose preferences are also subject to frequent change. Leaders must engage in agile strategies to remain in the market and satisfy the customers. A few organizations established in the same period as IKEA are still in existence. IKEA has earned the trust of consumers through consistency and competence so much that it has become a household name. Its major competitors, Target and Walmart, were established almost 20 years later.

Case Study 3: Nokia Phones

Anyone born before the 2000s got to know Nokia as a major player in the phone business. The brand was trusted for durable phones with longer battery life. However, as customer preferences evolved with digital technology, brands like Samsung and Apple phones offered functionality in other areas that were more suitable for consumer preferences. Nokia did not take the opportunity, banking on its market leadership to adapt to emerging trends; it refused to switch to making Android versions and kept with Symbian versions of phones. The implication of this decision is evident in its extinction from the phone market.

Analysis of Clutch Success/Failure

Diversification – the leadership of Nokia has focused on other aspects of business, offering technological solutions to enterprises, service providers, and even public agencies. Its technological solutions include network equipment, research, and patent licensing. Since it left the phone market, Nokia has made other significant contributions to the world of technology, including soft routers, photonic integrated circuits, self-organizing networks, and massive MIMO – a foundational technology in 5G network systems.

Inadaptability and Lack Of Innovation – The organization did not align itself with emerging technology trends despite being in a market prone to fast-paced disruptions. This is not indicative of clutch leadership and led to detrimental consequences. The decision led to a decline in the brand's trust among customers, investors, and other stakeholders.

Loss of Market Share – Nokia lost a significant market share to its competitors, who were more responsive to emerging digital trends.

Loss of mobile division: though the organization is still in existence, the failure to adapt resulted in subsequent market struggles, which ended with Microsoft selling off the mobile division – Nokia – in 2014 (Lamberg et al., 2021).

Overcoming Challenges

Emerging Trends – By not taking necessary measures to adapt to emerging trends, the organization suffered, highlighting the consequences of slow response in the present digital era. The organization's leadership failed to recognize an impactful market trend and did not take advantage of it. If it had promptly responded to this emerging trend, the market superiority of the brand at the time would have provided it with a significant competitive advantage. In its other aspects of business, where the organization adopted emerging technology and took advantage of the opportunities presented by digital transformation, it thrives (Nokia, 2025).

Leverage Strengths – Nokia's leadership saved the organization from total collapse by building on its expertise in digital communications to explore other business ideas. This strategic decision to divest into a connected but new line of business was essential in helping the company stay afloat and subsequently thrive in the marketplace. This bold and strategic decision portrays clutch leadership, showing adaptability and resilience to turn negative decisions around and achieve exceptional results.

Nokia's case makes a very compelling argument for the benefits of digital transformation and the effectiveness and need for clutch leadership in today's digital context. Through its failure and success stories, it highlights the positive results of clutch leadership as well as the detrimental consequences of failing to apply it.

Conclusion

With the leadership style of Tim Cook, Apple's market capitalization grew from $348 billion in 2011 to almost $2.5 trillion in 2021. This is attributed to various clutch strategies, including empowering employees, ensuring intimacy, and building competence and resilience by diversifying to other innovative products, yielding up to a triple increase in revenue and profits. Apple has maintained a competitive advantage despite the change in its leadership, surviving several high-pressure situations and keeping its employees satisfied and committed. With clutch leadership strategies, Ingka Group and IKEA have effectively navigated challenges, including changes in consumer demands, disruptions in the supply chain, and a global pandemic, which all represent high-pressure situations. This is evidently due to the innovative and agile strategies of its leaders.

Though Nokia's failure in the smartphone business illustrates the detrimental effect of the absence of clutch leadership, the organization made a strategic move by leveraging its existing telecommunications experience to provide network infrastructure and intelligent solutions, creating innovative opportunities in this digital landscape. Case studies demonstrate the profitability of clutch leadership in the digital era, highlighting the challenges of uncertainty in digital transformation and the need for effective leadership.

Trust and engagement are foundational factors to ensure employees' continual commitment to productivity that will help leaders respond promptly and implement agile strategies to disruptions. Leaders must prioritize the role of trust and engagement to ensure resilience and achieve business success. To build a sustainable business in this digital era, investing in innovation, employee empowerment, and sustainable growth strategies is essential.

The relevance of clutch leadership will become increasingly significant in this ever-evolving era of digital technology. Organizational leadership cannot ignore the need to adopt clutch leadership strategies to position themselves for success in this era. Recognizing employees' efforts within the team will transmit a sense of value and produce positive spillover effects that motivate other team members.

With continuously evolving technological and economic trends, the business landscape will present leaders with different challenges at each point. Leaders must adapt, innovate, and make strategic decisions to overcome these challenges and emerge stronger. The future of leadership is grounded in recognizing uncertainty and swiftly adapting to changing conditions with innovative strategies and practices. This is most effective in a work environment where trust and engagement are encouraged.

Employees must be motivated and supported to develop relevant skills and competencies, utilizing them to boost organizational productivity in today's digital era. Leaders must continually invest in learning and self-development to be empowered with leadership skills suitable for this evolving digital landscape. Being ignorant or lacking the appropriate skills required to adapt to emerging trends is detrimental. This chapter provides crucial insights on staying ahead of the leadership curve and driving organizations to thrive despite adverse market conditions, emphasizing the importance of a competent and adaptable leader.

References

Belasen, A. T. & Belasen, A. R. (2024). Signaling trust during disruptions: Perceived gender differences in trustworthy leadership traits. *Gender in Management: An International Journal*, 40(2), 197–214. https://doi.org/10.1108/GM-04-2024-0187

Clement, J. (2023). Revenue per employee of leading tech companies 2022. Available at: https://www.statista.com/statistics/217489/revenue-per-employee-of-selected-tech-companies/

Deci, E. L., Olafsen, A. H., & Ryan, R. M. (2017). Self-determination theory in work organizations: The state of science. *Annual Organizational Psychology And Behavior Review*, 4(1), 19–43.

Faria, J. (2024). Apple brand value 2006–2024. Available at: https://www.statista.com/statistics/326052/apple-brand-value/

Floridi, L., & Cowls, J. (2019). A unified framework of five principles for AI in society. *Harvard Data Science Review, 1*(1). https://doi.org/10.1162/99608f92.8cd550d1

Hinings, B., Gegenhuber, T., & Greenwood, R. (2018). Digital innovation and transformation: An institutional perspective. *Information and Organization*, 28(1), 52–61.

Hu, C., Wu, C., & Yu, L. (2023). Challenges and opportunities of digital transformation in enterprises. *Accounting and Corporate Management*, 5(12), 1–9.

Jobin, A., Ienca, M., & Vayena, E. (2019). The global landscape of AI ethics guidelines. *Nature Machine Intelligence*, 1, 389–399. https://doi.org/10.1038/s42256-019-0088-2

IKEA (2025). Back to 1965. Available at: https://www.ikea.com/global/en/stories/our-roots/1965-time-capsule-250117/

Korejan, M. M., & Shahbazi, H. (2016). An analysis of the transformational leadership theory. *Journal of Fundamental and Applied Sciences*, 8(3), 452–461.

Lamberg, J. A., Lubinaitė, S., Ojala, J., & Tikkanen, H. (2021). The curse of agility: The Nokia Corporation and the loss of market dominance in mobile phones, 2003–2013. *Business History*, 63(4), 574–605.

Matt, C., Hess, T., & Benlian, A. (2015). Digital transformation strategies. *Business & Information Systems Engineering*, 57, 339–343.

Nokia (2025). History. Available at: https://www.nokia.com/we-are-nokia/our-history/

Peachman, R. R. (2024). World's best employers forbes. Available at: https://www.forbes.com/lists/worlds-best-employers/

Richter, F. (2021). A decade of growth: Apple thrived under Tim Cook (online). Available at: https://www.statista.com/chart/25610/apple-growth-under-tim-cook/

Schweickle, M. J., Vella, S. A., & Swann, C. (2022). Was it a clutch performance? A qualitative exploration of the definitional boundaries of clutch performance. *Psychology of Sport and Exercise*, 62, 102238.

Stackpole, T. (2021). Inside IKEA's digital transformation (Online). Available at: https://hbr.org/2021/06/inside-ikeas-digital-transformation
Vial, G. (2019). Understanding digital transformation: A review and a research agenda. *Managing Digital Transformation*, 28(2), 118–144.

STRATEGIC DISRUPTION

E

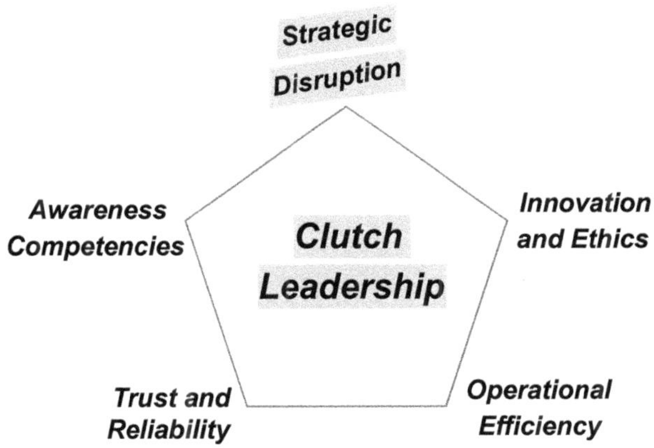

DOI: 10.4324/9781003629214-13

Chapter 9

Bold Leadership vs. Epic Failures: Insights from Global Supply Chain Challenges

Betul Lus and Sylwia E. Starnawska

Introduction

This chapter explores the critical dichotomy of bold leadership and epic failures within the context of global supply chain management by examining novel approaches to critical events such as consolidation, international expansion, diversification, and the acceleration of contingency plans. It expands the concept of first-mover advantage in supply chain management by incorporating technological, ethical, and risk dimensions. Additionally, environmental, social, and governance (ESG) practices along with sustainable development goals (SDG), a set of 17 universal goals adopted by the United Nations in 2015, will assist in addressing emerging challenges, including legal, environmental, and sociopolitical issues.

Through the analysis of exemplary case studies, the chapter illustrates the practical application of pioneering strategies, experimentation, and venturing

DOI: 10.4324/9781003629214-14

into new frontiers. It explores pathways to successful operational excellence, scrutinizing the integration of reliable solutions with flexible resources to create dynamic and agile organizations. The chapter also identifies the red flags of future potential business failures, offering valuable insights for proactive decision-making.

This chapter supports a functional perspective of leadership decisions with the vision of a future global business system driven by blockchain and AI technologies. The functional perspective focuses on behaviors and practices that promote effective forms of leadership. It is a transformative inspiration for clutch leaders preparing for urgent and instant interventions during times of disruption, driving global change (Belasen & Pfeffermann, 2024). Targeting professionals, educators, and students, the chapter emphasizes the critical role of leadership in balancing efficiency and resilience in a rapidly evolving global economy. Practical insights and actionable strategies offer a framework for addressing current and future challenges, making this chapter a vital resource for fostering sustainable and robust supply chain ecosystems.

First-Mover Advantage in Global Supply Chain

First-mover advantage in the global supply chain refers to the competitive edge that a company gains by being the first to enter new markets, adopt new technologies, or implement innovative supply chain practices or strategies. First-mover advantage can provide substantial benefits to a company, such as gaining larger market shares and higher returns, achieving economies of scale, establishing strong relationships with suppliers, securing lucrative contracts, and setting industry standards for new entrants.

While these benefits are enormous, first movers can also face significant challenges such as high capital investments in research and development, failure risks, and the potential of being dominated by more innovative competitors. Furthermore, rapid technological advancements and evolving global markets exacerbate these challenges, making it more difficult for first movers to sustain their competitive advantage in today's dynamic world. Therefore, first movers must effectively balance their relative advantages with challenges through continuous innovation, adaptation, and improved core competencies to create entry barriers for potential competitors.

Technological Advancements

Technological advancements revolutionize global supply chains through automation and autonomy, enhanced visibility and transparency, data-driven decision-making, and improved connectivity across supply chain networks, driving increased investment in technological innovation. According to the 2024 MHI Annual Industry report, 55% of supply chain leaders are ramping up their technology and innovative investments, with 88% planning to spend over $1 million and 42% allocating more than $10 million (MHI, n.d.).

Companies that early adopt and integrate these innovations gain a first-mover advantage by achieving operational and cost efficiencies, improving decision-making, and building strong industry and supplier partnerships, creating significant barriers to entry for competitors. According to a 2024 Accenture report, companies that lead in building capabilities in their supply chains using generative AI, advanced machine learning, and other evolving technologies for autonomous decision-making, advanced simulations, and continuous improvement are 23% more profitable when compared to others, and delivered 15% better total return to their shareholders between 2019 and 2023 (Blanchet et al., 2024).

Within global supply chain management, AI technology such as machine learning and advanced data analytics can be game changers and provide significant benefits. These technologies enable companies to forecast demand with higher accuracy, optimize scheduling, planning, inventory management, and logistics, and create more adaptive and resilient supply chains. As a result, companies can achieve greater levels of efficiency, reduced waste and costs, improved customer satisfaction, and build stronger supply chain relationships (Chan et al., 2024; Joel et al., 2024). Additionally, AI can enhance supplier relationship management by improving supplier selection, assessment, and monitoring through advanced analytics, enabling better risk mitigation, and ensuring better reliability and quality. It can also automate repetitive processes by leveraging machine learning and algorithms to perform tasks like contract management, allowing businesses to focus instead on more strategic initiatives (Kumar et al., 2024).

Blockchain is a decentralized and distributed digital ledger technology that securely records transactions across a network of computers in a transparent and immutable manner. Integrating blockchain technology into supply chains enhances transparency, visibility, and traceability by enabling real-time tracking and monitoring of transactions and product movements from end to end. Blockchain-enabled supply chains improve information sharing, coordination, integration, and collaboration, leading to various supply chain performance improvements, including better quality compliance, increased process efficiency, greater flexibility, decreased costs, and shorter process times (Nandi et al., 2020).

The role of blockchain in today's increasingly complex supply chains is critical as it enhances the transparency of transactions and traceability, reducing various supply chain and logistics risks and unethical practices. By providing a single source of information accessible to authorized stakeholders, blockchain fosters greater accountability and trust among supply chain partners. Furthermore, blockchain enhances sustainability efforts by enabling companies to verify the origin of raw materials, ensuring responsible sourcing and ethical labor practices.

Integrating AI with blockchain-enabled supply chains can further enhance blockchain's potential benefits. For example, AI can analyze data stored in the blockchain to identify patterns and improve demand forecasting, inventory management, and logistics.

Kumar et al. (2024) studied the impact of advanced technologies, such as AI, robotics, blockchain, and the Internet of Things (IoT), on optimizing supply chain management. The study included 15 corporations from the manufacturing, retail, and logistics sectors that aggressively integrate AI technologies into their supply chains and evaluated how this integration affected key performance indicators (KPIs). The results indicate significant improvements, including a 34% reduction in lead time, a 28% increase in inventory turnover, a 12.4% decrease in costs, and a 5.7% improvement in order accuracy. Furthermore, their findings highlight notable improvements in demand forecasting, inventory management efficiency, and logistics and transportation efficiency.

Extending the above, the integration of self-driving transportation, particularly drones, further enhances supply chain and logistics operations by improving delivery efficiency, reducing carbon emissions and energy consumption, mitigating road traffic congestion, and lowering costs (Li et al., 2022). In line with the SDG, these advancements not only optimize logistics performance but also reduce environmental and societal impact, contributing to a more sustainable supply chain.

Moreover, a report by PricewaterhouseCoopers embarked on an analysis of the drone delivery ecosystem and found that retailers and logistics companies can improve customer experience, expand their market reach, and enhance operational efficiency by leveraging drone delivery technology. While the use of drones is still in its early stages, the global value of goods delivered to consumers by drones is projected to grow exponentially from $251 million in 2024 to $65.1 billion in 2034, with a compound annual growth rate of 74%, offering a competitive advantage for early adopters (PwC, 2024).

Additionally, fully autonomous self-driving trucks are projected to hit the roads by 2027. This innovation will help alleviate the growing driver shortages and substantially rising transportation costs, contributing to an estimated $600 billion market in 2035 (Kelkar et al., 2024).

Ethical Considerations

The integration of advanced technologies in global supply chains presents new ethical considerations, particularly regarding data privacy, labor rights, and algorithmic bias. As companies increasingly utilize AI-driven advanced analytics and machine learning, they collect massive amounts of sensitive supply chain data from suppliers, employees, and customers. If not properly secured, this data can be misused, leading to privacy breaches and potential exploitation. Companies must ensure compliance with data protection regulations, such as the General Data Protection Regulation (GDPR) and the California Consumer Privacy Act (CCPA), and implement robust cybersecurity measures to prevent breaches and safeguard stakeholders' information (Owusu-Berko, 2025).

Furthermore, with the widespread adoption of AI-driven systems and automation, employees are concerned about losing their jobs, particularly in industries that heavily rely on manual labor. Without proper intervention, job displacement could disproportionately affect low-skilled and manual workers, worsening economic inequality. To address this issue, companies begin to invest in retraining and upskilling programs, creating pathways for workers to transition into new roles and maintain job security in an evolving supply chain landscape (Ok et al., 2025). Additionally, upskilling employees is crucial for the successful implementation of new technologies.

Regarding algorithmic bias, AI-driven procurement and supplier evaluation systems may unintentionally disadvantage smaller vendors or certain regions, reinforcing systemic inequalities. To promote ethical sourcing practices, companies must implement fair AI governance frameworks and conduct regular bias audits (Owusu-Berko, 2025).

Sustainability Considerations

Sustainability risks such as global warming, climate change, scarcity and misuse of resources, human rights abuses, and unethical practices have significantly increased in the past decade. As a result, consumers, investors, and governments have been paying growing attention to environmental, social, and governance (ESG) requirements. According to a 2023 Morgan Stanley survey, 77% of global individual investors are interested in sustainable investments, with this rate being 84% in the United States Furthermore, 82% and 77% of global investors want companies to address environmental and social issues, respectively (Morgan Stanley, 2024).

Additionally, a 2021 PwC survey found that 83%–86% of consumers are more likely to buy from companies that share their values across ESG factors (PwC, n.d.). The increasing interest in ESG factors forces companies to adcpt ethical and sustainable practices in their global supply chains. This can create valuable opportunities for first movers in responding to ESG requirements to attract a growing market of ethically conscious consumers and investors.

Notably, the United Nations' Sustainable Development Goals (SDGs) are increasingly being recognized as critical targets and standards to protect the environment and society. The SDG goals and trends highlight the key impact areas and provide a structured framework for companies to enhance their ESG reporting, ensuring that their ESG initiatives contribute to broader environmental and societal goals (Urbieta, 2024). Therefore, to improve their supply chain sustainability, companies must prioritize the ESG factors along with the SDG trends to effectively address the emerging challenges.

For example, sustainability initiatives such as optimizing transportation routes for fuel efficiency or powering supply chains with renewable energy sources help reduce carbon emissions and align global efforts to fight against climate change, according to the SDG of climate action. These initiatives will not only help companies meet the rising expectations of consumers and investors but also ensure compliance with increasing regulatory requirements, reinforce ethical business practices, strengthen stakeholder trust, and secure long-term competitive advantage.

Organizational Changes and Challenges

While first-mover advantage in global supply chains enables companies to gain a competitive edge through technology and sustainability leadership in today's dynamic global business environment, these advancements necessitate significant, diverse, and ongoing organizational changes to maintain competitiveness, profoundly impacting corporate supply chain management.

Globalization strategies with restructuring and regulatory compliance pressures pose challenges for supply chain management, such as increased complexity, cost fluctuations, and disruption risks. However, they also create opportunities for process reengineering, streamlining for optimization, and efficiency gains propelled by technological advancements and enhanced communication. Effective and proactive change management should incorporate innovative supply chain modifications with consideration of risk mitigation. The prevalence of challenges and underperformance in widespread international corporate merger and acquisition (M&A) transactions is often caused by operational failures and mismanagement of supply chain integration.

Global Consolidation

Firms increasingly engage in mergers and acquisitions (M&As) to improve their network positions and enhance performance. Merged firms tend to consolidate their supply bases (i.e., reducing the number of suppliers) while diversifying suppliers across multiple countries. This strategy was found to improve post-M&A operational performance, particularly in horizontal M&As (Yang et al., 2024).

Supply chain decisions in M&As can enhance post-M&A operational performance or limit the synergies if not properly done. Similarly, cross-regional horizontal collaboration supported by producers, grading and packaging shed owners, and wholesalers can improve the export supply chain (Akbar et al., 2020). Factors identified as affecting the potential success of horizontal collaboration involving companies sharing resources at the same level of the supply chain in export include product quality, access to market information, risk-sharing among supply chain stakeholders, leadership, and management skills. However, improved vertical coordination (which synchronizes production and marketing) or supply chain integration may also be required to increase the effectiveness of horizontal collaborations.

Although supply chain management plays a significant role in corporate strategy, intra-firm and inter-firm capabilities are central to its overall effectiveness. Firms can combine and leverage multiple capabilities to create a competitive advantage through stabilizing (building), enriching (developing), and pioneering (creating) (Madhavaram et al., 2023). Under-diversification bias in supply chain management can occur due to the tendency to overly rely on a single supplier or a limited number of suppliers, even when diversification could mitigate risks and improve resilience, often driven by the perceived benefits of lower costs and economies of scale. It is a cognitive bias where decision-makers prioritize cost-saving measures (like single-sourcing) over the potential benefits of diversifying their supply base. As per Goldschmidt et al. (2021), under-diversification bias is costly, and its causes are difficult to overcome, presenting firms with the daunting task of devising debiasing mechanisms that reinforce a supplier diversification strategy when the rarity of disruptions almost always renders supplier consolidation the ex post preferred strategy.

Meta-organizations can build new links across industries and sectors, enabling value chain reconfiguration and broader systemic transitions by transforming linear value chains toward circularity, with some challenges, like valorizing materials and building supply relationships. They facilitate sustainability transitions by mobilizing the collective action of members. The five key collective activities for reconfiguring value chains toward circularity through meta-organizing include setting material agendas, balancing membership openness and closedness, brokering new relationships among organizations, facilitating material-based platforms, and opening new material opportunities. Two significant outcomes observed were circular co-experimentation and localized circular supply chain development (Miller et al., 2025).

Industry 4.0 is underway and describes the current technological revolution and digital innovations, particularly in manufacturing and industrial processes. The Fourth Industrial Revolution is characterized by the integration of digital technologies like the Internet of Things (IoT), Artificial Intelligence (AI), and Big Data into manufacturing and industrial processes, leading to automation and interconnected systems.

Many companies embrace Industry 4.0 technologies to enable operational sustainability against increasing climate change effects, decreasing natural resources, and raising consumer awareness of environmental issues. Demir et al. (2023) explained how smartness (covering availability, integrity, and adaptability sub-dimensions) and sustainability items (including social, environmental, and economic sub-dimensions) create strengths, weaknesses, opportunities, and threats for the supply chain operations.

Okay et al. (2024) presented a pioneering sustainability assessment framework aimed at increasing transparency and accountability in global supply chains that seamlessly integrate with Industry 4.0 technologies across a range of sectors, enabling more dynamic assessments with insights from the Global Reporting Initiative (GRI). As supply chains are becoming less transparent, facing pressing sustainability challenges such as the inappropriate use of natural resources, poor working conditions, and environmental degradation, the model facilitates companies in measuring their own and their suppliers' sustainability performance and enhances their capacity to effectively communicate their environmental and social progress to stakeholders.

Machado et al. (2020) identified that small and medium-sized companies, in their production processes and their supply chain, need to go beyond the mandatory actions imposed by governments regarding environmental management. Further, the environmental demands of large companies may favor the consolidation of environmental management practices in small and medium-sized companies through collaboration, increased knowledge, and the development of responsible behavior.

International Expansion

International expansion, although challenging, may be a significant driver positively affecting the entire supply chain. Companies must deal with negative consumer perception, cultural differences, and barriers when entering foreign markets. Differentiation and localizing production with distinct production lines help establish a stable connection with local consumers with the support of local business distribution networks (Amin & Zaman, 2022).

Implementation of innovative servitization activities can facilitate how organizations generate, capture, and deliver value in the long run throughout their value chain. This development proves to be especially beneficial if conducted in collaboration with suppliers, employees, and customers based on a robust, total-quality culture. The servitization activities produced stronger customer emotional loyalty stimulated by social media networks and a strong brand image while enabling the growth of local suppliers, creating an excellent capacity for innovation and stability (Albors-Garrigos & de Miguel Molina, 2023).

Similarly, Nim et al. (2024) observed that deeper immersion in local digital marketing ecosystems can support global expansion efforts by providing MNEs with greater multinational flexibility in supply chain. This enables them to adapt their global strategies to navigate increasing complexities in global markets, such as trends toward growing protectionism and geopolitical disruptions. Additionally, a holistic understanding by managers of the complexity of global production networks, considering the interplay between firms, clusters, and institutions, is important. The expansionary entries of Emerging Market Multinational Enterprises (EMNEs) positively affect their performance, but the relationship is moderated by the institutional environments in host countries. Different cluster linkages affect the expansion strategy of EMNEs. Firm-cluster relatedness creates varied opportunities or limitations for firms to engage in global supply chains (Wu et al., 2023).

Suppliers are essential partners in innovative projects, as they own resources, knowledge, assets, and capabilities that complement those of buying firms. In today's competitive environment, firms may choose to collaborate with suppliers beyond dyads, forming triadic or three-party relationships. Using the theoretical lens of the relational view, Patrucco et al. (2022) explained how triadic relationships are governed, how they invest in relationship-specific assets, how they combine complementary resources, and how they exchange knowledge and information in each type of triad appropriate to different innovation project settings. Firms govern triadic supplier relationships in collaborative innovation projects by investing in relationship-specific assets made to enhance coordination between first- and second-tier suppliers. Knowledge exchange with and between first- and second-tier suppliers is critical, but the intensity of this knowledge exchange within the triad differs.

Although more resource-consuming, establishing a direct and formal relationship with the second-tier supplier enables satisfactory time performance. Firms choose different types of triads (or governance mechanisms), according to where complementary resources reside in direct or indirect suppliers to achieve their project objectives, depending on whether they are innovating high or moderate technological complexity products. Firms seek to keep certain suppliers close to them and, sometimes, with each other, according to how much technological capability they have themselves and how they manage the risks of spillovers through collaborating too closely. It influences the decisions for managers: which suppliers need to be involved in the project and under what circumstances; and how to engage suppliers and combine their resources into the projects.

One of the key strategic resources in the triads with supplies is new technology, such as AI. According to Kinkel et al. (2023), a cross-national survey of 676 manufacturing companies from 16 industrialized countries showed a positive effect of AI on companies' offshoring and backshoring decisions, although international concentration (locating business activities in only a few local or global locations) did not moderate the relationship between AI and production relocation strategies.

International Diversification

Product and international diversification strategies play an essential role in the firm's competitive advantage but also have a considerable influence on the operations manager's inventory decisions. It is evidenced by a U-shaped relationship between unrelated product diversification and inventory level and a partially inverted U-shaped relationship between international diversification and inventory level. Therefore, laser-focused strategic planning for diversification requires significant changes in the operations manager's inventory control policies to achieve the strategic fit between corporate diversification and inventory management (Qian et al., 2025).

To avoid disruption and hedge against supplier lead time uncertainty, companies rely on diversification, multisourcing, and safety lead times. In multisourcing, the buyer might order the same product (raw material) from different suppliers. The design of a robust and cost-efficient purchasing/ordering plan in multisourcing is a complex task which has a strong impact on the performance of the company. As per the model developed by Thevenin et al. (2022), an extremely risk-averse decision-maker selects a single supplier, namely the most reliable one, even if it does not offer the lowest price.

Based on a multi-industry sample of 2,715 firm-year observations, Murcia et al. (2021) demonstrated that firms with higher CSR performance tend to vertically integrate more (or outsource less). However, this tendency is weaker for firms that have higher degrees of asset specificity or international diversification. Firms can reconcile the tension between CSR performance and outsourcing by deepening their collaborations with suppliers.

A dark side of corporate international diversification related to the riskiness of global supply chains was evidenced in the study of firms from 73 countries over the period from January to December 2020, showing that a stronger financial system mitigated negative crisis returns, especially under stringent government responses. Real factors, such as the firm's supply chain and investments in human capital and research and development, were shown to exacerbate negative crisis returns (Guedhami et al., 2022). Consequently, as Lavassani et al. (2023) explained from a supply chain strategy perspective, businesses need to have a realistic map of their supply chain to show their dependencies on other firms, industries, and countries throughout multiple tiers.

Based on the supply chain network data, businesses can reliably use the data to conduct clustering analysis to identify the boundaries of their business ecosystem and their competitors' business ecosystems to pinpoint their vulnerability to random failures and intelligent attacks at various levels. The supply chain mapping provides opportunities to explore business expansion or continuity planning, sustainability, cybersecurity, and contingency plans. Replacing suppliers is not always feasible; it can be costly, time-consuming, and constrained by product redesign requirements or location, capacity limitations, or feasible options limited only to notable suppliers and customers.

Case Examples

This section examines companies that have demonstrated visionary leadership in navigating global supply chain complexities to gain a competitive edge and pioneer in their industries, as well as those whose failures led to significant disruptions. Reviewing these success and failure stories can reveal key lessons in effective supply chain management and strategic decision-making in a rapidly evolving global landscape.

The selection of cases is based on recent news, visibility, a long track record, substantial market size, international presence, a variety of sectors represented, worldwide recognition, and a significant presence in the industry or sector with market power. Each case features an identified unique and evident problem (the cause and how it could have been avoided or prevented) or a clear and sound solution (the origination and how the innovation was fostered). They are worthwhile to share because of their universal value for transferability and recognizing future challenges in the field of global supply chain management. Each case provides evidence for balancing efficiency and resilience, specific to the respective industry and situation.

Bold Leadership

In today's increasingly complex world, global supply chains face ongoing challenges including geopolitical tensions, natural disasters, visibility, rising costs, sustainability concerns, and evolving customer demands. Companies with bold leadership manage these challenges by embracing innovation, advanced technologies, digital transformation, resilient strategies such as diversification of suppliers and building collaborative partnerships, and sustainable practices such as reducing carbon emissions and investing in renewable energy, contributing to the United Nations SDGs. These companies turn potential challenges into competitive advantages, positioning themselves as industry leaders while maintaining supply chain efficiency and customer satisfaction in the challenging dynamics of the global environment.

Amazon

Amazon is a global e-commerce leader with a strong global presence, dominating both the online retail and cloud computing sectors. Amazon has revolutionized its operations and supply chain by leveraging AI, robotics, and computer vision, enabling the company to achieve greater efficiency and productivity while creating a safer work environment for employees and offering customers ever-faster delivery. The company has introduced a large fleet of AI-powered robots in its fulfillment centers to support storing and retrieving inventory, transporting items, sorting packages, and more (Greenawalt, 2024). Morgan Stanley analysts have reported that the AI-powered robots reduced fulfillment costs by 25% during peak hours, and the company's savings could exceed $10 billion a year by 2030 (Boughedda, 2025).

Amazon's commitment to achieving net-zero carbon across its global operations by 2040 is driving the company to focus on reducing its environmental impact through numerous initiatives. These include regionalizing fulfillment centers and investing in electric delivery vehicles to reduce logistics emissions, innovating with AI and cloud computing for energy-efficient solutions, and fostering industry-wide change through collaboration and investments in sustainable technologies (Darley, 2024).

Amazon's transformational leadership in supply chain management offers valuable insights and lessons. By integrating advanced technologies, the company has developed innovative solutions that can be adapted across various industries to enhance supply chain efficiency, resilience, and sustainability. Importantly, ongoing innovation and technological advancements are vital for Amazon to respond to evolving markets and to maintain its leadership position in the industry.

Coca-Cola Company

Coca-Cola Company has been a global leader in the beverage industry since its foundation in 1886, with a worldwide recognized brand identity. Coca-Cola has dominated global markets through its effective leadership in balancing global scale with local relevance/adaptation by leveraging strategic partnerships and M&As. Partnerships with local bottlers and distributors provided access to established logistics infrastructure and route-to-market, while acquisitions of strong regional beverage brands enabled entry to new consumer segments, local distribution networks, and innovation and technology capabilities (The Strategy Institute, 2024).

Coca-Cola leverages digital innovation to improve supply chain efficiency and responsiveness. The company migrated to a cloud-only infrastructure, modernized its network to enhance global connectivity with bottling partners, and created AI-driven predictive algorithms for optimized inventory management and sales performance. To support its ongoing digital transformation, the company created a cross-functional digital council to manage governance, prioritization, and strategic capabilities. Further, the company developed a modular operating structure that enables rapid experimentation of new technologies, localization, and scalable solutions that can be adopted across the Coca-Cola system to create real value for all stakeholders (Noyes, 2025).

Through strategic partnerships, M&As, advanced technologies, and localization strategies, Coca-Cola has established a highly adaptive and efficient global supply chain. This approach not only drives operational excellence and profitability but also reinforces Coca-Cola's leadership in global expansion.

Apple

Apple is a global leader in technology and consumer electronics with a strong global presence and a highly valued brand. The company is renowned for its groundbreaking technological innovations and strong supply chain capabilities. Apple's robust supply chain management provides a competitive advantage by diversifying its supplier base to minimize reliance on a single supplier, building strong relationships and connections with its supply chain partners, enforcing strict terms and high standards on its suppliers, and reinforcing its commitment to sustainability (Yan et al., 2022).

These strategies continue to solidify Apple's supply chain resilience to risks and disruptions, as well as its responsiveness to changing market conditions. For example, while recent geopolitical tensions between the United States and China have made Apple resilient to tariffs, the company started moving production of some devices to countries like Malaysia, India, Vietnam, Thailand, and Brazil, further diversifying its suppliers to mitigate the risk of potentially escalating geopolitical tensions (Gurman, 2025).

Apple has effectively integrated advanced technologies into its global supply chain through advanced data and predictive analytics, AI-driven automation, and robust IT systems to enhance visibility, efficiency, responsiveness, and adaptability. By leveraging these technologies, Apple can forecast demand, optimize logistics and inventory management, and identify and prepare for potential supply chain disruptions.

By utilizing Customer Relationship Management (CRM), Internal Supply Chain Management (ISCM), and Supplier Relationship Management (SRM) technologies, Apple gains a deep understanding of customer demands, effectively manages the flow of goods, information, and finances across the supply chain, fosters trust among supply chain partners, and promotes innovation and sustainability. Furthermore, it enables the company to effectively align its supply chain capabilities and strategies with the dynamics of the external environment, creating a strategic fit (Budiono & Ellitan, 2024).

Apple's supply chain model reinforces the company's position as an innovative technology leader and sets an example for other companies. Its focus on strategic alignment, technology integration, supplier collaboration, and customer-driven strategies provides a framework for companies striving to achieve innovation, efficiency, and resilience in dynamic markets and long-term competitiveness.

Procter & Gamble (P&G)

P&G is a global leader in consumer goods with a strong global footprint across five sectors: health care, fabric and home care, grooming, beauty and baby, feminine and family care. The company has demonstrated long-term leadership in supply chain excellence, continuously strengthening it for greater agility, flexibility, data transparency, scalability, and resilience (Procter & Gamble, 2024, p. vi).

With a culture of innovation, P&G has been committed to enhancing its supply chain's digital capabilities by leveraging artificial intelligence, advanced analytics, end-to-end data synchronization, and automation. These digital advancements have brought significant benefits to P&G, including faster deliveries and reduced costs. Some examples include the implementation of digital twin technology to improve warehouse operations at a factory in Guangzhou, China, resulting in 99.9% on-time deliveries, a 30% reduction in inventory costs, and a 15% reduction of logistic costs (Kaplan, 2023); the integration of data analytics and automation to streamline the supply chain in India, reducing touchpoints by 60%; and the implementation of an AI-driven ordering system to better predict distributor shipments and replenishment, contributing to an 8% average sales growth in India over the past three years (Procter & Gamble, 2024, p. vii).

To continue with successful digital transformation, P&G is investing in advancing capabilities in three key areas. First, it is upskilling the workforce to harness the power of AI and other digital tools through comprehensive training programs. Second, it is developing and scaling the deployment of AI platforms across the entire organization to enhance efficiency, optimize decision-making, and foster creativity and innovation. Third, it is building a future-ready supply chain to meet evolving customer demand by leveraging automation, real-time analytics, and a commitment to quality (Cohen, 2024).

Walmart

Walmart, a global leader in the omnichannel retail industry, has a strong international presence with an extensive network of stores and e-commerce platforms. The company has revolutionized its global supply chain by leveraging innovative practices and cutting-edge technologies, thus creating a significant competitive advantage. Indeed, Walmart's commitment to supply chain innovation was recently recognized when it was named the winner of the 2024 NextGen Visionary Award (NextGen Supply Chain Conference, n.d.).

Walmart is recognized as a pioneer in integrating advanced technologies into its supply chain for greater efficiency, responsiveness, and sustainability. For example, the company has invested in AI-powered logistics technology, an innovative solution for route optimization and efficient trail packing, enabling it to avoid 94 million pounds of carbon emissions by eliminating 30 million unnecessary miles driven (Walmart, 2024).

Walmart has made this technology available to all businesses, underscoring its strong commitment to environmental and supply chain sustainability. Another example of Walmart's innovative approach is its cutting-edge partnership with India's GreenPod Labs to pilot a creative solution to reduce food waste, ensure fresher products, and expand sourcing to new countries (Carlyle, 2025). Moreover, Walmart continues to expand automation across its supply chain, significantly improving the fulfillment and delivery processes. Warehouses powered by robotic technologies and automated distribution centers are accelerating store-fulfilled deliveries and enabling next-day and two-day shipping for customers, reducing the net delivery costs per order by nearly 40% year-over-year (Taylor, 2024).

Walmart's ongoing investments in technology and innovation position the company to successfully address future supply chain challenges. By leveraging AI, automation, and strategic partnerships, Walmart exemplifies how large retailers can adapt to and shape the future of global supply chain management.

United Parcel Service (UPS)

UPS is a global leader in logistics, providing premier package delivery services and supply chain management solutions to customers in nearly every country worldwide. The company has been at the forefront of the logistics industry with innovative supply chain initiatives to enhance efficiency and visibility, and to meet the evolving market demands.

UPS's commitment to offering innovative solutions is demonstrated by its recent investments in expanding healthcare logistics capabilities through cold-chain acquisitions. In addition to several previous acquisitions, UPS has recently acquired Frigo-Trans and its sister company BPL, the industry-leading, Germany-based complex healthcare logistics providers (Hilton, 2025). This strategic move expands UPS's end-to-end services to address the increasing demand for temperature-controlled and time-critical logistics solutions.

Furthermore, the company introduced UPS Premier services for critical healthcare shipments, offering real-time monitoring, temperature control, and priority shipping and handling. This reinforces UPS's leadership in the healthcare logistics industry by setting a new industry standard for visibility, control, and prioritization for the most critical medical shipments around the world (Berman, 2022).

As part of its commitment to enhance supply chain sustainability, UPS has been heavily investing in advanced technology solutions to eliminate fuel and energy usage within its operations. For example, its groundbreaking ORION platform that utilizes advanced algorithms and real-time data to optimize delivery routes saves UPS about 100 million miles and 10 million gallons of fuel, reducing operational costs by $300 million to $400 million per year. Furthermore, it reduces greenhouse gas emissions by 100,000 metric tons, aligning with UPS's sustainability goals (Torres, 2024).

UPS maintains its position as a global leader and sets a high bar for its followers in the logistics industry through groundbreaking advanced technologies, strategic acquisitions, customer-focused strategies, and a strong commitment to innovation and sustainability.

Epic Failures

Unfortunately, there are endless examples of catastrophic man-made supply chain disasters serving as lessons to be learned by any and every company, big or small. Complacency, greed, negligence, human error, ignorance, time pressure, computer glitches, and IT upgrade/integration challenges are common and destructive. Astonishingly, none of the companies saw the events coming, even though they should have. Most often, as evidenced, companies were stung by self-inflicted supply chain problems that had catastrophic results for their market share, stock valuation, and undermined business sustainability/solvency (Ashcroft, 2021). A wise man learns from the mistakes of others.

Boeing

Boeing is the United States' fourth-largest defense contractor and the world's second-biggest commercial airline producer with a long-established history and strategic importance for the United States (internally and as an exporter), focused on international supply chain efficiencies, cost savings, and increased combat capabilities.

Following two fatal plane crashes attributed to a software malfunction, the Boeing 737 Max crisis unfolded in 2018 and was settled with the US Department of Justice for deliberately deceiving the Federal Aviation Administration (FAA) about a critical system on board the aircraft, known as the Maneuvering Characteristics Augmentation System (MCAS). Further ongoing in-flight safety problems revealed aboard other Boeing-built aircrafts in 2024 caused Boeing to face major federal investigations into safety concerns and public trust erosion.

Leadership issues, outsourcing decisions after limiting vertical integration, design changes, cost-cutting decisions, insufficient supplier management and testing, and a litany of many other factors contributed to the resignation of Boeing CEO Dave Calhoun at the end of 2024. The crisis highlighted the criticality of integrated and effective multilevel quality control, a need for proper training and thorough testing in the development and deployment of complex technologies (Supply Chain Game Changer, 2023).

Volkswagen

Volkswagen, the iconic German automobile manufacturer, the onetime world's largest automotive manufacturer by global sales, was faced with an emissions scandal, also known as Dieselgate. Volkswagen's deliberate manipulation of emission tests revealed a systemic failure in the company's automotive supply chain. The emissions scandal of 2015, resulting from a cost-reduction imperative, led to substantial financial losses, legal consequences, and a decline in consumer trust. The corporate priority should have been subject to ethical practices, integrity, and regulatory compliance within supply chains, emphasizing the need for transparency and monitoring mechanisms (Supply Chain Game Changer, 2023).

Samsung

As a South Korean multinational major appliance and consumer electronics producer, Samsung was once ranked the world's second-largest technology company by revenue. It was the largest semiconductor company in the world (briefly dethroning Intel – the decades-long champion), and it is the world's largest manufacturer of smartphones by handset volume.

Samsung's Galaxy Note 7 smartphone experienced widespread battery explosions in 2016, leading to a global recall of the product and significant damage to Samsung's reputation. Manufacturing and design issues were blamed as these batteries were provided by one dominant supplier. Samsung had to quickly find and qualify alternative suppliers, which also experienced battery problems as these products were rushed to market (Supply Chain Game Changer, 2023). The Galaxy Note 7 smartphone recall and subsequent production halt resulted in an estimated $17 billion in financial losses for the company, including lost sales, recall costs, and damage to brand reputation.

Intel

Historically a frontrunner in chip production and innovation, Intel is facing serious supply chain management challenges at a pivotal juncture for the semiconductor industry, with significant changes driven by the rapid progression of AI, complex supply chain dynamics, and the evolving landscape of global technology partnerships.

In recent years, the global supply chain for chips has been deeply disrupted, with logistical bottlenecks, raw material shortages, and geopolitical conflicts affecting the timely production and delivery of key components, leading to production delays, impacting delivery times, and creating backlogs. Unable to successfully face fierce competition resulting in compressed profit margins, Intel's stock value declined significantly in recent years due to delays in rolling out new technologies.

Intel was not able to fully capitalize on the AI surge. It also suffered from the geographical concentration of manufacturing in Asia, which was negatively affected by natural disasters, increased company sustainability risk, outsourcing third-party dependency with overreliance on key partners supplying components, and cost increases under competing high demand pressures (Collins, 2024).

Nike

In 2001, the sports-gear giant Nike, the world's largest supplier of athletic shoes, went live with a new – and supremely complex – supply chain planning system, apparently without adequate testing. Programming bugs and integration challenges left the company with significant inventory shortages and excesses. Nike ended up slashing prices to get rid of the additional inventory, putting pressure on margins and profits. At a quarterly conference call, Nike cited "software problems" for causing a $100 million revenue shortfall, and Wall Street knocked 20% off its stock price (Ashcroft, 2021).

Over the years, the company has also been continuously facing increased scrutiny from its shareholders and lawsuits over concerns about forced labor, compromised worker well-being, and discriminatory practices in its supply chain at an unprecedented scale and lack of transparency (ignoring salient risks in the apparel and footwear sector), although expected to embrace its corporate responsibility to respect human rights by adopting the UN Guiding Principles on Business and Human Rights.

Toys"R"Us

By the 1990s, Toys"R"Us was the undisputed king of toy retailers in the United States. However, e-retail was heating up in 1999, and the online division of Toys"R"Us advertised heavily. They overpromised delivery for Christmas while swamped by tens of thousands of orders. The inventory was in place, but it simply couldn't be picked, packed, and shipped fast enough because of the bottleneck of the limited capacity of warehouse workers. Toys"R"Us sent out thousands of infamous "We're sorry" emails, telling customers their orders would not be arriving in time for Christmas.

Not planning correctly for seasonality and lack of human feasibility in logistics were obvious errors in entering the online business, even though historically, the company generated 40% of its net revenues during the fourth quarter in the brick-and-mortar distribution. Next, in the disrupted retail landscape, it was also an e-commerce failure when the company signed, in 2000, a convenient ten-year agreement with Amazon, in which Toys"R"Us was losing money due to wrong pricing, sourcing, and a limited/dated scope of product range.

Toys"R"Us was too late to catch Amazon or Walmart online when they bought Etoys.com a few years later. They rushed into e-commerce unprepared, without a thoughtful, long-term approach. This huge misstep opened the door to others and pushed the company to bankruptcy and liquidation, ending a 70-year run as one of America's iconic retailers (Ashcroft, 2021). They were left behind because they did not enter early enough and were not steady enough in moving forward without successfully pioneering their global supply chain.

Drivers, Disruptions, and Future Challenges

New challenges are emerging for global supply chain management due to increasing pressures. Supply chain management and logistics play a pivotal role in creating well-being outcomes that benefit society. Supply chain professionals encourage scholars to expand transformative and holistic research on 21st-century challenges that are relatively less addressed in operations management literature, such as corporate social responsibility, evolving customer expectations, resource scarcity, climate change, and civic and political unrest (Mollenkopf et al., 2024).

Geopolitical Tensions Limiting Capacity

Political instability, military conflicts, and geopolitical shifts are poised to significantly influence global supply chains by changing trade policies. Developing flexible supply chain strategies and maintaining strong relationships with global partners can help mitigate risks associated with these political changes (Extensiv, 2024; KPMG, 2022). Additionally, trade tensions and disputes are hindering the movement of semiconductor products, manufacturing equipment, and critical materials (McKinsey, 2024; QIMA, 2024).

Natural Disasters Reducing Efficiency

Climate change and extreme weather events are expected to intensify, affecting access to goods and their flow to final destinations. These disruptions can lead to port delays and reduced availability of containers and ocean freight (KPMG, 2022). Connectivity across global supply chains can threaten resilience because networks propagate individual shocks across the broader economy.

Deeply intertwined and fragile supply chains can turn micro disruptions into macro-level effects. For example, the primary reason US production suffered as a result of the 2011 Japanese earthquake was the inability of firms to substitute imported intermediates for domestic alternatives in the short term. Offshoring has increased risk in pharmaceutical supply chains, where firms' cost-cutting incentives outweighed the benefits of investing in resilience and extra capacity. Both domestic and international diversification are required to increase the resilience of supply chains (White House, 2023).

Cost Pressures and Demand Fluctuations

Global economic uncertainty, resulting from fluctuating oil prices, unpredictable inflation rates, and shifting trade policies, remains a significant challenge for supply chains worldwide, impacting cost structures and operational stability. 71% of global companies highlight raw material costs as their number one supply chain threat. Proactive financial planning and strategic global partnerships are key to adapting to these economic fluctuations while maintaining supply chain resilience (Extensiv, 2024; KPMG, 2022; QIMA, 2024).

Legal Compliance, Consistency in Quality, and Visibility (ESG-Related Regulations)

Navigating a complex web of new, existing, and varied regulations across different markets is daunting for supply chain managers. Automated systems that track and manage compliance data can significantly ease this burden. Staying proactive about regulatory changes with the assistance of legal experts and integrating legal constraints into business operations is crucial for smooth operations.

Sustainability initiatives, such as optimizing transportation routes to reduce fuel consumption as well as focusing on renewable energy sources and optimizing energy use, not only help businesses comply with increasing regulatory demands but also meet the rising expectations of consumers and investors who prioritize ESG metrics. Only 16% of businesses have comprehensive knowledge of their suppliers across all tiers, and nearly a third of respondents reported knowing less than 50% of their supply chain.

With obscure traceability causing inconsistent product quality, it is imperative to improve corporate transparency about environmental impact at every stage of the supply chain. This refers to end-to-end visibility of the supply chain to see where your goods move, the organizations that are moving them, and their sustainability credentials, as well as to adopt more sustainable logistics practices to meet broader ESG goals. Fifty-three percent of organizations plan to increase their focus on sustainable sourcing and shifting their manufacturing locations by friendshoring and nearshoring to avoid geographical vulnerabilities instead of just relying on inventory buffers (McKinsey, 2024).

Data-Driven Technology Implementation and Cybersecurity

Advanced analytics play a crucial role in understanding and anticipating consumer behaviors, allowing businesses to manage inventory more effectively and reduce waste. By integrating responsive logistics solutions, companies can not only satisfy current consumer demands but also adapt to future innovations and expectations related to fast service, transparency, customization, and sustainability. Sixty seven percent of organizations consider meeting customer expectations for speed of delivery a critical force impacting the structure and flow of their supply chains, leading to morphing retail and distribution supply chains.

Automation and artificial intelligence are becoming increasingly important, filling in gaps related to labor shortages (including truck drivers and warehouse workers) and enhancing productivity. Collaboration with IT security experts to continuously update and fortify security measures ensures that supply chains are protected against evolving cyber threats. Especially with supply chain digitization, the risks of cyber threats will grow. Regular audits and employee training on security best practices are also vital (Extensiv, 2024; KPMG, 2022; White House, 2023).

The holistic "smart" supply chain is well on its way to becoming the new normal, with cross-functional expertise and the critical role of reliable data in fully or partly automated through low-code platforms, which carry compounded cyber risk (KPMG, 2022).

Overcoming Supply Chain Challenges

There is no one-size-fits-all approach to supply chain planning, and the challenges will persist. Based on the previous discussion and references, it is recommended to:

- Foster supply chain resilience by remaining flexible to adapt quickly, adjust to new market conditions, and navigate fluctuations smoothly, keeping your business robust in the face of adversity.
- Prepare contingency plans by hedging against existing bottlenecks such as congested ports, busy routes, and strained warehouse capacity. Implement geographically dispersed inventory strategies to mitigate congestion and supplier inefficiencies.
- Embrace cutting-edge technology for order routing automation, real-time inventory management, and integrated warehouse management. Leverage predictive analytics for demand forecasting to fine-tune your inventory levels, meet consumer demands, and manage resources efficiently, reducing costs and maximizing profitability.
- Fortify cyber defenses to safeguard your data, systems, and supply chain management to ensure smooth operations and maintain your reputation.
- Diversify sourcing and fulfillment to build resilience against future shocks and mitigate risks associated with geopolitical tensions and trade policy shifts, such as material shortages and longer lead times in procurement. Cultivating partnerships enhances the supply chain flexibility and protects operations against disruptions and bottlenecks.
- Keep liquidity in your business with flexible access to capital and cash on hand, as well as a flexible line of credit that can be used to stock up on evergreen or perennial items in high demand and prioritize manufacturing/shipping.

Conclusion

Effective management of global supply chains requires achieving the right balance between efficiency and risk while fully recognizing the evolving international political, socioeconomic, and environmental landscape. Companies must embrace proactive development and continuous enhancement and adaptation, recognizing the serious challenges of the 21st century. Integrating advanced technologies like AI, robotics, and data analytics into supply chains is vital in today's highly complex and dynamic environment to enhance visibility, efficiency, responsiveness, and resilience. These innovative technologies enable real-time monitoring, rapid response to disruptions, and data-driven decision-making, ensuring seamless operations and sustained competitive advantage.

However, reliance on novel and disruptive technologies requires an explainable, rational, and rigorous approach to verifiability, transparency, and contingency planning. Corporate objectives must always prioritize the reliability and control of supply chain architecture and systems under all circumstances. If not carefully managed, organizational changes can lead to under-diversification of supply chains and underestimation of the severe disruption risks.

M&As and strategic partnerships are essential for companies in expanding into new markets, allowing them to gain access to established networks, new resources, and local expertise while accelerating growth and competitive advantage. Furthermore, pioneering and experimentation need to become "the first nature" of the evolution of the global supply chain, logically embedded in the corporate culture.

Companies should actively solicit new ideas and perspectives from across global business management and rigorously test solutions before full implementation. Time, geography, and human factors will remain critical dimensions in the supply chain evolution. New industry leaders will emerge as some first movers experience erosion of their competitive advantage in the supply chain with intensifying ethical scrutiny.

Additionally, companies must implement sustainable practices in their supply chains to reduce environmental impact, enhance social responsibility, address growing stakeholder expectations, and create long-term value. By fostering innovation and resilience, companies can navigate uncertainty while maintaining a competitive advantage.

Clutch leadership plays a critical role in navigating the complexities of global supply chains, particularly as organizations face disruptions from technological innovations, geopolitical tensions, and evolving international political, socioeconomic, and environmental landscapes. Clutch leaders anticipate and respond promptly to these challenges by fostering adaptability, resilience, and strategic collaboration across their supply networks. They leverage advanced technologies and data-driven insights to enhance decision-making, optimize operational efficiency, and improve agility (Belasen & Pfeffermann, 2024). Furthermore, they cultivate strong relationships with key supply chain partners to maintain flexibility and sustain competitive advantage in a highly unpredictable global business environment.

Clutch leadership is also vital in navigating the fast integration and implementation of novel and disruptive technologies such as AI, robotics, automation, blockchain, cybersecurity, and data analytics into global supply chains. Today's highly complex and dynamic environment requires that clutch leaders adopt structured approaches that emphasize explainability, verifiability, and robust contingency planning. Through continuous testing and iterative improvement, they ensure seamless implementation, risk mitigation, and legal compliance with sustainability standards.

By leveraging technology to improve visibility, traceability, and efficiency, clutch leaders drive responsible supply chain transformations that minimize environmental impact, enhance social responsibility, and maintain a competitive edge. In doing so, they harness complexity to create opportunities across the entire supply chain system.

References

Akbar, D., Rahman, A., Rolfe, J., Kinnear, S., Schrobback, P., & Bhattarai, S. (2020). Models of horizontal collaboration in agrifood export supply chain: The case of Queensland's mango industry. *Australasian Journal of Regional Studies, 26*(3), 211–238.

Albors-Garrigos, J., & de Miguel Molina, M. (2023). The servitization of innovation in the retail grocery sector: The case of Mercadona. *Journal of International Entrepreneurship, 21*(2), 245–270. https://doi.org/10.1007/s10843-023-00336-3

Amin, M. K., & Zaman, M. H. (2022). Tapping into middle eastern markets for soft drinks industry of Bangladesh. *Emerging Economies Cases Journal, 4*(2), 84–88. https://doi.org/10.1177/25166042221146634

Ashcroft, S. (2021, December 7). Top 10: Worst supply chain disasters in history. *Supply Chain Digital.* https://supplychaindigital.com/supply-chain-risk-management/top-10-worst-supply-chain-disasters-history

Belasen, A. T. & Pfeffermann, N. (2024). What makes a brilliant leader? The new leadership mindset, Chapter 1. In A. T. Belasen & N. Pfeffermann (Eds.), *Brilliant leadership – unlocking the power of innovation-communication*, pp. 1–20. Routledge.

Berman, J. (2022, July 19). *UPS Healthcare heralds new features for UPS Premier offerings.* Modern Materials Handling. https://www.mmh.com/article/ups_healthcare_heralds_new_features_for_ups_premier_offerings

Blanchet, M., Meyer, S., & Pawlowski, B. (2024). *Next stop, next-gen. Tap into new value with advanced supply chain capabilities.* Accenture. https://www.accenture.com/content/dam/accenture/final/accenture-com/document/NextStopNextGen-2.pdf

Boughedda, S. (2025, February 3). *Amazon saving up to $3b a year after introducing 6 new warehouse robots: Analyst.* Investing.com. https://www.investing.com/news/stock-market-news/amazon-saving-up-to-3b-a-year-after-introducing-6-new-warehouse-robots-analyst-3845465

Budiono, K., & Ellitan, L. (2024). The efficiency and performance of Apple's supply chain management. *ULIL ALBAB: Jurnal Ilmiah Multidisiplin*, *3*(5), 46–67.

Carlyle, K. (2025, February 10). *Innovation in action: New partnerships push walmart's supply chain to the cutting edge*. Walmart. https://corporate.walmart.com/news/2025/02/10/innovation-in-action-new-partnerships-push-walmarts-supply-chain-to-the-cutting-edge

Chan, L., Zhang, P., Kowtha, R., & Lee, C. S. (2024). Artificial intelligence for Supply Chain Management (SCM): A thematic literature review. *International Journal of Business & Management Studies*, *5*(11), 8–18. https://doi.org/10.56734/ijbms.v5n11a2

Cohen, S. (2024, November 20). *3 keys to successful digital transformation*. Procter & Gamble. https://us.pg.com/blogs/keys-to-successful-digital-transformation/

Collins, G. (2024, December 5). Intel's leadership shakeup amid semiconductor challenges. *Supply Chain Digital*. https://supplychaindigital.com/technology/intels-leadership-transition-amid-semiconductor-challenges

Darley, J. (2024, October 29). Amazon's CEO shares top five sustainability initiatives. *Sustainability Magazine*. https://sustainabilitymag.com/articles/amazons-ceo-shares-top-five-sustainability-initiatives

Demir, S., Gunduz, M. A., Kayikci, Y., & Paksoy, T. (2023). Readiness and maturity of smart and sustainable supply chains: A model proposal. *Engineering Management Journal*, *35*(2), 181–206. https://doi.org/10.1080/10429247.2022.2050129

Extensiv. (2024). *Supply chain challenges in 2024 & how to overcome them*. https://www.extensiv.com/blog/supply-chain-management/challenges

Goldschmidt, K., Kremer, M., Thomas, D. J., & Craighead, C. W. (2021). Strategic sourcing under severe disruption risk: Learning failures and under-diversification bias. *M&SOM: Manufacturing & Service Operations Management*, *23*(4), 761–780. https://doi.org/10.1287/msom.2020.0907

Greenawalt, T. (2024, October 9). *Meet the 8 robots powering your Amazon package deliveries*. Amazon. https://www.aboutamazon.com/news/operations/amazon-robotics-robots-fulfillment-center

Guedhami, O., Knill, A., Megginson, W. L., & Senbet, L. W. (2022). The dark side of globalization: Evidence from the impact of COVID-19 on multinational companies. *Journal of International Business Studies*, *53*(8), 1603–1640. https://doi.org/10.1057/s41267-022-00540-8

Gurman, M. (2025, February 10). Apple's China focus thrusts it into center of geopolitical fight. *The Seattle Times*. https://www.seattletimes.com/business/apples-china-focus-thrusts-it-into-center-of-geopolitical-fight/

Hilton, L. (2025, January 28). UPS acquires European healthcare cold-chain logistics providers. *Packaging Digest*. https://www.packagingdigest.com/pharmaceutical-packaging/ups-acquires-european-healthcare-cold-chain-logistics-providers

Joel, O. S., Oyewole, A. T., Odunaiya, O. G., & Soyombo, O. T. (2024). Leveraging artificial intelligence for enhanced supply chain optimization: a comprehensive review of current practices and future potentials. *International Journal of Management & Entrepreneurship Research*, *6*(3), 707–721. https://doi.org/10.51594/ijmer.v6i3.882

Kaplan, I. (2023, May 22). *Why manufacturers should use digital twins for sustainability not just productivity.* World Economic Forum. https://www.weforum.org/stories/2023/05/digital-twins-manufacturing-sustainability/

Kelkar, A., Heineke, K., Kellner, M., Möller, T., Brennecke, R. & Chauhan, S. (2024, September 25). *Will autonomy usher in the future of truck freight transportation?* McKinsey & Company, Automotive & Assembly. https://www.mckinsey.com/industries/automotive-and-assembly/our-insights/will-autonomy-usher-in-the-future-of-truck-freight-transportation#

Kinkel, S., Capestro, M., Di Maria, E., & Bettiol, M. (2023). Artificial intelligence and relocation of production activities: An empirical cross-national study. *International Journal of Production Economics, 261*, n.p. https://doi.org/10.1016/j.ijpe.2023.108890

KPMG. (2022). *The supply chain trends shaking up 2023.* https://kpmg.com/us/en/articles/2022/the-supply-chain-trends-shaking-up-2023.html

Kumar, P., Kant, K., Mishra, N., Babu, V., & Chander, N. (2024). AI for optimizing supply chain management. *International Journal of Research in Applied Science & Engineering Technology, 12*(11), 549–560. https://doi.org/10.22214/ijraset.2024.65059

Lavassani, K. M., Boyd, Z. M., Movahedi, B., & Vasquez, J. (2023). Ten-tier and multi-scale supply chain network analysis of medical equipment: Random failure & intelligent attack analysis. *International Journal of Production Research, 61*(24), 8468–8492. https://doi.org/10.1080/00207543.2022.2152892

Li, Y., Liu, M., & Jiang, D. (2022). Application of unmanned aerial vehicles in logistics: A literature review. *Sustainability, 14*(21). https://doi.org/10.3390/su142114473

Machado, M. C., Vivaldini, M., & de Oliveira, O. J. (2020). Production and supply-chain as the basis for SMEs' environmental management development: A systematic literature review. *Journal of Cleaner Production, 273*, n.p. https://doi.org/10.1016/j.jclepro.2020.123141

Madhavaram, S., Manis, K. T., Rashidi, S. S., & Taylor, D. F. (2023). Capability bundling for effective supply chain management: An integrative framework and research agenda. *Journal of Business Logistics, 44*(2), 170–197. https://doi.org/10.1111/jbl.12329

McKinsey. (2024). *Supply chains: Still vulnerable.* https://www.mckinsey.com/capabilities/operations/our-insights/supply-chain-risk-survey#/

MHI. (n.d.). *The 2024 MHI annual industry report.* https://og.mhi.org/publications/report

Miller, E. M., Patala, S., & Ovaska, J.-P. (2025). *Forging the future: Reconfiguring value chains through circular economy meta-organizing.* Organization & Environment. https://doi.org/10.1177/10860266241297340

Mollenkopf, D. A., Esper, T. L., Stolze, H. J., & Ozanne, L. K. (2024). Transformative supply chain research: A new frontier for SCM scholars. *Journal of Business Logistics, 45*(3), 1–10. https://doi-org.sunyempire.idm.oclc.org/10.1111/jbl.12389

Morgan Stanley. (2024). *Sustainable signals understanding individual investors' interests and priorities.* Morgan Stanley Institute for Sustainable Investing & Wealth Management. https://www.morganstanley.com/content/dam/msdotcom/en/assets/pdfs/MSInstituteforSustainableInvesting-SustainableSignals-Individuals-2024.pdf

Murcia, M. J., Panwar, R., & Tarzijan, J. (2021). Socially responsible firms outsource less. *Business & Society, 60*(6), 1507–1545. https://doi.org/10.1177/0007650319898490

Nandi, M. L., Nandi, S., Moya, H., & Kaynak, H. (2020). Blockchain technology-enabled supply chain systems and supply chain performance: A resource-based view. *Supply Chain Management: An International Journal, 25*(6), 841–862. https://doi.org/10.1108/SCM-12-2019-0444

NextGen Supply Chain Conference (n.d.). *Awards.* https://www.nextgensupplychainconference.com/awards/

Nim, N., Pedada, K., & Hewett, K. (2024). Digital marketing ecosystems and global market expansion: Current state and future research agenda. *International Marketing Review, 41*(5), 872–885. https://doi.org/10.1108/IMR-04-2024-0108

Noyes, K. (2025, February 11). Scaling AI at Coca-Cola: From marketing to supply chain and beyond. *The Wall Street Journal. Deloitte.* https://deloitte.wsj.com/cmo/scaling-ai-at-coca-cola-from-marketing-to-supply-chain-and-beyond-2d81e110

Ok, E., Aria, J., Jose, D., & Diego, C. (2025). Ethical considerations and challenges of AI in supply chain management. https://www.researchgate.net/publication/389255282

Okay, N. C., Sencer, A., & Taskin, N. (2024). Quantitative indicators for environmental and social sustainability performance assessment of the supply chain. *Environment, Development & Sustainability*, 1–21. https://doi.org/10.1007/s10668-024-05210-3

Owusu-Berko, L. (2025). Advanced supply chain analytics: Leveraging digital twins, IoT and blockchain for resilient, data-driven business operations. *World Journal of Advanced Research and Reviews, 25*(2), 1777–1799. https://doi.org/10.30574/wjarr.2025.25.2.0572

Patrucco, A., Harland, C. M., Luzzini, D., & Frattini, F. (2022). Managing triadic supplier relationships in collaborative innovation projects: A relational view perspective. *Supply Chain Management, 27*(7), 108–127. https://doi.org/10.1108/SCM-05-2021-0220

Procter & Gamble. (2024). 2024 annual report. https://s1.q4cdn.com/695946674/files/doc_financials/2024/ar/2024_annual_report.pdf

PwC. (2024). *Drone deliveries: Taking retail and logistics to new heights.* https://cee.pwc.com/pdf-nf/PwC_DPS_Global_Drone_Deliveries_Report.pdf

PwC. (n.d.). *Beyond compliance: Consumers and employees want business to do more on ESG.* https://www.pwc.com/us/en/services/consulting/library/consumer-intelligence-series/consumer-and-employee-esg-expectations.html

Qian, Z., Wang, C. X., & Yang, H. (2025). Association between corporate diversification strategies and inventory performance: A firm-level investigation. *International Journal of Operations & Production Management, 45*(1), 88–113. https://doi.org/10.1108/IJOPM-03-2023-0199

QIMA. (2024). *2023's top supply chain challenges extend to 2024: Gaps in visibility pose obstacles for global supply chains.* https://blog.qima.com/traceability/2023s-top-supply-chain-challenges-extend-to-2024

Supply Chain Game Changer. (2023). *10 catastrophic man-made supply chain disasters!* https://supplychaingamechanger.com/10-catastrophic-man-made-supply-chain-disasters/

Taylor, G. (2024). Walmart boasts 'nearly 40 percent' cuts in delivery costs. *Sourcing Journal.* https://sourcingjournal.com/topics/logistics/walmart-automation-fulfillment-center-delivery-costs-cut-40-percent-robotics-e-commerce-store-pickup-next-gen-522762/

The Strategy Institute. (2024, April 19). *Coca-Cola's global dominance - Decoding the beverage giant's business strategy.* https://www.thestrategyinstitute.org/insights/coca-colas-global-dominance-decoding-the-beverage-giants-business-strategy

Thevenin, S., Ben-Ammar, O., & Brahimi, N. (2022). Robust optimization approaches for purchase planning with supplier selection under lead time uncertainty. *European Journal of Operational Research, 303*(3), 1199–1215. https://doi.org/10.1016/j.ejor.2022.03.029

Torres, A. (2024, March 1). *The science of winning.* ORMS Today, Informs. https://pubsonline.informs.org/do/10.1287/orms.2024.01.09/full

Urbieta, L. (2024). Firms reporting of Sustainable Development Goals (SDGs): An empirical study of best-in-class companies. *Sustainable Development.* https://doi.org/10.1002/sd.2944

Walmart. (2024, March 14). *Walmart commerce technologies launches AI-powered logistics product.* https://corporate.walmart.com/news/2024/03/14/walmart-commerce-technologies-launches-ai-powered-logistics-product

White House. (2023). *Issue brief: Supply chain resilience.* https://www.whitehouse.gov/cea/written-materials/2023/11/30/issue-brief-supply-chain-resilience/

Wu, S., Huang, X., Fan, D., Su, Y., & Li, Y. (2023). Cluster linkages in the global production networks: Exploring the impacts on the expansion of emerging market multinationals. *Transportation Research Part E: Logistics & Transportation Review, 171*, n.p. https://doi.org/10.1016/j.tre.2023.103039

Yan, P., Bai, X., & Shen, Z. (2022, April). Operations and supply chain analysis of the smartphone industry: Comparing Apple and Huawei. In *2022 7th International Conference on Social Sciences and Economic Development (ICSSED 2022)* (pp. 1523–1526). Atlantis Press.

Yang, S. Y. S., Chae, S., Yan, T., & Linderman, K. (2024). Consolidate? Diversify? Post-M&A supply base structural changes and operational performance. *Decision Sciences*, 1. https://doi.org/10.1111/deci.12631

IN PERSPECTIVE F

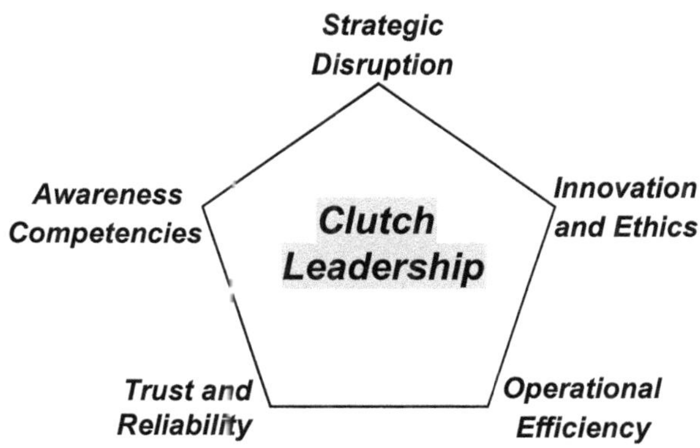

DOI: 10.4324/9781003629214-15

Chapter 10

Harnessing the Power of Character, Intuition, and Empowerment of Clutch Leaders

Barry Eisenberg and Alan T. Belasen

Introduction

What does one basketball shot have to do with over 150 million pairs of sneakers? The answer is at the very heart of this book on clutch leadership. First, some context before we share the answer.

In 1982, basketball superstar Michael Jordan was in his rookie season at the University of North Carolina at Chapel Hill (UNC). UNC made it to the national championship in a game that would pit them against rival Georgetown, a powerhouse with strong chances to capture the national title. Dean Smith, the UNC coach, had earned a reputation for being unable to win the "big one," having lost two national championship games in the recent past. For him, this was more than a game. It was a mission.

It wasn't common for rookies to be in the starting lineup of championship matches, let alone hold a prominent role. But Smith saw something special in

DOI: 10.4324/9781003629214-16

18-year-old Jordan. Not just his masterful athletic ability and basketball prowess, but his cool demeanor in pressure situations.

The game was close throughout. Fans were on the edge of their seats. With about half a minute to go, Georgetown took the lead by one point. The team rejoiced, believing that with its solid defense, it could hold on to win. UNC took a timeout during which they devised a play. The Georgetown players and coaches, not to mention every spectator in the arena as well as the national audience watching the game on television, were sure that UNC's highly talented James Worthy, who was playing his final college game before moving on to the pros, would be tapped to take the shot.

But as the ball was inbounded, it became clear that Worthy would function as a decoy, and instead the ball would go to the rookie Jordan, who was calling for the ball on the far side of the court. The video of those few seconds, as Jordan gestures for the ball, is revealing. He appears composed and confident, ready to take charge; neither cocky nor timid, his assuredness is driven by a keen self-awareness of his skills and his ability to execute in the most tension filled of circumstances.

As the clock ticked down to 20 seconds remaining in the game, the ball was lobbed to Jordan. He immediately turns his body toward the basket. As Georgetown defenders frantically rush away from Worthy and toward Jordan to try to smother his shot attempt, Jordan rises and methodically releases the ball. The Georgetown defenders watch helplessly as the ball passes cleanly through the rim, its arc so perfect as to barely unsettle the net on its descent.

UNC held off their Georgetown rivals for the remaining seconds of the game and captured the national championship. With his reputation on the line, Coach Smith built that crucial play around Jordan. He believed that the team's best chances to win the game of his life lay with this rookie rather than players who had already been tested under pressure and had far more experience under their belts.

Michael Jordan's performance in that remarkably pressure-packed moment is as clutch as it gets. And as the world knows, he would go on to have countless moments like that as a professional basketball player.

And the 150 million pairs of sneakers? That is the number of Air Jordan sneakers Nike had sold since signing a contract with Jordan in his rookie season with the Chicago Bulls in 1984. And it was his performance in the championship game against Georgetown that brought Jordan to Nike's attention. The Nike executives would eventually report that as impressive as that winning shot was, it was Jordan's self-confidence, maturity, and poise in the seconds before the shot that mattered most. It was his apparent belief in himself that convinced them of his greatness (Convery, 2023).

What the Nike executives saw paid off well beyond expectations. Between 2018 and 2023 alone, Nike earned $19 billion from the sale of Air Jordan sneakers (Hyperbeast, 2023). Jordan himself became a billionaire in 2014 from royalties from the product line, along with other business investments. A decade later, in the post-COVID-19 era, in the second quarter of 2024, Nike reported a disappointing revenue of $51.4 billion, a mere 0.3% increase over the previous fiscal year. However, Jordan's brand was the strongest performer of Nike's divisions, with a 6% sales gain to $7 billion, compared to Men's (1%), Women's (0%), and Kids (1%).

But assigning the label of "clutch" to that singularly enthralling moment of basketball heroics, while completely understandable because it's impossible not to be riveted to its brilliance, may miss all the hard work it took to make that moment possible. Indeed, Michael Jordan is widely considered the "clutch GOAT" (Greatest of All Time) due to his exceptional ability to perform in critical moments of the game, particularly during the playoffs and NBA Finals. And when the character trait of *dedication* is added to that extensive preparation and skill refinement, any aspiring leader, like Michael Jordan, will have a chance to shine. When their clutch moment arrives, when the straits become unexpectedly turbulent and their navigational capacity is harshly tested, they too find a way out of the storm. This book endeavors to give definition and contour not just to the clutch episode, but to all that undergirds it. The most clutch among us convert a crisis into an opportunity.

In "Clutch Leadership," *we* explored important skills and traits necessary for successful leadership during crises. It is thematically organized around the *Pentagon Framework* (see Chapter 1, Figure 1.6), which consists of five interconnected areas that build from a focus on self and personality to environmental conditions and culminate in strategy development. Accordingly, the Part 1 of the book, "Awareness Competencies," inquired into how a leader's commitment to evidence-driven decision-making and transparency is central to building trust, without which the odds of failing in a crisis can escalate dramatically.

Part 2, "Trust and Reliability," consists of two chapters that expand on self-awareness while beginning to pivot to organizational factors relevant to crisis situations. Chapter 3 demonstrated how leadership empathy can facilitate successful crisis management. In this regard, empathy is the glue that binds employees to the organization's purpose and heightens members' willingness to commit their full energies toward a positive outcome. Chapter 4 highlighted the notion that crises can pose significant threats to all organizations, including High Reliability Organizations (HROs).

While HROs are designed to be resilient and prepared for disruptions, crises such as the COVID-19 pandemic or economic downturns can disrupt their operations, potentially leading to serious challenges and setbacks. HROs like airlines and hospitals have special obligations to protect their members and stakeholders against high risks, preventable adverse events, and costly errors. This chapter also presented the benefits of learning from military training to prepare potential leaders for the challenges associated with crises. Military training programs offer a wealth of transferable skills that can be valuable in civilian life. As illustrated in the chapter, these skills include leadership, teamwork, communication, problem-solving, and resilience, which are highly sought by HROs.

Part 3, "Operational Efficiency," continued the shift from the inner (self) to the outer (environment) by exploring the transformative impact of AI on operations management and highlighting the importance of integrating innovation into leadership vision. Inspiring a vision that embraces creativity and generative AI, while also fostering a culture where risk-taking, learning, and collaboration have been shown to be key success factors in achieving measurable outcomes.

Part 4, "Innovation and Ethics," synthesized material from the previous sections by demonstrating the revolutionary power of AI and digital transformation on all facets of commerce and industry. The section employed the healthcare industry as an extended example of how such disruptive technology may be harnessed but must be tempered to avoid the unleashing of potentially profound ethical misuse of AI in healthcare, which includes data bias leading to unfair or discriminatory outcomes as well as a lack of transparency in AI decision-making.

Part 5, "Strategic Disruption," broadened the environmental perspective to a global scale. It demonstrated how the worldwide supply chain, because of its highly interdependent nature and complexity, is particularly susceptible to disruption, creating vulnerabilities if one part of the chain fails. Yet, as also presented in the section, opportunities for clutch leaders to thrive can materialize from smart choices, a sound assessment of environmental conditions, and a vision for a winning outcome, along with the skills to bring it to fruition.

This final chapter brings the book full circle, right back to where it began, by focusing on the individual who has in their hands the central responsibility for managing a situation teeming with challenges. In so doing, this chapter integrates critical concepts from the contributions of this book's authors while advancing the proposition that clutch leadership is an amalgam of preparation, skill, and determination. This chapter is also, and even primarily, about character, that seemingly intangible force that gives each of us distinctiveness. In the context of this chapter, it relates to the synergistic interplay of our moral and mental impetuses that drive our choice-making goals and fuel our tenacity to achieve them.

If we just glance at a given clutch experience, the groundwork that made success possible may be easily and understandably obscured by the dazzle of the performance at that moment. But, as noted, preparation is central to that moment. That is where "clutch" actually resides – less in the last-second basketball shot than in the tireless hard work that made it feasible. Michael Jordan's relentless commitment to practice is well-known in the basketball community. He was often the first player to the gym and the last to leave. As he said, "No one is going to prepare more than me. No one is going to practice more than me" (deciphr, n.d.). That is character.

In bridging the clutch performance with all that is required to make that performance fruitful – preparation, skill, and determination – this concluding chapter specifically explores (1) the relationship between rational and intuitive approaches to decision-making, (2) the critical relationships among organizational structure, culture, and strategy, and (3) the motivational foundation necessary to mobilize stakeholders during periods of disruption.

Rational VS. Intuitive or Rational *and* Intuitive Decision-Making

Simply put, it is easier to categorize than synthesize. Take virtually any organization, say an average-sized hospital that has about 350 beds and employs 2,500 people. Every day, they prepare over 1,000 meals, perform over 3,000 lab tests, and administer over 5,000 medications. One would think a well-oiled machine must be at play, with all parts of the operation completely in sync, humming the same tune.

Wrong!

Estimates of the cost associated with operational inefficiency are jaw-dropping. A meta-study conducted by Shrank et al. (2019) compiled 71 estimates from 54 studies and concluded that approximately $50 billion was wastefully spent due to the failure of effectively coordinating the provision of care. Additionally, $265.6 billion was squandered on administrative complexity. Those two areas of waste alone account for about 8% of the total US expenditure on healthcare.

Instead of hospitals functioning as highly integrated systems with well-defined and well-executed interconnections among the various components, they tend to function more on a "silo basis" (Belasen et al., 2024). This is not surprising. Nor is it unique to healthcare. After all, employees in any organization tend to gravitate toward and identify with those with whom they spend the most time, have similar or overlapping professional responsibilities and training backgrounds, share common purposes for how the institution's priorities are ordered, and even identify with those having similar sociocultural and socioeconomic backgrounds.

Finding a compelling explanatory framework for the workings of a complex organization, one which demands the interlinking of a multiplicity of parts, can direct us to rational or behavioral decision-making models. The former presupposes that people – and by extension, organizations – approach decision-making situations with an underlying logical evaluation of the costs, benefits, and risks associated with potential choices and that the final decision is based predominantly on its capacity to maximize the desired outcomes. In its archetypal form, rational decision-making involves collecting facts in an orderly fashion and using that fact pattern to build a case for addressing a problem. From a rational decision-making perspective, the coordination of interdependent functions in an organization would begin with a systematic analysis of how those functions operate efficiently. By way of example, and again, in a hospital, the Physical Therapy Department must coordinate with the Imaging Department so that a patient is not booked for both at the same time. And the transporters who bring patients to these departments must also coordinate with them to ensure the efficiency of operations.

This does not differ from a warehouse in which inventory management, stocking, shipping, and payments for goods must be highly interlaced to make sure there are no inefficiencies, that is, no time wasted in the transitions among the processes associated with a given activity. In each of these cases, evidence-based processes would be pursued, with a methodical calculation of how to align scheduling and capabilities to ensure that available resources are efficiently and effectively utilized to achieve organizational goals.

Seems easy, doesn't it? And logical? Yet, inefficiency across the business economy in the US generally stands at an astounding 20% to 30% (Candito, 2016). Inefficiency is most commonly related to poor data quality, ineffective interdepartmental communication, outdated technology, and poor performance. Thus, it is understandable that significant fees are paid to efficiency specialists by companies to help identify areas for improvement, implement new processes, and optimize workflows in an effort to increase efficiency and reduce costs. In fact, of the roughly $300 billion spent annually on management consulting, strengthening operations accounts for the largest share at 28.4% (PRNewswire, 2019).

In contrast to the rational decision-making model is the behavioral model, sometimes referred to as the intuitive model. Whereas the rational model posits an optimal method for decision-making, intuition provides context for how decision-making actually occurs by integrating cognitive, psychosocial, emotional biases and related psychological elements into decision-making activity. Thus, rationality and intuition have complementary relationships and, when used jointly, lead to better quality outcomes (Thanos, 2023).

We may look to Michael Jordan's championship-winning basketball shot to demonstrate how the rational and behavioral perspectives are unified, transcending the seemingly discrete nature of these perspectives on decision-making.

It is in those very special high-pressure moments that their integration becomes most apparent.

Jordan, as noted, was a notoriously well-practiced professional. According to his personal trainer, Tim Grover, his routine would consist of highly specialized training that included weightlifting, calisthenics, stretching, running, and, of course, basketball playing, all for several hours each day (Wong, 2017). He would invariably shoot between 100 and 500 free throws in grueling practice sessions, concentrating on technique perfection rather than the outcome. He reasoned that if the technique was perfect, the outcome would follow. This highly programmed approach epitomized discipline, and the repetitiveness of the activity translated into significantly effective and reliable performance on the basketball court.

But then there is that pressure-filled moment during an actual close game, that "clutch" moment. The term "clutch" was originally used in 1929 in the *New York Times* to describe a baseball player who was able to get on base at an opportune time (Safire, 2005). Over time, the term has served as an adjective for the tense situation or for the performer who faces it. The qualities that Michael Jordan brought to those situations struck a balance between three pairs of seemingly competing character traits: determination and self-regulation; self-confidence and belief in the team; and risk and caution. These are the balances that lead to successful clutch performance in any context.

Determination balanced against self-regulation. Determination is a key ingredient in the effective management of pressure situations. We may think of it as an unwavering resolve, an unrelenting commitment to face a challenge. But unchecked, determination, especially in the face of disruption, can shift from a productive and essential quality into a destructive force. This is where self-regulation comes into play. As Catanese (2024) notes, "Self-regulation is the act of controlling your behaviors, thoughts, emotions, choices, and impulses." It serves as a guardrail, imposing limits on behavior that might otherwise be destructive to the self or to others.

In the case of an athlete, self-regulation functions to maintain performance goals in an achievable domain. In clutch moments, it restrains the basketball player from launching low-percentage, unwise flings toward the basket. In the case of an organization, it restrains the decision-maker from adopting extreme measures that could exacerbate the crisis rather than restore stasis. Absent self-regulation, determination could lead to decisions that hold the potential for dramatic benefit, but they have a very low probability of success.

Self-confidence balanced against belief in the team. Self-confidence, at its core, involves belief in one's abilities to succeed in a given situation. Most would agree that self-confidence is important when it comes to facing high-pressure circumstances. But in moments of serious challenge, self-confidence that goes unchecked could result in the leader drawing all the decision-making calculus into their realm. Much like a vacuum, self-confidence, absent constraint, would suck in all the decision-making energy, relegating those around them irrelevant.

Respect for the team is a vital countervailing force, promoting empowerment based on the recognition that no single individual holds the all-encompassing knowledge necessary to decide. Reid Hoffman, who built LinkedIn from a modest networking platform, turning it into a global enterprise, cautioned, "No matter how brilliant your mind or strategy, if you're playing a solo game, you'll always lose out to a team" (Alaili, 2023).

In periods of disruption, when decision-making time is compressed, the self-confidence that a leader must have, tempered by a belief in the ability of others to contribute, will have an edge over the leader whose uncurbed self-confidence has morphed into a self-perception of invincibility and infallibility. As Michael Jordan himself observed, "Talent wins games, but teamwork and intelligence win championships" (Freeland, 2018). As the stakes rise, so does the value of the contributions around the decision-maker, the clutch leader.

Risk balanced against caution. Risk is a singularly powerful and essential precondition for exploring, adapting to evolving circumstances, innovating, and serving others more capably. It is the very trait that emboldens a leader to dispense with caution – *some* caution – to engage in discovery and pursue invention. Risk is what allows curiosity to manifest in learning, exploration, and experimentation. The failure to do so leads to stagnation, and failure to do so is as much a choice as is the choice to act. As Rene Descartes observed, "If you choose not to decide, you still have made a choice" (Gibby-Brown, 2020).

But what is the difference between calculated risk and recklessness? Tilting too far toward risk could lead to carelessness. It could result in a thoughtless bet, one lacking a sound or even reasonable rationale. Tilting too far toward caution by becoming risk-averse (e.g., favoring safe investments over high-growth options) could impair an organization's competitive position. Risk-averse behavior can impede progress and opportunity by causing decision-makers to avoid beneficial actions due to the fear of potential losses or setbacks.

In a crisis, the stakes for achieving that balance are magnified. In a crisis, not all "unknowns" can be converted into knowns. Without having the luxury of time for investigation and deliberation, the effective leader uses whatever time might be available in the most strategic of ways to assess the probabilities of success across option avenues. The effective leader neither gambles away the organization's future in a crapshoot nor hides behind a safe wall in the hopes that the crisis will pass. Michael Jordan's last-minute shots in close games were not blind heaves from midcourt, but rather calculated and reasonable shot attempts that he believed would provide the opportunity to put his team ahead (Sarlis et al., 2024).

Blink

Crises help us to understand the highly integrated relationship between the rational and intuitive perspectives on decision-making. The rational dimension explains much of what lies below the surface. The intuitive dimension explains those seemingly amorphous psychosocial influences on the logical antecedents that frame decision-making choices.

In his bestseller *Blink*, Malcolm Gladwell (2005) captures the relationship between the dual perspectives through the use of a compelling example. He describes the Getty Museum's interest in the early 1980s in purchasing a seven-foot marble statue of a male youth purportedly carved in the 6th century BC. Before investing in the statue, the museum's curators invited groups of experts to assess its authenticity. They used the most up-to-date scientific tools to do their work, including the use of "electron microscopes, electron microprobes, mass spectrometry, X-ray diffraction, and X-ray fluorescence" (p. 4). Geologists confirmed that the statue's materials could indeed have come from that era.

After 14 months of evaluating the statue, the Getty was prepared to execute the approximately $10 million purchase. But two people had misgivings. Frederico Zeri, who had been a member of the Getty board, confessed that something didn't look right, though he couldn't put his finger on it. Evelyn Harrison, a world-leading expert on Greek sculpture, also examined the statue. There was something about it that appeared "off," but she was not able to define it. Zeri and Harrison had hunches, though neither could immediately translate their hunches into a coherent explanation. Juxtaposed against their suspicions was the fact that the statue had undergone the most rigorous scientific tests, all of which seemed to confirm its authenticity.

Thomas Hoving, who had been the director of the Metropolitan Museum of Art in New York City, was then asked to examine the statue. He, too, felt something was amiss, suggesting that perhaps the statue's appearance was too "fresh." Again, just a hunch.

Enough red flags had been raised for the Getty to dig deeper into the statue's authenticity. They shipped it to Greece, where among those examining the statue was Angelos Delivorias, director of the Benaki Museum in Athens. Delivorias instantaneously declared it a fake, emphasizing that his immediate reaction was based on "intuitive repulsion." The Getty had invested considerable time, effort, and money in a scientific analysis which had led to the determination that there was a high probability that the statue was genuine. And now they were faced with growing counterarguments grounded in something that seemed antithetical to science: *intuition*.

Following additional and quite extensive investigations of not only the statue, but of the circumstances leading to the seller's pitch to the museum, it was determined that the statue was a fraud – an exceptionally well-crafted fraud, but a fraud, nevertheless. In recounting the story, Gladwell raises the question of how, after two seconds of looking at the statue, Ziri, Harrison, and the others got it right and a year's worth of scientific investigation got it wrong. They were all certain of their belief, but could not pinpoint why, at least not at first.

Gladwell employs the statue example to demonstrate the ostensible logical-intuitive divide and how that relationship influences our approach to decision-making. The well-known gambling study from the University of Iowa provides the basis for the explanation (Bechara, 1994). Subjects were asked to select cards from multiple decks in which the cards were ordered in a complex fashion, though the subjects were not informed that they were arranged in a pattern. Incentives were provided for selecting certain cards. On average, it took respondents about 50 selections to gain an understanding of the pattern.

However, the researchers observed that at about the 10th card, subjects exhibited certain physiological changes, including the onset of sweaty palms, and that their choice-making patterns were beginning to change. These changes occurred well in advance of their awareness of the pattern.

The researchers concluded that two decision-making currents were operative: logical and intuitive. The logical component, more fully associated with conscious fact-finding and cognition, took longer to develop, while the intuitive dimension operates more quickly and resides outside the conscious sphere. Of course, that intuitive dimension may prove less reliable. But – and this is of great importance – the more capable their logical strategizing prowess, the more effective the decision derived from the intuitive function. The logical, of course, takes more time because of its fact-finding nature. It needs to assemble evidence and identify links between information elements. The intuitive operates from the notion that we are approaching a decision before our mind even understands that a decision is approaching. With intuition, only a limited range of information is available, too limited for the logical process to work toward completion.

Clutch leaders aren't those who process the most information or spend the most time deliberating, as the rational model posits. Rather, clutch leaders are those who have perfected the art of "thin-slicing" – focusing on the vital few factors that matter the most from an overwhelming number of variables. They use intuition to derive feasible courses of action. When uncertainty is high and time is of the essence, clutch leaders rely on gut feelings, especially in high-pressure situations where quick decision-making is crucial. This reliance on intuition, or "gut instinct," can be a powerful tool for leaders, allowing them to act quickly and decisively without getting bogged down in analysis paralysis. Daniel Wegner (2002) coined and defined the term *adaptive unconscious* as a set of mental processes that is able to affect judgment and decision-making but is out of reach of the conscious mind. He advanced the proposition that such a trait is foundational to survival, largely because situations involving survival vulnerability often require decision-making that cannot consider all relevant information.

Crises, by definition, would properly be categorized as potential loss of survival phenomena. Crises can bring organizations to the edge of viability, threatening something of great value, whether assets, reputation, standing in a community of importance, or even their existence. The more capable the adaptive unconscious, the greater the ability to withstand the test of a crisis. Central to the interdependence of logic and intuition with respect to decision-making is that adaptive capabilities will prove effective to the extent that the logical processes, which include all the Michael Jordan-like preparation, have been undertaken. It is exactly the same for the art experts who declared the statue a fake. Their intuition was not separate from their expertise. It was made possible because of their expertise. It just arrived more quickly than their complex cognitive computations.

Intuition is not a substitute for hard work; quite critically, it is that very hard work that makes effective intuition possible. Neither alone could solve a crisis. But together, they offer the decision-maker more than a fighting chance.

The Essential Interplay of Organizational Strategy, Structure, and Culture

On August 19, 2016, Samsung launched its new model Galaxy phone, the Note 7. Hopes for brisk sales were justifiably high given that its predecessor, the Galaxy 6, was very popular. Less than one week later, on August 24, a Note 7 exploded in a fiery eruption. Stories about the phone's flaw spread rapidly as more and more explosions occurred.

Naturally, Samsung initiated investigations, quickly discovering what they believed to be the defective parts. They corrected the problem and conducted a highly visible campaign to encourage owners of the phone to replace it with the upgraded version. However, shortly after the exchange program got underway, there were widespread reports that the "fixed" Note 7 phones were also exploding. Airlines banned all Samsung Galaxy Note 7 phones from their flights. Sales of the phones plummeted. The crisis was potentially perilous for Samsung. The problem had not been corrected, despite assurances that it had; thus, Samsung faced the risk of broader and long-term reputational damage, which had now grown exponentially higher.

Fast forward one year. Samsung's brand had more than rebounded, and its Galaxy S8, a successor to the Note 7, generated record profits for the company

(Martin & Jeong, 2017). What occurred in that year is a testament to the company's extremely effective management of the crisis. Their performance is a lesson in the essential synchronicity among organizational *strategy*, *structure*, and *culture*; absent their congruity, recovery may have proven elusive.

With respect to strategy and culture, Samsung was proactive, accepted accountability, and remained steadfast in its commitment to a comprehensive and tireless investigation. Being proactive meant that the customer comes first, not with lip service or hollow platitudes. It meant that the number one priority would be customer safety. As DJ Koh, President of Mobile Communications Business for Samsung Electronics, said, "Technology innovation is important to Samsung, but our customer's safety is more important. We want to reinstate trust in the brand" (Lopez, 2017).

That commitment was translated into action. Following extensive engineering assessments of all components of the phone, it was determined that the culprit was the battery. Samsung worked with other telecommunications companies that would send messages to the Note 7 phones to disable their charging mechanism, rendering the devices useless. They did not wait for the investigation to conclude; rather, they took this action in anticipation that other explosions could occur while the fact-finding was in progress. They also recalled all the Note 7s at a cost of $6 billion (Team Pepper, 2022).

With respect to accountability, Samsung immediately communicated to the public that the faultiness of the phone was their responsibility and theirs alone. They were neither defensive nor opaque, but forthright and apologetic. At the same time, they committed to a spare-no-expense effort to find the problem and remedy it. While they may not have had sufficient information at the time to convey reasonable suppositions about the nature of the problem, they left no doubt that they would not stop until they found it.

But proactivity and accountability are more than strategies. Let's face it, it is not uncommon for organizations to declare their faithfulness to those precepts. By investing considerable capital in the buyback, and in leaving no doubt about their culpability and responsibility, Samsung demonstrated something vital to winning back trust – *sincerity*. Rebuilding trust would be virtually impossible if proactivity and accountability are not core elements of organizational culture. After all, stakeholders look to deeds, not words, to judge sincerity. In the case of Samsung's crisis response, the range of deeds was expensive, including not only the buyback, but also forfeiting opportunities to take legal action against companies that contributed to the battery's manufacture, and undertaking a very wide-ranging and expensive investigation.

Moreover, in communicating straightforwardly and frequently, Samsung left no doubt about its liability belonging exclusively to them. The decision-making culture that had been in place prior to the crisis did not suddenly change on the day the crisis erupted. It would not be possible to re-engineer an organization's culture overnight.

Consider that organizational cultures take time to develop; they are built around shared values and beliefs that are cultivated, woven into the fabric of everyday organizational life, embedded in unspoken assumptions about how business will be conducted, how customers are viewed, and how employees feel about their affiliation with the organization. In this way, proactivity and accountability cannot magically appear or be summoned by the will of the executives. If those critical elements were not in place the day prior to the crisis, they would not be in place on the day of occurrence.

Organizational structures are akin to Goldilocks and the Three Bears. Too top-heavy typically results in micromanaging and disempowered employees. Too lean typically forces managers to devote excessive attention to day-to-day operations and not enough planning. The trick for organizational leaders is to get the structure "just right." The ability to do that is an important leadership skill. "Just right" varies from company to company and industry to industry. And "just right" goes beyond manager-to-staff ratios and span of control, encompassing a broad range of variables, much of which boils down to whether the chief decision-maker has at their disposal a full complement of expertise that is relevant to the challenges at hand. It also means being prepared to adapt the structure to shifting circumstances.

Among the most cataclysmic of shifting circumstances is a crisis that will surely test organizational structures in ways that normal times do not. In this regard, Samsung responded. The company created a laboratory for the testing of batteries. It was built on an existing organizational platform but was greatly expanded. Samsung assembled a team of 700 engineers and researchers and provided them with an inventory of 30,000 batteries to test across a wide variety of environmental conditions to determine the cause of overheating. Ultimately, they discovered that the size of the battery compartment was insufficient relative to the size of the battery and could not contain the residual heat produced by the battery.

The relationships between strategy, structure, and culture in an organization can be assessed in many ways. But an outsider looking in can get a sense of those relationships by examining two elements: communication and empowerment. In the Samsung example, the responsibility for determining the cause of the phone failure was immediately handed over to those with relevant expertise. The leadership's charge to that engineering group was to go where the facts led. They were empowered, with a free hand, to engage in a process of discovery without preconditions, without constraints that could have otherwise been self-serving to management. And the public, their employees, and the industry were kept fully abreast of the activities undertaken by the company to determine the cause of the problem and their pledge to not only rectify it but to learn from it in the spirit of quality improvement.

Leaders of many healthcare organizations faced a monumental challenge when the COVID pandemic hit. They had responsibility for mobilizing their organizations around the Herculean task of managing patient care in the face of a staggering public health emergency. This involved channeling the full measure of their institutional activity toward a common goal in an atmosphere of uncertainty about patient volumes and severity of illness, shortages of essential staff, supplies, equipment, and employee anxieties about their own health and the welfare of their families.

Among the most important insights derived from studies of hospital performance is that those facilities which already had sound and effective communication cultures in place fared better during the pandemic (Belasen et al., 2024). An effective communication culture served as a foundation for constructive coordination and collaboration, critical elements in the fast-moving and stress-laden atmosphere (Díaz-Agea et al., 2022). To the extent that work processes occurred with greater efficiency and reliability, the flow of important information to decision-makers was smoother and quicker; as such, decision-making about institutional strategy and operational effectiveness led to better organizational performance and improved care for patients.

As with communication, empowerment is critical for the successful management of an emergency or crisis. We need to rely on others to get the job done quickly, competently, and reliably. But empowerment does not come about easily or automatically, and it certainly cannot materialize overnight. If an organization's practice had been to micromanage, staff would not have had the opportunity to gain the necessary knowledge and skills when a crisis hits, let alone the confidence to execute. Organizations that understand the importance of encouraging employee growth, learning, and skill development during normal times will find a more capable workforce when times get tough, as when an emergency occurs.

In short, healthcare organizations whose cultures were characterized by egalitarian, transparent, evidence-based, and trustworthy leadership orientations, but with a capability for decisiveness, had an edge during the pandemic. These cultural conditions cannot exist without a complementary strategy and structure to bring it to fruition, especially during disruptions. And evidence from COVID-19 related research proves this linkage to be of utmost importance for organizational performance.

As the COVID-19 pandemic continued to disrupt hospitals' performance due to lockdown policies and suspension of elective surgeries, stay-at-home orders, and demand for telemedicine, it also provided a unique opportunity for linking a strong, supportive culture with successful strategy implementation.

Structure, which outlines how the hospital is set up and processes designed to improve efficiency, streamline operations, and help hospitals achieve their strategic goals, also needs to be aligned with both the strategy and the culture to ensure efficient resource utilization and patient satisfaction (Belasen, Eisenberg, & Huppertz, 2016).

In a recent study, researchers (Belasen et al., 2023) examined the strategy-structure-culture linkage as a function of hospitals' CEOs' professional training and performance. They found that while the COVID-19 pandemic generated greater demand for inpatient beds, physician-led hospitals improved their capacity utilization compared to those led by traditional hospital CEOs and governing boards that recruit trustees and executives whose expertise is based on business experience. Notably, the absence of physicians on the board was associated with a decrease of three to five percentage points in three of four measures of care quality. Contrast this with evidence that physicians who received leadership or management training were found to perform well in executive leadership roles, including driving system-wide care delivery transformation, employee engagement, and physician alignment (Belasen, 2022). Hospital settings with physicians that fit the clutch leadership model discussed in this book saw an average increase of 7.1% in the Hospital Consumer Assessment of Healthcare Providers and Systems (HCAHPS) ratings of patients who strongly agreed to recommend the hospital to friends and family members.

Strategy, of course, relates to the processes and plans associated with goal achievement. In a culture that values empowerment and communication, strategy development emerges not just from the top but from all corners of the organization; each employee is encouraged to contribute. Thus, when a crisis hits, there is a prevailing or overriding expectation that leaders are equipped with the "Pentagon" qualities and traits of clutch leadership, where everyone takes ownership of the new commitments through joint accountability and transparency. By demonstrating clutch behaviors, leaders can encourage employees to follow suit and feel empowered to take initiative and own their work. This also fosters a sense of trust and collaboration, leading to more efficient and successful outcomes. In such an environment, hierarchy may be critical to ensure decisiveness, promptness, and orderliness of decision-making, but it does not mean that idea generation is confined to those who have titles of authority (Belasen & Eisenberg, 2023).

When structure, culture, and strategy align well during usual times, the organization will have a great advantage going into an unusual time. It will be better prepared and able to rely more fully on members whose efforts, productivity, motivation, and stamina are most needed. It is important, however, to be mindful that such alignment does not come simply by wishing for it, but by devoting much effort and continuous nurturing. When it does occur, it is a testament to the compelling vision, character, and skills of clutch leaders.

Motivating for Mobilizing

> This is a story told about four people named Somebody, Everybody, Anybody, and Nobody. There was one important job to be done. Everybody was sure that Somebody would do it, but Nobody did it. Somebody got angry about it because it was Everybody's job. Everybody thought Anybody could do it. Nobody realized that Everybody wouldn't do it. It ended up that Everybody blamed Somebody when Nobody did what Anybody could have done.
>
> **(Lindquist, n.d.)**

Contrast the above with the story of President Kennedy and a janitor. In 1961, President Kennedy made a visit to the NASA space center. As the story goes, as he was going on a tour in the evening, he noticed a janitor and walked over to him. The president introduced himself and they shook hands. President Kennedy then asked the janitor about his job. He replied that his job was to help put a man on the moon.

Considering each of the two scenarios above, imagine a crisis which required an all-hands-on-deck response. It may be a natural disaster, like a flood or a lightning strike, or faulty equipment that imperils life or property, or the loss of vital funding, or an industry-changing invention from a competitor. Which employee would organizational leadership want to provide critical help in the effort – Somebody? Everybody? Anybody? Nobody? Or the janitor? While the answer is probably clear, what may be less clear is what led each of those employees to respond in the way they did.

One explanation might be that the first organization had the rotten luck of hiring four people who shared an inherent trait of indifference, while NASA had the good fortune of finding a highly engaged person to work as a janitor.

Possible, but hardly likely.

The more plausible explanation is that leadership in the first organization did little, if anything, to cultivate a belief on the part of the employees that, regardless of their particular jobs, they each, individually, have an important role in contributing to the mission of the organization. Conversely, the leadership in NASA managed to inculcate a feeling that the janitor's purpose as an employee, no matter the nature of the tasks, was to contribute to the organization's goal of successful space travel. NASA probably helped the employees feel that every job is connected to one another by a shared objective, and that if any position is plucked from the equation, that objective would be that much harder to achieve.

It takes much time and effort to make sure employees feel inherently and inextricably connected. After all, whereas institutional leaders may always have one eye on organizational strategy and mission achievement, that is, the "big picture," employees spend much of their time on repetitive tasks whose relationship to the whole may not be easily discernible.

The goal of leadership is to ensure the discernment of that relationship to the whole, thereby infusing meaningfulness into the employee's day-to-day functions. The challenges to accomplish this, of course, can seem formidable. How can the biller who works remotely for a telecommunications giant come to feel that their work is contributing something of value? How can the inventory clerk in a large retailer come to feel that their work makes a difference? If it seems reasonable to conclude that it would be almost impossible for those employees to appreciate the value they provide, reflect on how a night shift janitor at NASA believes he is helping to put a man on the moon.

When leadership communicates that everyone is part of the same team and working toward the same goals with sincere messaging, reinforced through words and deeds, and modeled from the top down, the organization appears cohesive and fully aligned. This alignment is evidenced by clear communication, a shared understanding of objectives, and a sense of collective ownership.

The organization that views labor predominantly as an expense rather than an investment may end up spending more on the very labor whose costs it seeks to contain. This is because a demotivated workforce comes with a price: lower productivity, higher turnover, more absenteeism and replacement costs associated with hiring, training, and orienting replacements. And that price is astonishing. According to Gallup (2024), low employee engagement costs the global economy $8.9 trillion, a whopping 9% of global GDP, with engagement defined as the extent to which employees are committed to contributing to the organization's success and actively participating in the organization's culture.

The message at the heart of this book is that engaged employees are more inclined to contribute during disruptions. When employees trust their leaders, they tend to be more loyal, motivated, and productive, leading to higher levels of commitment and greater motivation to exert extra effort. These employees are typically more resilient, dedicated to a successful outcome, and adept at and more willing to adjust to shifting, even in highly challenging and potentially perilous circumstances. Such employees are less intimidated by the prospect of change because they trust their leaders; and, quite critically in relation to a crisis, that trust translates into a greater willingness to take risks in support of the organization (Eisenberg, et al., 2025).

Moreover, the most significant predictor of engagement is empowerment. As Donovan (2022) explains: "There is a strong behavioral aspect of empowerment, which enables employees to have control over their work, make decisions, and determine importance of tasks and processes to complete their work" (p. 141). Again, achieving high levels of motivation requires concerted efforts and significant investments in core values that shape members' identity by fostering a sense of belonging, purpose, and collective action.

This book has advanced a framework for doing so, including strategies for building trust, role modeling behavior grounded in ethics, keeping employees informed and involved, inviting their contributions, and demonstrating how their work relates to the mission. One hospital CEO reported that she invited the billing clerks, whose offices were about a mile from the hospital, to occasionally make patient rounds with doctors and nurses. It was an opportunity to feel directly connected to the goal of the organization – to take care of people. And, by extension, by being invited to participate in that activity, they felt valued by the organization. But it went beyond symbolism. During those rounds, the billers were encouraged to provide patients with their business cards and to let them know they should call them directly if they ever have questions about their bill. The billers were empowered to interact directly with patients. They were grateful to work in an organization in which they were trusted by management.

That same CEO had hospital residents (recent medical school graduates) lie on gurneys to be transported throughout the hospital. He wanted them to experience the vulnerability of lying there, staring up at the ceiling as they were wheeled through the maze-like, disorienting hospital corridors into the operating room. He hoped that this visceral experience would help the residents understand the anxiety patients might feel as they headed into surgery.

When a crisis strikes, those billing clerks and residents, and of course the NASA janitor, will be more willing to head to the front lines and do all that it takes to support the organization's efforts to right the ship. While these employees will give it their all, Somebody, Everybody, Anybody and Nobody will give it 50%, if you're lucky. Who would you want in your corner?

Conclusion: The Clutch Leader in *You*

When we hear the term leader, our mind may take us to the classic tableau of the person sitting at the head of a long table in the C-suite having the last say. Much of this book has focused on the roles, responsibilities, and skills that leaders display when the pressure is turned way up.

Woven throughout this book is the underlying message that such a leader resides in all of us. One's formal organizational title need not constrain those very qualities and traits from emerging. In fact, as we have discussed throughout the book, organizational leaders – those with the formal authority – who are most successful are also those who understand the value of empowerment and give their blessing to employees to exercise it. That is perhaps the great irony of power, that it surges in those who dispense it. And when the feeling of empowerment drives the relationship the employee has with the organization, when it is firmly established as the bedrock of organizational culture, that organization is far more poised to come out on the other side of a crisis not merely intact but stronger.

We began this book with the Pentagon Framework's focus on self-awareness. It concludes in the same place, with an inward look. Somebody, Everybody, Anybody and Nobody looked within and simply did not care enough to do the task. They didn't *own* the task. This doesn't forgive or excuse personal accountability. But upon discovering that the task was not done, the immediate reactions of each were to finger-point and dodge responsibility. Getting the job done was less important than making sure they were not held to account for failing to do so. Defensiveness, rather than initiative, can emerge as the principal employee mode of conduct when leadership fails to respect employees' agency.

When disinterest in the task prevails, things fall through the cracks. It may manifest as a decline in service quality, an ethical breach, a safety lapse, a financial breakdown, or employee discontent.

By contrast, the janitor *owned* his job. He took responsibility for it and felt pride in a job well done. He understood its relationship to all other jobs in the organization. Not necessarily in the technicalities of those jobs, but in what they had in common. By owning the job, he owned the mission.

The most successful clutch leaders create cultures which encourage employees to look inward, to connect their character to the values of the organization, and to understand that those values are the most central and binding element in employees' relationships with the organization. If, during a worst-case scenario, a rocket malfunctions, the janitor would not wait to be asked how he could help. That is the spark of character which is as valuable as any asset an organization can have at its disposal. The organizational leader who nurtures it will always have it, especially during a crisis, when it is needed most. In the end, clutch leadership is less about the grand effort under pressure and more about the capacity to rebalance their traits and behaviors, play to their strengths, demonstrate strong self-awareness and emotional intelligence skills, and make them aware of their own biases and how they impact others, especially when stakes are high and winning is on the line.

And when employees are empowered and inspired all along, they will also be there, ready to give their maximum effort when the clutch moment calls for it. Ultimately, clutch leadership is a test of character. And as we believe, everyone has it within themselves to be a clutch leader. In Michael Jordan's legendary words: *Talent wins games, but teamwork and intelligence win championships.*

References

Alaili, A. (2023). *Entrepreneur Post.* https://www.entrepreneurpost.com/2023/05/27/no-matter-how-brilliant-your-mind-or-strategy-if-youre-playing-a-solo-game-youll-always-lose-out-to-a-team-reid-hoffman/#google_vignette

Bechara, A., Damasio, A. R., Damasio, H., & Anderson, S. W. (1994). Insensitivity to future consequences following damage to human prefrontal cortex. *Cognition*, 50(1–3), 7–15.

Belasen, A. T. (2022). *Resilience in Healthcare Leadership: Practical Strategies and Self-Assessment Tools*, New York, NY, Routledge.

Belasen, A. T., Belasen, A. R., & Feng, Z. (2023). The physician CEO advantage and hospital performance during the COVID-19 Pandemic: Capacity utilization and patient satisfaction. *Journal of Organizational Healthcare Management*, 37(3), 313–326. https://doi.org/10.1108/JHOM-04-2022-0126

Belasen, A. T., & Eisenberg, B. (2023). Building trust for better crisis communication: Lessons for leadership development, Chapter 7. In N. Pfeffermann & M. Schaller (Eds.), *New Leadership Communication - Inspire Your Horizon*, pp. 93–110, Switzerland, Springer. https://doi.org/10.1007/978-3-031-34314-8_7

Belasen, A. T., Eisenberg, B., & Borgos, J. (2024). *Transforming Leadership, Improving Patient Experience: Communication Strategies for Driving Patient Satisfaction*, New York, NY, Routledge.

Belasen, A. T., Eisenberg, B., & Huppertz, J. W. (2016). *Mastering Leadership: A Vital Resource for Health Care Organizations*, Burlington, MA, Jones & Bartlett Learning.

Candito, N. (2016). How inefficient processes are hurting your company. *Entrepreneur.* https://www.entrepreneur.com/growing-a-business/how-inefficient-processes-are-hurting-your-company/286084

Catanese. L (2024). *Self-Regulation for Adults: Strategies for Getting a Handle on Emotions and Behavior*, Harvard Medical School, Harvard Health Publishing. https://www.health.harvard.edu/mind-and-mood/self-regulation-for-adults-strategies-for-getting-a-handle-on-emotions-and-behavior

Convery, A. (2023). *Air.* https://deadline.com/wp-content/uploads/2023/11/Air-Read-The-Screenplay.pdf

decipher (n.d.). Michael Jordan driven from within. https://www.deciphr.ai/podcast/213-michael-jordan-driven-from-within

Díaz-Agea, J., Orcajada-Muñoz, I., Leal-Costa, C., Adánez-Martínez, M., De Souza Oliveira, A. and Rojo-Rojo, A. (2022). How did the pandemic affect communication in clinical settings? a qualitative study with critical and emergency care nurses. *Healthcare (Basel)*, 10(2), 373. https://doi.org/10.3390/healthcare10020373

Donovan, C. (2022). Examining employee engagement amid a crisis: reactions to mandatory stay-at-home orders during the COVID-19 pandemic. *Psychology of Leaders and Leadership*, 25(2), 114–143. https://doi.org/10.1037/mgr0000127

Eisenberg, B., Hall, C., Unangst, L., & Eisenberg, A. (2024). The convergence of empathy and authenticity in brilliant leadership. In A. Belasen & N. Pfeffermann (Eds.), *Brilliant Leadership: Unlocking the Power of Innovation-Communication*, New York, NY, Routledge.

Freeland, G. (2018). Talent wins games, teamwork wins championships. *Forbes*. https://www.forbes.com/sites/grantfreeland/2018/06/01/talent-wins-games-teamwork-wins-championships/

Gallup. (2024). *State of the Global Workplace: The Voice of the World's Employees*. https://www.gallup.com/workplace/349484/state-of-the-global-workplace.aspx

Gibby-Brown, S. (2020). 60 Rene Descartes quotes on truth, science, and more. *Everydaypower*. https://everydaypower.com/rene-descartes-quotes/

Gladwell, M. (2005). *Blink: The Power of Thinking Without Thinking*, New York, NY, Little, Brown and Co.

Hyperbeast. Michael Jordan's brand has reportedly earned Nike $19 Billion USD in the past five years. https://hypebeast.com/2023/1/michael-jordan-brand-helped-nike-earn-19-billion-usd-past-five-years-report

Lindquist, R. (n.d.). That's not my job. *Life Engineering*. https://lifeengineering.com/thats-not-my-job-poem/

Lopez, M. (2017). Samsung explains Note 7 battery explosions, and turns crisis into opportunity. *Forbes*. https://www.forbes.com/sites/maribellopez/2017/01/22/samsung-reveals-cause-of-note-7-issue-turns-crisis-into-opportunity/

Martin, T., & Jeong, E. (2017). Samsung posts record profits on back of strong Galaxy S8 sales. *MarketWatch*. https://www.marketwatch.com/story/samsung-posts-record-profits-on-back-of-strong-galaxy-s8-sales-2017-07-26

PRNewswire. (2019). *Management consulting market to reach $295 billion by 2020*. Beroe, Inc. https://www.prnewswire.com/news-releases/management-consulting-market-to-reach-295-billion-by-2020-says-beroe-inc-300943883.html

Safire, W. (2005, May 8). Go to! *The New York Times*. https://www.nytimes.com/2005/05/08/magazine/go-to.html

Sarlis, V., Gerakas, D., & Tjortjis, C. (2024). A data science and sports analytics approach to decode clutch dynamics in the last minutes of NBA games. *Machine Learning and Knowledge Extraction*, 6(3), 2074–2095. https://doi.org/10.3390/make6030102

Shrank, W., Rogstad, T, Parekh, N. (2019). Waste in the US health care system: Estimated costs and potential for savings. *JAMA*, 322(15), 1501–1509. https://doi.org/10.1001/jama.2019.13978

Thanos, I. C. (2023). The complementary effects of rationality and intuition on strategic decision quality. *European Management Journal*, 41(3), 366–374. https://doi.org/10.1016/j.emj.2022.03.003

Team Pepper. (2022). How did Samsung overcome the Galaxy Note 7 crisis? *Team Pepper*. https://www.peppercontent.io/blog/samsung-galaxy-note-7-crisis/

Wegner, D. (2002). *The Illusion of Conscious Will*, Cambridge, MIT Press.
Wong, A. (2017). The oral history of the 1996 Chicago Bulls: The story of the NBA's greatest season ever (1995–1996). *Complex.* https://www.complex.com/sports/a/alex-wong/oral-history-96-bulls

Index

For Product Safety Concerns and Information please contact our EU
representative GPSR@taylorandfrancis.com
Taylor & Francis Verlag GmbH, Kaufingerstraße 24, 80331 München, Germany

www.ingramcontent.com/pod-product-compliance
Ingram Content Group UK Ltd.
Pitfield, Milton Keynes, MK11 3LW, UK
UKHW022117190926
475702UK00013B/1502

* 9 7 8 1 0 4 1 0 4 6 3 7 0 *